The Industrial
Revolution

The Industrial Revolution

The Birth of the Modern Age

Peter Lane

BOOKS
10 East 53d St., New York 10022
(a division of Harper & Row Publishers, Inc.)

© Peter Lane 1978

Published in the USA 1978 by
Harper & Row Publishers, Inc.
Barnes & Noble Import Division

Library of Congress Cataloging in Publication Data

Lane, Peter.
    The Industrial Revolution.

    Bibliography: p.
    Includes index.
        1. Industry—History. 2. Economic history.
I. Title.
HD2321.L35   338'.09   78–17537
ISBN 0–06–494034–9

Printed and bound in Great Britain

To my wife Teresa,
of whom, Genesis ii. 18

Contents

Illustrations

Tables

Figures

Preface

My original, almost inherent, interest in the Industrial Revolution has its roots in my own origins. Born in industrial South Wales, to a father born in the Merthyr of the Crawshays and Guests, himself the child of Irish immigrants attracted to Wales by the prospects of employment in the booming iron industry, I could hardly have been other than interested in the development of that process and system which had produced the physical environment and social climate in which I grew up. I was fortunate in that parents and teachers helped stimulate that inborn interest and that my career has enabled me to enjoy the pleasure of continually studying the subject.

Along with all other students of the Industrial Revolution I have benefitted from the work of a number of outstanding historians. I have acknowledged my debt to some of them in the course of the text when I have quoted from their work. In the bibliography I have listed the works which I have read in preparing this book. I am particularly grateful, as all students must be, to Professor T. S. Ashton for having made what might be a complex study appear so simple and attractive. Along with all modern students I am indebted to B. R. Mitchell and Phyllis Deane for their compilations of statistics on which all of us are able to draw. In *The First Industrial Nation* (Methuen, 1969) Peter Mathias used the work of Mitchell and Deane when constructing the figures and tables which I have used on pp 55 and 183.

If Ashton provided us with a comparatively simple framework within which to work, R. M. Hartwell has been one of the leaders in the modern campaign which aims at forcing us to re-examine some of the well entrenched opinions that have held ground for so long. I am grateful for the spur which he has given to my study of this subject. Finally I am grateful to my students over the past twenty years whose demands, arguments and work has given me constant new insights into the story of the birth of modern Britain.

Introduction

The first, and still the classical, examination of the Industrial Revolution was made by Arnold Toynbee in a series of lectures given at Oxford in 1880/1, in which he emphasized the nature and degree of change that took place in England after 1760. This precise dating of the onset of the Industrial Revolution as well as Toynbee's emphasis on the fundamental changes which took place after that date were generally accepted by historians and scholars for about fifty years. The actual term 'Industrial Revolution' had been used earlier in the nineteenth century by Robert Owen in Britain and by Louis-Auguste Blanqui, a French economist, who claimed that the changes brought about by the economic revolution were as fundamental in their effect on British life as were those wrought by the political revolution which had changed French life after 1789.

Owen, Blanqui and to a lesser extent Toynbee tended to emphasize the very rapid change which had taken place in a short period of time. As C. Beard wrote in 1901: 'England of the first part of the eighteenth century was virtually a medieval England, quiet, primeval, and undisturbed by the roar of trade and commerce. Suddenly, almost like a thunderbolt from a clear sky, were ushered in the storm and stress of the Industrial Revolution.' If Toynbee was the first great historian of the Industrial Revolution, the second was undoubtedly Paul Mantoux, a Frenchman who in 1906 wrote a major work in which he claimed that 'in spite of the apparent rapidity of its development, the industrial revolution sprang from far-distant causes.' An American historian, J. U. Nef traced the beginnings of large-scale industry back to the sixteenth century, claiming that

> the rise of industrialism in Great Britain can be more properly regarded as a long process stretching back to the middle of the sixteenth century and coming down to the final triumph of the industrial state towards the end of the nineteenth, than as a sudden phenomenon associated with the late eighteenth and early nineteenth centuries.

However if Mantoux had shown that the developments of the eighteenth century were a culmination of movements already well under way, he also claimed the Industrial Revolution as an eighteenth-century phenomenon. This theme was taken up by the third of the great historians of the Industrial Revolution, T. S. Ashton. In 1948 he produced *The Industrial Revolution, 1760–1830*, and in his introduction to the twelfth edition of Mantoux's *The Industrial Revolution in the Eighteenth Century* (1961), he wrote:

> After 1782 almost every available statistical series of industrial output reveals a sharp upward turn. More than half the growth in the shipments of coal and the mining of copper, more than three-quarters of the increase of broad cloths, four-fifths of that of printed cloth and nine-tenths of the exports of cotton goods were concentrated in the last eighteen years of the century.

Ashton and Mantoux did not merely put the Industrial Revolution firmly back into an eighteenth-century context. They also brought to their study the skills of economists as opposed to those of historians and so introduced the element of economic analysis into the study of the subject, from which all subsequent students have benefited.

So we have two apparently contradictory standpoints. One is taken by historians such as Nef who wish to trace everything back to a Tudor past. Such historians would deny the validity of the use of the word 'revolution'. As George Unwin wrote:

> When, on looking back we find that the revolution has been going on for two centuries, and had been in preparation for two centuries before that, when we find that both in its causes and consequences it affects the lot of that three-quarters of the human race who are still farmers and peasants as profoundly as it does that of the industrial worker, we may begin to doubt whether the term . . . has not by this time served its turn.

The other standpoint is that taken originally by Toynbee and emphasized by Ashton in the title of his own work. However the differences between these two schools of thought are not as great as might first appear. Nef and his supporters do not deny the rapidity of change in the late eighteenth and early nineteenth centuries. Nor do Ashton and his supporters claim that these changes had their roots in the eighteenth century. Ashton wrote:

> The word 'revolution' implies a suddenness of change that is not, in fact, characteristic of economic processes. The system of human relationships that is sometimes called capitalism had its origins long before 1760, and attained its full development long after 1830; there is a danger of overlooking the essential fact of continuity. But the phrase 'Industrial Revolution' has been used by a long line of historians and has become so firmly embedded in common speech that it would be pedantic to offer a substitute.

In the course of this book I hope to show that the great changes of the Industrial Revolution would not have taken place if there had not been a pre-existing platform from which the take-off could be launched. I also hope to show why the take-off did take place when it did and why it took place in Britain rather than in say France or Holland. Finally I hope to outline the nature of the fundamental changes in agriculture and industry which altered the structure of the economy so that industrial production began to expand at a higher and sustained rate.

1. Population and Society in the Eighteenth Century

In 1910 the great historian J. H. Clapham wrote: 'Even if the history of "the industrial revolution" is a thrice-squeezed orange, there remains an astonishing amount of juice in it.' During the seventy years since those words appeared there has been an almost continual flow of learned monographs and detailed studies as well as more general surveys of the Industrial Revolution which has long been recognized as one of the 'great discontinuities' of history, marking the division between a world in which population, output and incomes rose slowly, if at all, and the modern world where populations, output and real incomes per head of population grow very quickly. There have been other such discontinuities – the Renaissance and the French Revolution for example, and all such great developments have always roused people's interests. Why did they take place? Why then and not at an earlier date? What were the processes which helped the development along? What did contemporaries think of the changes which were taking place around them?

Britain was the first country to undergo the transformation which is masked by the term Industrial Revolution. Other Western countries underwent a similar transformation at a later date, and in our own time hitherto underdeveloped countries in Africa, Latin America and Asia are doing as best they know how to race along the path towards industrialization, hoping to find – as Britain found – that industrialization brings with it a rising national income, opportunities for social development and a massive rise in general living standards. Economists, politicians and others anxious to help these underdeveloped countries look to the British experience as a classical model, hoping that by studying it they may be better fitted to promote what they consider a desirable change in the underdeveloped regions of the modern world.

If we wish to begin to understand what happened in Britain during the Industrial Revolution we do well, as R. M. Hartwell reminds us, to follow Macaulay's maxim: 'One of the first objects of the enquirer, who wishes to form a correct notion of the state of a community at a given time, must be to ascertain of how many persons that community existed.' We might add that it would be well to know how these 'persons' earned their livings, how well or badly they lived and the nature of the social and intellectual climates in which they lived.

Gregory King 1695

Our knowledge of the size of the British population at the beginning of the seventeenth century is based on the work of Gregory King (1648–1712), who was employed at the College of Heralds and later in government financial offices. King produced two major tracts. One, which was compiled in 1688, will be considered in Chapter 2. The second was completed in 1695 although it was not published until 1802 under the title *Natural and Politicall Observations and Conclusions upon the State and Condition of England.*

King's main purpose in this particular tract was to estimate the size of the population of England and Wales – Scotland being a separate kingdom not yet united with her southern neighbours. King took the returns 'charg'd in the books of the Hearth Office at Lady Day 1690' as the basis of his work. Every household had to pay a hearth tax and, one must assume, government tax collectors would have seen to it that every household (or hearth) would have been counted. There were, it appeared, 1,319,215 houses in England and Wales on 25 March 1690. Allowing for the building which had taken place between then and 1695, and also for some houses being empty (although charged for hearth tax,) King estimated that in 1695 there were 1,300,000 inhabited houses in England and Wales which 'we . . . shall thus apportion':

London	105,000
The other cities and market towns	195,000
The villages and hamlets	1,000,000
In all	1,300,000

King then examined the assessments for the tax on marriages, births and burials which was first imposed in 1695, in order to get an estimate of the number of people living in different sorts of houses in different parts of the country, made allowances for the probability that such returns were faulty, added figures for seamen, soldiers and vagrants, 'viz. hawkers, pedlars, crate carriers, gipsies, theves and beggars', who might not have figured in official returns and concluded that the population of England and Wales in 1695 was 5,500,000.

It is not surprising that modern historians have examined King's work very carefully; it was after all the first attempt at a population count and tells us a great deal about the nature of the country in which the first Industrial Revolution took place. It is now generally agreed that King's work was scholarly, thorough and fairly reliable, although it may be necessary to amend the figures slightly – by about 5 per cent so that in the opinion of the latest researchers the population of England and Wales in 1695 was probably about 5,200,000.

It is worth while considering the figure for a moment. Those of us who live in modern Britain with its population – for England and Wales – of about 45,000,000 will find it hard to grasp the concept of a population of about 5,200,000. We would have to do away with about eight in every nine people in present-day

England and Wales to arrive at this figure. Again in modern Britain we tend to live in urban areas or in massive conurbations. In King's time people lived in the main in 'villages and hamlets' where there were in total 1 million houses or about five-sixths of all the houses in England and Wales at the time. London had a population of about 500,000, or one-tenth of the total population. It exerted a very powerful economic influence – on agriculture for the surrounding countryside, on industry in London itself (food-processing, furniture-making, clothing and so on) and on industry elsewhere, since London's own industry required iron products (nails, domestic pots and pans), timber and other goods and materials.

After London the next largest towns were Norwich with about 29,000 inhabitants, Bristol with 25,000 and Birmingham with 12,000. There were no other towns with populations above 10,000. In 1697 and 1698 Celia Fiennes kept a travel-diary during her 'Great Journeys' to different parts of England. From this diary we get a vivid reminder of the nature of English towns in 1698:

> Manchester looks exceedingly well at the entrance, very sub-stantiall buildings, the houses are not very lofty but mostly of brick and stone, the old houses are timber work, there is a very large church all stone and stands high soe that walking round the church yard you see the whole town . . . which is large as alsoe the other town that lyes below it called Salfor, and is divided from this by the river Irwell over which is a stone bridge with many arches. Leverpool which is in Lancashire is built just on the river Mersy, mostly new built houses of brick and stone after the London fashion; the first original was a few fishermens houses and now is grown to a large fine town and but a parish and one church, tho' there be 24 streets in it.

King provides us with one firm figure of population. For an estimate of the population of Scotland we have to rely on the work of Alexander Webster who in 1755 was trying to work out a pension scheme for the widows of Scottish clergy. In that year he asked each parish clergyman to send him a return of the population of their parishes. While some of the individual returns may be challenged, it is generally accepted that Webster's estimate of the population of Scotland in 1755 as 1,265,000 is fairly reliable.

John Rickman 1801

During the latter part of the eighteenth century there was a good deal of public controversy about the size of the British population. There were those who sided with Cobbett and argued that it was stagnant while others, notably an Anglican clergyman, Thomas Malthus, argued that it was rising, and rising too steeply so that economic hardship was, it seemed, inevitable.

During this public debate there were proposals that the government should organize a proper census of the population. This it was argued would settle the matter once and for all. But in the public mind there was a deep suspicion of such proposals. King had used tax returns when he made his estimates; even though his work was not yet published, there was a link in people's minds between government-controlled counts of hearths, official returns of births, marriages and deaths – and government-imposed taxes. This helps to explain why there was no agreement on the organizing of a census until 1800 when John Rickman was put in charge of the operation due to take place in 1801.

This very first census gives us a fairly reliable figure for the population of Britain in 1801 although modern research has shown that there was undercounting of about 5 per cent so that the 1801 figures have been revised to show that the population of England and Wales was about 9,300,000 while in Scotland there were about 1,670,000 people. Not only was this first official census undercounted; it was also very limited in the information that it sought. Not for the people of 1801 the complicated forms of the modern census. We know only the numbers of each sex, the geographical distribution of the population, and only broad divisions as to age and occupation. It was not until much later that more sophisticated questions were asked which enable us to know more about the age-distribution of the population and the occupation-composition of the working people. However students have reason to be grateful for the second major landmark in the study of population. If King gives us one figure for 1695 (and so for the beginning of the eighteenth century), Rickman's census gives us a second for 1801 (and the end of the eighteenth century).

Rickman's estimates of eighteenth-century changes

However the two landmarks of themselves tell us relatively little beyond the fact that during the eighteenth century the population went up by about two-thirds. We need to know much more than that. Was the growth constant throughout the century or did it take place in a small number of larger than usual increases at various times during the century? Why did the population take off during the eighteenth century when for about two centuries it had increased by less than 1 per cent per decade? Was the increase caused by the industrial changes which we know were taking place during this century, or was the Industrial Revolution itself caused by the increase in population? Was the increase due to non-economic factors altogether, or do we have to link the increase with economic change?

These questions are not merely historians' attempts to arrive at the truth – valuable though that would be *per se*. The modern interest in the demographic changes which took place in eighteenth-century Britain is especially strong among economists with interests in the problems of countries endeavouring to 'break through' into industrialization. Answers to some of the questions posed above might provide guide-lines for underdeveloped and developing countries as to the right sort of population policy.

As part of his work John Rickman compiled estimates of

population figures throughout the eighteenth century. He wrote to all the parish clergy to ask them to provide him with all the entries in their baptism and burial registers firstly for each ten years between 1700 and 1780 and secondly for each year from 1781 to 1800. He then made an allowance for incomplete returns and then produced his *Parish Register Abstract*. For many years historians used this *Abstract* as the basis for their writing on eighteenth-century population.

However modern research has shown that little reliance can be placed on Rickman's figures. Indeed he himself was aware of the weakness of his material. In 1801 he wrote to the poet Robert Southey of 'the incredible inaccuracy of the returns under the Population Act'. Today we have some idea of the degree of that inaccuracy. Professor Chambers has compared the totals of births, marriages and burials in three parishes in Nottingham with the totals published for these parishes in Rickman's *Abstract*. Chambers writes of 'some disturbing discrepancies. . . . On nine occasions between 1760 and 1800 the totals given in the registers differ by [between] fifteen to thirty-three per cent from those provided in the *Abstract*.' D. V. Glass, a leading figure in population studies, has shown that at least 20 out of 85 known births in two London parishes at the end of the seventeenth century were omitted from baptism registers. We know that Cornish parish registers recorded an infant mortality rate of only 60 per 1,000 in 1800 whereas even as late as 1900 the figure was 140 per 1,000 for the whole of England and Wales. This suggests that at least half the infant deaths in Cornwall were simply not recorded, and it appears that clergymen in general did not enter the burials of unbaptized infants.

Even in Rickman's time there were many parishes not only where records were badly kept, but also where registers were vandalized, pages being torn out to be used as pot-handles, spills, wrapping-paper and firelighters. Then there was the tendency not to enter the births or burials of Nonconformists. One conscientious vicar at Wigston Magna in Leicestershire did record, although separately, the baptisms of Nonconformist children between 1707 and 1720. His records show that there were 89 such baptisms compared with 470 Anglican baptisms registered in the same period. For this village at this period Nonconformist families had about 16 per cent of all children born. But few vicars took the same trouble – some entering births to Nonconformist parents at one time and not at another, some never entering such births at all. It is therefore impossible to find any sort of multiplier which might be used to amend Rickman's figures which are therefore obviously unreliable guides to the changes which took place in the British population during the eighteenth century.

In part this unreliability is a reflection of the inefficiency of the Anglican clergy. During the early part of the century there was increasing pluralism and parochial organization became increasingly weaker. Towards the end of the century, with the growth of larger industrial towns, the Anglican Church became even more unrepresentative of the British people, failing to establish sufficient churches in the industrial and mining areas. This allowed the Nonconformists to increase their influence – and to make Rickman's figures less reliable. Alongside the growth of Nonconformity there was also present the onset of religious indifference, so that we know that many births were never reported to the local vicar. Private burial grounds grew in number, and many burials were never recorded in parish returns which took account only of the burial of baptized Anglicans.

The unreliability of Rickman's figures was also in part the result of the request that he made – that returns should be submitted for each decennial year from 1700 to 1780. We now know that certain of those years (1710, 1720 and probably 1740) were years of exceptionally high mortality due to epidemics. These high figures do not show what was happening in the period as a whole. They also gave rise to the belief that there was a sudden sharp fall in the death rate after 1781 – when yearly figures were available to Rickman.

Modern beliefs

So Rickman's figures are no longer accepted as they once were. Modern research shows that we know too little about eighteenth-century demographic changes to be as confident as previous historians were. However there is a measure of agreement on three major items. It is now clear that during the sixteenth and seventeenth centuries the population was increasing very slowly, and that during the nineteenth century it was increasing very rapidly, doubling between 1810 and 1851 and doubling again between 1851 and 1901. Therefore it is generally agreed that during the eighteenth century there was a change in the population pattern; we pass from a period of slow, almost negligible growth to one of rapid growth.

The second item on which most modern researchers are agreed is that on available evidence it appears that this eighteenth-century growth did not start to take place until after 1740 and did not take off until after 1770. The accepted pattern of population growth is shown in the table:

Table 1 *Population Growth in England and Wales*

1701–41	From *c.* 5.8 million to *c.* 6 million
1741–51	$3\frac{1}{2}\%$ growth
1751–61	7% growth
1761–71	7% growth
1771–81	10% growth
1781–91	10% growth
1791–1801	11% growth
1811–21	17% growth (the peak rate)

The third item on which historians are agreed is that this population explosion was not a peculiarly English phenomenon. There were similar population growths in most Western European countries and, in the British Isles, in Ireland as well. There is then no magical relationship between an increase in population and industrialization. Some historians used to write glibly that 'the increased population needed feeding and this led to the Agrarian Revolution. It also had to be clothed and housed which led to the Industrial Revolution'. Such a simplistic explanation begs the question as to why Ireland did not undergo a similar experience as did Britain, or why India and Pakistan have not managed the same simple follow-on in this century.

The increase in population and the death rate

The slight but historically rapid increase between 1700 and 1750 was similar to 'surges' which had taken place in the past. However there was something different about the eighteenth-century increase. Previously an increase in the population had led to pressure on the other available economic resources, in particular on the land-supply. One of two things had then happened. Either diminishing returns had set in and under economic pressure the rise in population was halted or – and this happened frequently – a single year's poor harvest, epidemic or plague had been enough to wipe out the increase of perhaps a decade or more. This time the surge was not merely maintained but accelerated as the century advanced.

Many historians believe that the major reason for the increase in population was a fall in the death rate. It is true that a fall in the death rate has a more immediate effect on population figures than the other possible reason for the increase – namely a rise in the birth rate. We have seen this for ourselves in the ever increasing populations of India and countries in Latin America. A fall in the rate of infant mortality has an especial influence on population figures not only because fewer deaths means that the population for a particular year goes up, but also because there are many more potential child-bearers who will then influence the population figures for future generations.

For a long time it was assumed that it was just such a fall which could be held to explain the rise in population in the eighteenth century. Furthermore historians put forward the thesis that this decreased death rate could be explained by advances in medical knowledge. It was left to medical historians to show that this explanation was invalid. There were few hospitals built in the eighteenth century and most of these built in large towns, so that their effect, if any, was not felt by the population at large. And even these hospitals were it appears sources of disease rather than centres of cure. Even as late as the 1870s a senior surgeon at University College Hospital, London advised his students that 'a woman has a better chance of recovery after delivery in the meanest poorest hovel than in the best conducted hospital furnished with every appliance that can add to her comfort and with the best skill that a metropolis can afford.'

There is evidence that there was some improvement in medical knowledge and that there was a gradual acceptance of the need for more hygienic methods of treatment which may have had some effect on the rate of maternal and of infant mortality. But the vast majority of mothers would not have come into contact with any of the few wiser, better-educated, medical practitioners. There is also some evidence that smallpox, hitherto a scourge, was on the decline even before the spread of inoculation and vaccination, although it is questionable whether the decline in the incidence of this disease helps to explain the fall in the death rate, since many of those who were saved from smallpox might well have died, at the same age, from some other of the many killer diseases.

If then there was a fall in the death rate, we have to look to non-medical causes for the change. We now know that between 1730 and 1755 Britain experienced an unusual number of bumper harvests so that huge quantities of grain were exported during most of those years. This abundance of food had a threefold economic effect. Firstly there was a sharp fall in food prices, secondly there was a high demand for labour to get the harvests in and finally there was a rise in real wages. All this was clear to Malthus when he wrote:

During the last 40 years of the 17th century and the first 20 of
the 18th, the average price of corn was such as, compared with
the wages of labour, would enable the labourer to purchase
with a day's earnings, two-thirds of a peck of wheat. From 1720
to 1750 the price of wheat had so fallen, while wages had risen,
that instead of two thirds the labourer could purchase the whole
of a peck of wheat with a day's labour.

An increase in real wages enabled the people to buy a better
and more varied diet. More fresh vegetables were bought and the
potato introduced into the working-class diet. Recent medical
research indicates that the potato is a most valuable staple food,
something which Adam Smith appreciated as long ago as 1776,
when he wrote in his *Wealth of Nations*:

The chairmen, porters, and coalheavers in London, and those
unfortunate women who live by prostitution, the strongest men
and the most beautiful women perhaps in the British dominions,
are said to be, the greater part of them, from the lowest rank of
people in Ireland, who are generally fed with this root. No
food can afford a more decisive proof of its nourishing quality,
or of its being peculiarly suitable to the health of the human
constitution.

Better diet, more cheap clothing, the slow replacement of
wattle-and-daub walls by brick, of thatch by tiles, of rushes by
carpet or wooden floors, all had an effect on death rates. In
particular the better diet would have affected the rate of maternal
mortality as well as the rate of infant mortality and this, as we
have seen, would have had a cumulative effect on future
generations.

There is also some evidence that the fall in the death rate was
due to a sudden end of some at least of the epidemics and plagues
which had swept the country from time to time. Writing of the
death rate in eighteenth-century Nottingham Professor Chambers
says:

It is not a question of . . . a steady decline under the influence of the ameliorating factors of diet and environment but rather of a sudden and temporary plunge downwards as a result of the absence of a factor which had made the preceding period one of exceptionally high mortality, followed by a return almost to the death rates of the pre-epidemic period.

He goes on to conclude: 'As far as Nottingham was concerned the age of massacre by epidemic was over.' There are several possible explanations for this change, which was evident throughout Western Europe as a whole. Smallpox became less of a killer and the plague which had so virulently attacked the British population in the 1660s was almost absent after the 1720s. The disappearance of the plague was due it seems to the displacement of the small domestic black rat, which liked living in human settlements and which carried the free-wandering and plague-carrying flea, by the outdoor brown rat with its nest-living flea. This new species reached England in the late 1720s and drove out the smaller, plague-carrying rat – and so helped lower the death rate.

The increase in population and the birth rate

It is now generally agreed that there was a fall in the death rate from about 1730 onwards. This was bound of itself to have led to a rise in the birth rate since there would be more potential child-bearers as the 'saved' infants grew to maturity. But there are other explanations for a rise in the birth rate. In pre-industrial England a high percentage of people did not get married at all. Those who did tended to get married at a relatively high age. When times were particularly bad – during famine or when epidemics made life more than usually difficult – marriages were postponed. After 1740 the economic forces tended to promote earlier and more marriages; there was plenty of employment and higher real wages as inducements to marriage. There was a decline in the system of apprenticeship with the need for the workman to live in with the employer. The setting up of a home at an earlier age became more common.

Marrying at an earlier age meant that more women married while their child-bearing potential was at its highest. There is some evidence that in pre-industrial Britain women tended to put off having successive children – perhaps by breast-feeding their children until they were two years old, perhaps by practising *coitus interruptus*. With the improved economic position in which they found themselves after 1740, more women tended to have their children in quicker succession, knowing that they were going to be able to provide for them and that in time the child would be able to get some employment and to contribute to the household income. The better diet enjoyed by the mothers would have had its effect on the rate of miscarriage and so on the number of children born, and on the rate of still-births and infant mortality.

We have evidence then that after 1740 there was a steady rise in the birth rate and, given that this was a cumulative process, we ought not to be surprised that after 1770 there should be a take-off since the increased number of infants born in the 1740s and 1750s became the parents of the 1770s.

Regional variation in birth rates

The link between economic development and the birth rate was well expressed in the report of the Swedish population commission of 1761:

It is obvious that crop failures and hard years prevent many persons from marrying. But it is also easy to understand why, at the same time, existing bridal beds will be less fruitful if it is remembered that an increase of a couple of daler in the price of corn will immediately result in an addition to all the burdens imposed on farmers, compelling them to cut down their other expenses in order to fill their own stomachs. . . . In 1747 and 1748 the price of corn was 30 to 28 daler per Tina in most parts of Sweden. In 1749 the price of corn fell to 25–26 daler, but in 1750 the price was only 17 daler. At once girls and boys were ready for the bridal bed and for married couples love began to burn more vigorously.

This is the basis for the Malthusian argument – that there is a correlation between incomes and births. Adam Smith wrote: 'The reward of labour must necessarily encourage in such a manner the marriage and multiplication of labourers, as may enable them to supply that continually increasing demand by a continually increasing population.' Malthus himself wrote: 'What is essentially necessary to a rapid increase of population is a great and continued demand for labour.' Arthur Young asked: 'Is it not evident that demands for hands, that is employment, must regulate the numbers of the people?'

We know that in the second half of the eighteenth century there was a continual and rapid growth in the population of England's industrial towns. In the past this rise has been explained by 'a migration of labour from the countryside to the town in search of employment'. We know now that there was little such migration; indeed we know that the population of the rural areas did not decline at the time when the population of the industrial centres was rising. What appears to have happened is that there was a higher than average increase in the birth rate in the industrial centres. In part this was due to earlier marriages. In the earlier part of the century the average age at marriage seems to have been about 27; in the textile and mining areas in 1800 the average age was 20 as compared with an average of 24 for rural areas. This it seems was a direct response to economic forces. In the industrial towns a man earned an individual wage, as distinct from the payment made to the head of the family by the putter-out in the domestic system. This made it easier to set up a home. Children were less of a burden in industrial towns where there was employment for them from an early age.

An increasing population and the economy

An increasing population meant more hands and perhaps cheaper labour. Some people have seen a direct link between the demands made by the increased population and the onset of the Industrial Revolution. The growth in population, it is argued, was a stimulus to industrialization. To accept this view is to ignore what happened in nineteenth-century Ireland with its Great Hunger and mass emigration. Indeed there is a good case to be made for the argument that an increase in population may actually retard industrialization. Why should an industrialist adopt labour-saving and expensive devices if there is a plentiful supply of labour available? This was the case in weaving in the late eighteenth and early nineteenth centuries when the introduction of power-weaving was held back because there was a plentiful supply of handloom-weavers (see Chapter 11).

An increase in population may also be a severe handicap to a country embarking on the road to industrialization. If that population has to be fed by imported food, the nation's balance of trade and balance of payments may be thrown out of gear, and essential imports of capital equipment and raw materials may have to be cut, so hampering the nation's efforts. Britain was fortunate in her Industrial Revolution in that she was able to feed her increasing population and did not have to divert any of her effort to pay for food imports. India today would no doubt like to be in the happy position of not having to pay for food imports and of having sufficient food to enable her to export the surplus. A foreigner visiting England in 1748 noted:

> We noticed ... several large rye-fields. I asked the people if they were in the habit of baking bread of this crop, or why they sow it. They answered that no others but poor people use it for bread; but the principal reason why they sow it is that they carry it to London where they sell it to merchants, who ship great quantities of it abroad, to be sold there.

There was, as Smith, Malthus and Young were aware, an increasing demand for labour. What they did not stress was that this was a fairly universal demand, not merely a demand for labour in the industrial towns. In Chapter 4 we shall see that there was an increasing demand for labour in rural England. The increased population of eighteenth-century England was fortunate. It was gainfully employed; it was fed, clothed and housed – because of the Industrial Revolution. Professor Ashton has written:

> The central problem of the age was how to feed and clothe and employ generations of children outnumbering by far those of any earlier time. Ireland was faced by the same problem. Failing to solve it, she lost in the 'forties about a fifth of her people by emigration or starvation and disease. If England had remained a nation of cultivators and craftsmen, she could hardly have escaped the same fate and, at best, the weight of a growing population must have pressed down the spring of her spirit. She was delivered, not by her rulers, but by those who, seeking no doubt their own narrow ends, had the wit and resource to devise new instruments of production and new methods of administering industry. There are today on the plains of India and China men and women, plague-ridden and hungry, living lives little better, to outward appearance, than those of the cattle that toil with them by day and share their places of sleep by night. Such Asiatic standards, and such unmechanized horrors, are the lot of those who increase their numbers without passing through an industrial revolution.

To eighteenth-century observers the employers appeared as the answer to the Malthusians who argued that an increasing population must inevitably suffer starvation, pestilence or some other such 'preventive check'. During the eighteenth century the population went up by about 66 per cent. During this time output of goods and services rose by 250 per cent, making England the richest country in the world, on its way to being 'the workshop of the world'.

2. A Map of Society 1688

In producing the first reliable estimate of the population of England and Wales in 1695 Gregory King provided future historians with a much-used document. In 1688 King had produced another equally significant tract, a table of the income and expenditure of each social group in England and Wales in that year. King undertook this compilation to provide an idea of the economic strength of the country at the time of the Glorious Revolution in which James II was deposed and replaced by the Protestant rulers William III and Mary II.

Modern research suggests that many of the figures in this estimate are suspect. For example it is probable that King underestimated the number of people in each of the families of 'cottagers and paupers'. It is also important to note that when King used the words 'families' in the second column and 'family' in the third column he meant 'members in the household' which included servants, apprentices, living-in workmen and labourers. Again King's estimate of the total national income has to be treated with great care; he has not included such income as was received by the Crown, the Church, trading companies, charities or trusts.

But the table gives us a rough idea of the society in pre-industrial Britain. We can see that this was an agricultural society with 75 per cent of the people gaining their livelihood in agriculture. England and Wales in 1688 were in roughly the same position as are most underdeveloped countries in the twentieth century. King estimated that there was a little under £2.2 million available for savings throughout the country. Of this he claims freeholders (£910,000), landed classes (£445,000) and farmers (£187,500) provided over half, with merchants (£400,000) and persons in the law (£210,000) providing the remainder. If there was to be any new investment in industry, transport, town-development or shipping it was the rural community which would have to provide the bulk of such investment. It was the land which was the source of this wealth (in rent, profits and wages); agriculture was the greatest employer, paying the largest share of the nation's wages bill. Agriculture supplied industry with much of its raw material – corn for brewer and miller, hides for the leatherworker and wool for spinners and weavers. The rural population also made most demands of industry – for tools and equipment, for such food and drink as was not produced locally, as well as for clothing and consumer goods. The bulk of such industry as did exist was organized on a cottage basis. Textile workers in particular, but nail-makers and other metal-workers also, did their work in their cottages when free from work in the field.

Further examination of the table shows that England and Wales was a hierarchical society. There were roughly 153,500 in an upper class (marked A in the table), about 516,000 in what may be called a middle class (marked B in the table), 1,730,000 wage-paying farmers (marked C in the table) and 2,575,000 in classes which earned wages or eked out a subsistence as 'cottagers and paupers'. However this situation was not static. The upper class has been best compared to passengers in a bus or train, some of whom get out at stops along the way while others climb aboard before the vehicle moves on. In the eighteenth century merchants, bankers, lawyers and industrialists who were successful could buy a country estate and turn themselves into gentry. As Defoe wrote:

> Fate has but little Distinction set
> Betwixt the Counter and the Coronet.

Table 2 *Gregory King's Estimate of the Population and Wealth of England and Wales, Calculated for 1688*

Rank	Number of families	Heads per family	Persons	Yearly income per family £	Yearly expenditure per family £	Total income of group £
Temporal Lords	160	40	6,400	2,800	2,400	448,000
Spiritual Lords	26	20	520	1,300	1,100	33,800
Baronets	800	16	12,800	880	816	704,000
Knights	600	13	7,800	650	498	390,000
Esquires	3,000	10	30,000	450	420	1,350,000
Gentlemen	12,000	8	96,000	280	268	3,360,000
Clergy, superior	2,000	6	12,000	60	54	120,000
Clergy, inferior	8,000	5	40,000	45	40	360,000
Persons in the Law	10,000	7	70,000	140	119	1,400,000
Sciences and the Liberal Arts	16,000	5	80,000	60	57 10s	960,000
Persons in Offices	5,000	8	40,000	240	216	1,200,000
Persons in Offices	5,000	6	30,000	120	108	600,000
Merchants by sea	2,000	8	16,000	400	320	800,000
Merchants by land	8,000	6	48,000	200	170	1,600,000
Shopkeepers, Tradesmen	40,000	4½	180,000	45	42 15s	1,800,000

Naval Officers	5,000	4	20,000	80	72	400,000
Military Officers	4,000	4	16,000	60	56	240,000
Freeholders (better sort)	40,000	7	280,000	84	77	3,360,000
Freeholders (lesser)	140,000	5	700,000	50	45 10s	7,000,000
Farmers	150,000	5	750,000	44	42 15s	6,600,000
Artisans, Handicrafts	60,000	4	240,000	40	38	2,400,000
Common Seamen	*50,000*	*3*	*150,000*	*20*	*21 10s*	*1,000,000*
Common Soldiers	*35,000*	*2*	*70,000*	*14*	*15*	*490,000*
Labouring people and servants	*364,000*	*3½*	*1,275,000*	*15*	*15 7s*	*5,460,000*
Cottagers and paupers	*400,000*	*3¼*	*1,300,000*	*6 10s*	*7 6s 3d*	*2,600,000*
Vagrants	*—*		*30,000*	*2*	*3*	*60,000*

Persons increasing the wealth of the country
2,675,520

Persons decreasing the wealth of the country
2,825,000 (italicized in the table)

Total income of persons in the country £44,394,800

Total expenditure of persons in the country £42,205,400

In another publication Defoe noted:

> Trade is so far here from being inconsistent with a gentleman,
> that in short Trade in England makes gentlemen, and has peopled
> this nation with gentlemen; for . . . the tradesmen's children, or
> at least their grandchildren, come to be as good gentlemen,
> statesmen, Parliament-men, privy-councillors, judges, bishops,
> and noblemen, as those of the highest birth and the most ancient
> families. . . . We see the tradesmen of England, as they grow
> wealthy, coming every day to the Herald's Office, to search for
> the coats of arms of their ancestors, in order to paint them upon
> their coaches, and engrave them upon their plate, embroider
> them upon their furniture, or carve them upon the pediments of
> their new houses.

We will consider the significance of this movement into (and out
of) the upper class in Chapter 3.

King's tables show that over half the population were unable to
live by their incomes and had to rely on charity and poor relief.
King described these as 'decreasing the wealth of the nation'. They
were a mass of people who worked as best they could and yet
could not make ends meet. The high level of abject poverty which
King revealed again reinforces the view that England and Wales
were underdeveloped countries, facing many of the problems
which such countries face in our own time. Underemployment
and seasonal unemployment were common in a country which
relied on a fairly primitive agricultural system. Britain overcame
this problem as a result of the Industrial Revolution which changed
the nature of the economic system, increased output per head and
so enabled an increase in the general standard of living. It is not
surprising that modern underdeveloped countries wish to imitate
Britain's example.

But King's table also shows that England and Wales were more
advanced than are most modern underdeveloped countries. A
long history of commerce had led to the emergence of a large
number of merchants, tradesmen, shopkeepers, artisans and handi-

craftsmen. England was already a well-established commercial economy, had a more complex social mix than did most other countries in contemporary Europe and certainly was more developed than are the majority of modern underdeveloped countries.

King's table also shows that there was a three-runged structure in rural society. There were those who owned land (from temporal lords through gentlemen down to freeholders). There was also a prosperous class of lesser freeholders whose income was barely above that of artisans. But there was also a large class of 150,000 tenant-farmers who rented land and employed labour. This was quite unlike the structure found in Ireland and throughout Europe as a whole, where the scene was dominated by a landless peasantry. In England there was a prosperous rural community which was already well versed in the problems of producing for a market economy as opposed to the European peasant who produced largely for his own subsistence. The significance of this will become clearer when we examine the development of commerce and trade in Chapter 7, where we shall see that the domestic market (primarily a rural market) was the largest outlet for the products of industry.

King probably underestimated the degree of 'savings' by including under the heading of 'expenditure' some spending which would have been made on making the farm more productive, on new machinery in industry and agriculture and so on. However, even allowing for this and for the omissions already noted, we can see that according to King the *per capita* national income was about £8 *per annum*. If we take account of what that money might buy at the time, and if we further try to make an estimate of how £8 in 1688 should be represented in the late 1970s, we shall find that in 1688 the *per capita* national income of England and Wales was in very rough terms perhaps six, eight or ten times greater than the *per capita* income of modern underdeveloped countries. There is little point in trying to make comparisons over such long periods of time and between economics of different regions. But it is of some significance that as late as 1750 Britain was exporting corn equal to the subsistence requirements of about one quarter of the total population (see Figures 1 and 2 on page 55), was consuming over 7 million gallons of spirits (or about $1\frac{1}{2}$ gallons per head of the population per year) and three times as much tea as the rest of Europe put together, and was in other ways providing evidence of having an economic surplus, even if – as in the case of gin-drinking – this was spent in an unhealthy way.

There was a small section of society which enjoyed a very high standard of living. In 1774 Parson Woodforde had a 'very elegant dinner' at Christ Church, Oxford, of which he wrote:

> The first course was, part of a large cod, a chine of mutton, some soup, a chicken pye, pudding and roots [root vegetables] etc. Second course, pidgeons and asparagus, a fillet of veal with mushrooms and high sauce with it, rosted sweetbreads, and lobster, apricot tart and in the middle a pyramid of syllalub [junket] and jellies. We had a desert of fruit after dinner, and Madeira, white Port and red to drink as wine. We were all very cheerful and merry.

At the other end of the social scale there were those who suffered from unemployment, low and irregular wages, and were the victims of disease and hunger. These were the people who took part in food riots, lived in squalor in town or countryside and whose lives give the lie to the confident claims that 'the eighteenth century was neat, well dressed and nicely appointed', as the Hammonds claim. Even the employed labourer was little better off. Arthur Young described an ideal diet for a labourer – an ideal which many never reached and yet one which we might find grimly poor:

> *Day One:* Two pounds of bread, made of a mixture of wheat, rye and potato. Two ounces of cheese. Two pints of beer.
> *Day Two:* Three portions of soup made from lean beef, pease,

mealy potatoes, ground rice, onions, celery and salt and water.
Day Three: Rice pudding made with half a pound of rice, a
little sugar and two quarts of skim milk.
Day Four: Quarter of a pound of fat beef and a quarter pound
of potatoes baked together. Beer.
Day Five: Rice pudding.
Day Six: Bread, Cheese and beer.
Day Seven: (Sunday) Fat beef, potatoes, cheese, beer.

So much for the 'roast beef of olde Englande'. And yet the
average Englishman in the eighteenth century was better off than
his European counterpart. Young went to France in the late 1780s
and reported that the French labouring classes 'are 76 per cent
less at their ease; worse fed, clothed and worse supported than the
same class in England'.

Perhaps this helps to explain why there was little resentment
among the English people in the eighteenth century. They lived in
what seemed to be fairly static society – at least until the 1750s.
People writing in the 1740s illustrated their arguments on the
economy by quoting from what they knew of King's work
which had been compiled fifty or more years before. In the pre-
industrial society, with its low standard of living and economic
stagnation, there was no 'rising expectation' that things would
change other than slowly and spasmodically, while they might
very well get worse as the result of plague or a series of bad
harvests. And yet it was this society which was to experience the
great changes which are summed up in the term 'Industrial
Revolution'.

3. The Changing Face
of the Countryside
in the Eighteenth Century

Land magnates

Gregory King's table (see Table 2, pages 24–5) shows the variety of people involved in the agricultural industry. The great land-owners tended to regard an estate more as a source of income than as a unit of production. It is true that most estates had a home farm which produced the food required by the 'big house' and its dependants. But the greater part of the estate was rented out to tenant farmers, and it was the rent-income rather than the produce of the home farm which was of prime interest to the magnates whose rent-roll might be as little as £1,000 a year or, as in the case of the Duke of Bedford in 1732, as high as £31,000.

We have already seen that there was a flow of new entrants into the ranks of the landowners. Many of the newcomers had made their first fortunes in industry, trade or commerce. Others had enriched themselves at the public expense: the second Earl of Nottingham was a Secretary of State for four years during which time he made £37,000 for himself; Robert Walpole spent £500,000 on building palaces and homes for himself, at the same time spending £25,000 a year on personal expenses. James Brydges was the fourth son of an impoverished Herefordshire gentleman. While Paymaster-General of the Forces, he made enough to build himself a palace at Canons sufficiently large to back up his new title of Duke of Chandos, while he also had £25,000 in stocks and shares and an income of £10,000 from his estates.

Whether they came from politics, law, trade or commerce the new owners brought to their landowning the habits of money-making and profit-seeking which had enabled them to amass their fortunes in the first place. Merchants and traders in particular brought to the business of agriculture the habit of ploughing back some at least of its profits, so ensuring that their estates remained prosperous and a safe investment for the family wealth.

The newcomers bought their estates from one or other of the older landed families who had fallen on hard times. For if there was a constant flow into the ranks of the upper class there was also a similar flow out. One or two spendthrift, gambling successors might easily run through the family wealth and be unable to meet even the interest on the mortgage, so that they might have to sell up. A larger than usual number of daughters, each of them taking part of the estate as a dowry, might cut down an estate to the point where the owner would be forced to sell the rest.

Freeholders and tenants

The people who owned smaller estates and the freeholders in the villages, as well as the tenant-farmers, regarded their land not merely as a source of income but as a unit of production – which also of course brought in their income. Some tenant-farmers rented land from more than one owner; some might see one landlord sell out to be replaced by one of the newcomers, but their own work would go on much as before. A change of landowner need not have affected the use of the land or the techniques being employed. However if the new owner was an active and efficient businessman–owner then the whole estate was affected. A Coke of Holkham or a vigorous Duke of Bedford organized the enclosure of farms, the drainage of vast areas and other general improvements which required a vast capital outlay but ensured increased output as well as increased productivity per acre and per workman. The landowner might then gain from higher rents while the tenant gained from the sale of the increased output. Coke raised the rentals from his Norfolk estates from £2,200 a year to £20,000 a year within forty years and Townshend also multiplied his rent-income by ten by the adoption of many of the new farming techniques discussed in Chapter 4.

The wage-earners

At the base of the rural hierarchical structure were the wage-earning labourers who owned no land and had few rights on common land. King's table showed that in 1688 the members of this class depended on charity or poor relief since their income was less than their expenditure. The bulk of this expenditure was on food and drink. A fall in food prices if accompanied by stable or perhaps rising wages meant a rise in real wages. This rise made this class a very large group of consumers eager to buy some of the consumer-durables which the better-off already enjoyed – pots and pans, clothing and shoes, furniture and ornaments. It was the demands of this group of rural labourers that helped stimulate industrial change.

The land market

Between 1680 and 1740 there was a change in the pattern of landownership as the possessors of already large estates took over more and more land from the owners of smaller estates. One explanation for this take-over was that the owners of the larger estates – often members of the peerage and of the House of Lords – enjoyed long periods in political office and so were able to amass the money needed to buy out the smaller gentry, whose political ambitions tended to find outlet in local affairs where the chance of making money was much less. Robert Walpole's son Horace drew £$\frac{1}{4}$ million from various government jobs and neither he nor his fellows thought that at all strange. Lord Hardwicke regarded public office and its rewards as a sort of rich man's Poor Law system. He wrote: 'I look upon such pensions as a kind of obligation upon the Crown for the support of ancient noble families.' This was to ignore the fact that few of the families were at all ancient, and the 'pensions' were large enough to enable the recipients to go on amassing larger estates, where better-qualified stewards and other officials would be employed to ensure that the rent-income continued to rise and that tenants used their land well.

Estates also grew because of marriage. The Bedfords, the Pelhams and many other families arrived at their greatness as a result of the gradual and patient seeking out of wives who would bring an estate if they were heiresses, or at least a portion of an estate as dowries. The head of a landed family was often merely the titular landowner. The legal devices of strict settlement and entail prevented him from selling any part of the estate except in the case of complete bankruptcy. This gave him an income for life, but also ensured that the estate was handed down in its entirety – or indeed, if there had been later acquisitions, even augmented in size.

The high land-tax during the long years of the anti-French Wars of 1690 to 1715 had a greater effect on the income of the owners of small estates who had no other source of income from which to pay the tax than it had on those owners who could pay the tax out of their income from trade, commerce, law or politics. When the level of tax fell during peacetime, the fall in prices affected the incomes of the owners of small and probably less efficient estates, and was another factor in the process of forcing some to sell up to larger and more efficient owners.

There was also a great extension of the system of land mortgage which enabled an owner to raise a mortgage on his land and, provided the interest on the loan was paid each year, prevented the creditor from compelling the owner to sell his land to repay the original loan. A mortgage became in effect a long-term loan. There were many businessmen willing to make such loans, particularly since there was a guarantee that a good estate would always be able to pay the interest, while there were always investment-seekers willing to take up the loan should the first creditor wish to get his hands on his money again. This mortgage system provided owners of large estates with a method of obtaining the money needed for dowries without having to part with any of the estate; younger sons, unable to get any portion of the estate because of entail and strict settlement, were also provided with capital from such mortgages. Very often the dowry money was used by the new husband to buy land to add to an existing estate. Thus the mortgage system led to the creation of more and larger estates. It also provided the capital required for the conspicuous consumption of the landed magnates who built lavish homes, furnished them grandly and spent vast sums on the 'Grand Tour' of Europe.

The Georgian upper-class had several advantages over their Stuart forefathers. The professions of architect and furniture designer had grown and become even more sophisticated; the rich had grown accustomed to living in style and opulence – which had been a novelty for some of their fathers – and their expectations of what was grand or upper-class were even greater and grander. One of the hallmarks of the upper class has always been lavish expenditure. One is reminded of the Rolls Royce advertisement: 'If you have to ask the price, then this car isn't for you.' The upper class has never had to ask the price of anything – its members have always spent as freely as Robert Walpole did when he built a palace for himself at Houghton in Norfolk. The house took thirteen years to build and involved moving a whole village which detracted from the view. William Kent designed the furniture and decoration, Michael Rysbrack the chimney-pieces and statuary, while Europe was scoured to find the pictures to adorn the walls. The cost is unknown but must have approached that of Audley End (£190,000). Walpole was also building the Old Lodge at Richmond Park (£14,000) and renting a London house in Arlington Street for £300 a year. The upkeep of all these houses was enormous: at Houghton he employed seventy-seven weeders in the gardens, his wine bill was £1,000 a year and his personal expenditure between 1714 and 1717 was £90,000.

But the mortgage system had a great effect indirectly on land-usage and on farming techniques. When an owner mortgaged off only a small portion of his estate, the interest payment would have been relatively small. As he mortgaged off even more, and perhaps finally arrived at the point where he had mortgaged the whole estate, the interest charges were more of a burden. At the same time there was a steady rise in the expenditure of families learning to live the good life. There were then twin pressures to ensure that the estate yielded as high a rent-income as was possible. This led to a search for new techniques of farming (see Chapter 4), and for tenants prepared to pay higher rents for short-term leases of farms which had to be made more productive to enable the tenant to pay those higher rents.

But another effect of the twin sisters – entail and mortgage – was a drying up of the land-market towards the middle of the eighteenth century. Merchants, eager to acquire land and build grand houses, found that there was less land coming on to the market after 1750 than 'at any time in the two previous centuries', according to Professor Mingay in *English Landed Society in the Eighteenth Century* (1963). Merchants, traders and others who might otherwise have invested their money in land and an estate were then compelled to look elsewhere for outlets for their invest-ments. If the availability of investment capital is one essential factor in enabling a country to take off into industrialization, then it has to be said that the changing pattern of landownership was indirectly at least a factor in making such capital available to borrowers in the mid-eighteenth century.

Searching for incomes from the estate

We have seen that there were increasing pressures to raise the income being derived from landed estate. One method of so raising income was to make the estate that much more efficient as a farming unit.

Not all English landowners took part in the development which has earned the title of the Agrarian Revolution. Some were too old, others not interested enough in changing the traditional methods which had brought them wealth. But the changes that taken together made up that Agrarian Revolution were in part the work of the upper classes. In the 1720s the Duke of Somerset took a keen interest in his tenants' farming and kept a notebook on matters of special interest. Sir Robert Walpole, although Prime Minister from 1721 until 1742, always opened the letters from his steward or gamekeeper before reading the state papers. His brother-in-law Lord Townshend was not the first to use turnips, as his nickname seems to suggest, but he did extend their use on his estates and tried to make popular the four-course rotation method which helped to make farms both more productive and more profitable.

At Wentworth the Marquess of Rockingham farmed 2,000 acres himself, and was personally involved in experiments to see how lime and manure improved turnip yield. He had two model farms, one using Kentish methods and one using methods popular in Hertfordshire. Lord Howe wrote a paper for the Board of Agriculture's report on the West Riding; in 1722 Lord Sheffield founded at Lewes in Sussex a society for the 'encouragement of agriculture, manufacture and industry'.

A later generation of climbing middle classes would have shared the opinion of Gwendoline Fairfax who in Oscar Wilde's *The Importance of Being Earnest* said that she was 'glad to say I have never seen a spade'. The rural upper class however was best represented by the Countess of Circumference in Evelyn Waugh's *Decline and Fall*. Her axiom, 'dig it and dung it', echoing round the school sportsfield was a piece of down-to-earth advice which the upper classes would have understood. George III, giving the royal lead to his upper-class followers, enjoyed his nickname of 'farmer George', while the Earl of Leicester (Coke of Holkham), the Duke of Bedford (at Woburn Abbey) and Lord Althorp were prominent in developing new and profitable methods of stock-breeding.

Parts of estates consisted of land on which new urban developments might be promoted. This was a major feature of estate development in the nineteenth century. In 1826 Lord Grosvenor (who was also Duke of Westminster and Viscount of Belgrave) induced Parliament to pass an act to allow him to exploit the building possibilities of his estate at what is now Belgravia. Not many people realize as they walk around the shops in Grosvenor Place and the other parts of Belgravia that they are treading on the estate of one of the country's richest families, part of whose income comes from the rents they get from the valuable properties which they have built themselves or allowed other people to build on their land.

Such estate development has a long history. John Evelyn wrote in 1665 about the development of the Bloomsbury area by the Earl of Southampton. On the site now occupied by the British Museum the Duke of Montagu had a vast house while the Bedford family's developments of their estate can be traced in the family names which dominate part of this area. Russell, Tavistock, Bedford, Woburn are all remembered in streets, squares or roads, and all bring in the large income required by the upper classes. They made their first development in 1775 when they built Bedford Square; now the once grand houses are offices for architects and publishers. They also owned the Covent Garden area and from 1630 onwards they had begun to develop that area north of their own town houses on the Strand.

Similar developments added to the incomes of families such as the Butes. While the Marquis lived in Cardiff Castle and watched that fishing village grow first to a town and then to a city, he also supervised the development of the land which he owned and on which he built, or allowed to be built, docks, railway stations, hotels, shopping centres and houses – all providing him with a rental of hundreds of thousands of pounds *per annum*. The Durham family were similarly fortunate in that the Industrial Revolution's demand for coal could be satisfied only by the development of coal-seams on its estates. The sort of income it enjoyed can be indicated by the 'radical' Lord Durham's statement in the 1830s that a man could 'jog along on £40,000 a year', and this when the average workman earned about 50p a week. No wonder he was known after this as 'King Jog'.

Other landowners promoted the local turnpike trust or canal as methods of improving access to their estates and to the minerals on those estates, so helping make the produce of the estate (agricultural and mineral) more readily available to the nearest town. In the eighteenth century the Duke of Bridgewater increased his income by about £40,000 a year by building a canal from his coal-mines at Worsley to the developing town of Manchester. In 1773 the Earl of Thanet built the Skipton Canal to carry lime and limestone from his estates. The Marquess of Stafford cut a canal to serve his ironworks in Shropshire. The development of the Welsh coal valleys owed a good deal to the Bute family whose name is commemorated in the docks and estates in Cardiff bearing the family name.

Few English landowners would have been as stupid or unenterprising as the Youssoupoff family in Russia. In the eighteenth century the head of the family Prince Nicolas Youssoupoff, commenting on the commercial activities of the English aristocracy, declared of his estate- 'Archangeleskoie is not run for profit.' Such a cavalier attitude to investment-opportunities continued to be the hallmark of the Russian nobility. The last of the Youssoupoffs in possession before the revolution swept their class away was Prince Felix. He recorded: 'One of our estates on the Caucasus stretched for one hundred and twenty miles along the Caspian Sea; crude petroleum was so abundant that the soil seemed soaked with it, and the peasants used it to grease their cart wheels.' An English milord would have known how to develop such a vast potential in the age which made multi-millionaires of oil magnates such as the Rockefellers.

After 1750 there was a rise in corn prices. These provided the tenants with a higher income and the landowner with a chance to charge higher rents when leases were renewed. These higher incomes for tenant and landlord provided the investment-capital which both of them required to make the estate more productive than it had been before.

Changing the face of the countryside

The almost continual increase in agricultural output was achieved through a combination of changes in land-usage. Gregory King estimated that about 10 million acres – or one quarter of the country – were uncultivated in 1688. In 1795 the Board of Agriculture estimated that there were less than 8 million acres left uncultivated, most of it being wastes and moors which required to be drained before it could be brought under cultivation. But during the eighteenth century over 2 million acres were brought into production and this helped boost the total figures of production.

There was also a change from the open-field system to one of consolidated and enclosed farms. The open-field system had disappeared many years ago in some areas, notably in those covered by the old Danelaw of the tenth century. In other areas enclosure had taken place on a large scale during Tudor and Stuart times when the high demand for English wool made sheep-farming very attractive and encouraged landowners to enlarge their farms by enclosing what had once been commons and wastes, and by ejecting tenant-farmers. But in the south and parts of East Anglia the system of open-field farming still prevailed at the beginning of the eighteenth century.

Under this system the land around a village was divided into three major 'fields'. Each farmer – whether freeholder or tenant – was allocated a number of strips. In one of the three fields Farmer Jones might have been allocated anything from three to 200 strips, each separated from the other by the strips allocated to other farmers. This scattered distribution of land in the one field ensured that no one farmer received all the well-drained land while another had only the stony land. In the Christian traditions of the countryside it seemed fair that each should have a share of the good along with a share of the less desirable. Farmer Jones would have another allocation of scattered strips in Fields B and C. He and all his neighbours wasted a good deal of time in moving their ploughs from one strip to another when cultivation got under way. There was also a great deal of wasteland since each strip was separated from its neighbour by wide, grassy, uncultivated banks known as *balks*, on which grew all kinds of grasses and weeds, seed from which might then spread among the nearby strips under cultivation.

Village agriculture under this open-field system followed a traditional three-year cycle of crop rotation. In year one a field was ploughed and wheat sown; in year two a crop of peas would be sown; while in year three the field was left to lie fallow so that nature might restore the soil. Here again was a great waste of resources, in that about one-third of all the agricultural land was left uncultivated each year.

It is not surprising that this system had many critics among the commentators on agricultural affairs from the sixteenth century onwards. Time and land was wasted on quite a large scale in a system where tradition ruled, and where traditional patterns of land-usage made it almost impossible for an enterprising farmer to introduce any innovations such as the planting of root crops.

When the harvest had been gathered in, the wheatfields were thrown open as pasture land for the animals and the land manured as a result. Until artificial fertilizers were invented there was no other way of manuring the land. But the throwing together of all the animals of a village in field and on common meant that it was easy for disease to spread among herds and flocks, while it was almost impossible for an innovator to introduce any of the new ideas of stock-breeding.

In addition to the three large 'fields' each village had its commons and wastes where every villager had the right to pasture animals and collect wood for fuel, as well as to gather nuts and berries as an addition to the poor diet. These commons covered vast areas of up to 7,000 acres in a village and 265,000 acres in the West Riding of Yorkshire, which made of England a green – if not always a pleasant – land. But the existence of such large tracts of uncultivated land meant that a good deal of England's main source of wealth, the land, was being underused.

All this was slowly changed during the eighteenth century by a continuous and accelerating process of enclosure, which was one of the necessary conditions of agricultural improvement, as Young made clear: '... no small farmer would effect such great things as have been done in Norfolk. Inclosing, marling, and keeping a stock of sheep large enough for folding, belong absolutely and exclusively to great farmers. ... Split them into tenures of an hundred pounds a year, you will find nothing but beggars and weeds in the whole county.'

Enclosure

In 1700 about half the arable land of the country was cultivated under the open-field system. By 1830 almost all agricultural land was enclosed. Sometimes the largest landowner in the village might persuade the other farmers to agree to private enclosure, and negotiations would take place by which strips were exchanged so that our mythical Farmer Jones had all his landholding consolidated in one farm. During these negotiations some tenants might have lost their right to farm – perhaps because their leases had run out, perhaps because they were unable to prove any legal claim to the land although their family had traditionally been allocated a certain acreage. In some villages the larger landowner might have bought out some if not all of the freeholders as well as the leases of some of the tenant farmers. This would allow him to have a large, consolidated farm at his disposal – either for working under the management of his own bailiff or for renting out to one efficient tenant.

We have no record of the number of such private arrangements, which did not require any parliamentary approval. We do know that from 1700 onwards there was an increasing use of private acts of Parliament, brought in by landowners as a method of enforcing enclosure. The table shows that the number of such private acts increased dramatically after 1760 by which time prices were rising:

Table 3 *Private Enclosure Acts Passed 1710–1810*

Date	Private Acts
1710–10	1
1710–20	8
1720–30	33
1730–40	35
1740–50	38
1750–60	156
1760–70	424
1770–80	642
1780–90	287
1790–1800	506
1800–10	906

We know that the bulk of these parliamentary enclosures took place in the corn-growing districts of the East Midlands, the east and north-east, whereas previous enclosures tended to be concentrated in the pastoral and mixed farming districts of Leicestershire and Buckinghamshire where, wrote Defoe, 'All the gentlemen hereabouts are graziers, though all the graziers are not gentlemen.' After 1760 it was the rising price of corn which stimulated landlords.

Some Enclosure Acts were concerned only with the enclosure of what had been common land or wastes which perhaps had been considered worthless when the price of corn was low but which became marginally valuable as the price of corn rose. Other acts were concerned with the enclosure of arable fields cultivated under the open-field system (in which common land was also involved).

An enclosure act

If a landlord decided to go for a private act he was obliged to call a meeting of the freeholders of the land in the parish or village and get the consent of the owners of four-fifths of the land involved before taking any further step. Such agreement was not too difficult to obtain where the landowner himself may have owned something approaching four-fifths or where an enterprising owner let it be known that he was prepared to buy out any freeholders who objected to enclosure.

When agreement had been reached, a notice to this effect had to be fastened to the church door telling the rest of the villagers what had been agreed. The various tenants – leaseholders, copyholders, cottagers and so on – were then invited to make known their objections to the freeholders within three weeks. There are some examples of angry villagers tearing down such notices, but in general the social discipline of the village was sufficiently strong to ensure that the will of the largest landowner would prevail. The smaller tenants were also aware that they probably had in-sufficient influence socially and politically to be able to stop the proceedings which would then get under way.

The freeholders then applied to Parliament for a private act. We can trace the progress of one such application, for the village of Stillington, as it made its way through the House of Commons:

January 17 1766
   A Petition of Stephen Croft, the Younger, Esquire, Lord of the Manor of Stillington, in the County of York, and Owner of several Estates, within the said Manor and Parish of Stillington;

of the Reverend James Worsley, Clerk, Patron of the Vicarage
of Stillington, of the Reverened Lawrence Sterne, Clerk, Vicar
of the said Parish, and of William Stainforth Esquire, and of
several other Persons, whose Names are thereunto subscribed,
being also Owners of Cottages, Estates, and other Properties,
within the said Parish; was presented to the House and read;
Setting forth, That, within the said Manor and Parish is a
Common called Stillington Common, and also several Open
Fields which, in their present Situation, are incapable of Improvement; and that it would be of great Advantage to the
Persons interested if they were inclosed and divided into specific
Allotments, and all Right of Common in the said Parish, were
extinguished, or if the said Common was so inclosed, and a
Power given to the several Proprietors and Owners of Estates
to inclose the same; and after inclosing, all Right of Common
was to cease: And therefore praying, that Leave may be given
to bring in a Bill for the Purposes aforesaid . . .
Ordered, That Leave be given to bring in a Bill, pursuant to the
Prayer of the said Petition: And that Mr. Cholmley, Sir George
Savile and Sir Joseph Mawbey, do prepare, and bring in, the
same.

February 3 1766
   Mr. Cholmley presented to the House a Bill for inclosing and
dividing the Common, Waste Grounds, Open Fields, Open
Meadows, Grounds, within the Parish of Stillington, in the
County of York: And the same was received, and read the First
Time.
Resolved, That the Bill be read a Second Time.

February 10 1766
   A Bill for inclosing and dividing the Common Waste
Grounds, Open Fields, Open Meadows, Grounds and Ings,
within the Parish of Stillington, in the County of York, was
read a second time.

February 27 1766

Mr. Cholmley reported from the Committee, to whom the Bill for inclosing and dividing the Common Waste Grounds, Open Fields, Open Meadows, Grounds, within the Parish of Stillington, was committed. That the Committee had examined the Allegations of the Bill; and found the same to be true; and that the Parties concerned had given their Consent to the Bill, to the Satisfaction of the Committee, except the Proprietors of Sixty Acres of Land, in the said Fields, and Ings, who refused their Consent to the Inclosure, and the Proprietors of Twenty-seven Acres, who were not at Home when Application was made for the Consents; and that the whole of the said Fields contain Six hundred Acres, or thereabouts; and also, except the Proprietors of Eight Common Rights, who refused to consent, and the Proprietors of Seven Common Rights, who were from Home, when Application was made for their Consents; and that the whole Number of Common Rights are Eighty-nine; and that no Person appeared before the Committee to oppose the Bill; and that the Committee had gone through the Bill, and made several Amendments thereunto; which they had directed him to report to the House; and he read the Report in his Place; and afterwards delivered the Bill, with the Amendments, in at the Clerk's Table: Where the Amendments were Once read throughout; and then a Second Time, One by One; and, upon the Question severally put thereupon, were agreed to by the House; and several Amendments were made, by the House, to the Bill.

Ordered, That the Bill, with the Amendments, be ingrossed.

March 3 1766

A Bill for inclosing and dividing the Common Waste Grounds, Open Fields, Open Meadows, Grounds, within the Parish of Stillington, was read the Third Time.

Resolved, That the Bill do pass. . . .

Ordered, That Mr. Cholmley do carry the Bill to the Lords, and desire their Concurrence.

Gains and losses

When land was enclosed the more enterprising landowners were able, if willing, to introduce the new methods of arable farming and stock-breeding, either on their own farms or on tenants' farms. Coke raised the income from his estates and Young wrote: 'If the melancholy wastes and commons are enclosed and drained then land yielding at present 3s. 6d. or 4s. 6d. an acre can be made to yield 10s. an acre.'

So among the gainers were the owners of enclosed land whose rent-income rose. In the case of the small freeholder of a consolidated farm or in the case of the successful tenant-farmer there was also a gain in that their incomes rose – from the sale of produce from their more productive farms. Sometimes this increased income was spent in a form of conspicuous consumption which Young condemned:

> I see sometimes, for instance, a pianoforte in a farmer's parlour, which I always wish was burnt; a livery servant is sometimes found and a postchaise to carry their daughters to assemblies. Those ladies are sometimes educated at expensive boarding schools, and the sons often at the University to be made parsons, but all these things imply a departure from that line which separates these different orders of beings, let all those things and all the folly, frippery, foppery, expense and anxiety that belongs to them remain among gentlemen.

Some people lost by enclosing. A freeholder with a small allocation might find that the cost of hedging plus his share of the costs of promoting the passage of the Enclosure Act might have left him too poor to be able to afford to invest in new buildings, machinery or stock. Some of these sold out and made their way to the nearest towns; others sold out and became labourers in the countryside. But the greatest and most immediate loss was felt by the rural poor, who had no right to land before enclosure, but had traditional rights on common and waste, where they pastured an animal or two, and found wood for fuel, and extra food in the form of rabbits, or fish from the nearby stream. There is a good deal of evidence that the diet of this large group of people was poorer after enclosure than it had been before. A contemporary poet, William Howitt, noted:

The enclosure system has been conducted upon the principles that 'Unto him that hath shall be given and from him that hath not shall be taken away even that which he hath', the consequence being that our poor population, stripped of all their common rights, have been thrown upon the parish, their little flock of sheep, their few cows, their geese, their pigs are all gone and no help left them to eke out their small earnings.

These people would also have been badly affected by the rise in bread prices resulting from the higher price of corn after 1760, a price which rose even higher during and immediately after the Napoleonic Wars. In 1815 the price of a four-pound loaf was 1s 2d (7p) although the agricultural labourer's wage was only 8s (40p). People who had once despised rye-bread were all the more resentful when they were unable to afford the wheaten bread to which they had become accustomed. When on top of this the government imposed the Corn Laws in 1815 to prevent the importation of cheap foreign corn, cottagers and wage-earning labourers were particularly badly affected, as a contemporary poem made clear:

> Ye coop us up and tax our bread
> And wonder why we pine;
> But ye are fat and round and red,
> And fill'd with tax-bought wine.
> Thus, twelve rats starve, while three rats thrive,
> (Like you on mine and me)

> When fifteen rats are caged alive,
> With food for nine and three,
> Why are ye call'd 'my lord' and 'squire'
> While fed by mine and me,
> And wringing food and clothes and fire
> From bread-tax'd misery?

Arthur Young was a firm believer in the new methods of farming. But even he was critical of some of the effects of enclosure. He wrote:

> Go to an alehouse kitchen of an old enclosed country, and there you will see the origin of poverty and poor rates. For whom are they to be sober? For whom are they to save? (Such are their questions) For the parish? If I am diligent, shall I have to leave to build a cottage? If I am sober, shall I have land for a cow? If I am frugal, shall I have half an acre of potatoes? You offer no motives; you have nothing but a parish officer and a workhouse! Bring me another pot [of ale].

In 1799 England had already been at war with France for six years and had also suffered the first of what was to prove to be a series of bad harvests. An Anglican clergyman, Revd William Warren, wrote:

> 'Ah, Sir,' said my new acquaintance, 'time was when these commons enabled the poor man to support his family, and bring up his children. Here he could turn out his cow and pony, feed his flock of geese, and keep his pig. But the Enclosures have deprived him of these advantages. The labourer has now only his 14d per day to keep himself, his wife, and perhaps five or six children, when bread is 3d per pound, and wheat 14s per bushel. The consequence is, the parish must now assist him. Poor-rates increase to a terrible height. The farmer grumbles, and grows hard-hearted. The labourer, knowing that others must maintain his family, becomes careless or idle, or a spendthrift, whilst his

wife and children are obliged to struggle with want, or to apply to a surly overseer for a scanty allowance.'

In Parliament there were those who spoke only of the gains, as did Sir John Sinclair, who declared in 1795:

The difference between the size of cattle and sheep now and in the reign of Queen Anne when half the stock of the Kingdom were fed on commons is hardly to be credited. In 1710 the cattle and sheep sold at Smithfield Market weighed, on average, as follows:—

Cattle, 370 lb; Calves, 50 lb; Sheep, 28 lb; Lambs, 18 lb.
Now they weigh:—
Cattle, 800 lb; Calves, 143 lb; Sheep, 80 lb; Lambs, 50 lb.

The increase is to be attributed to the improvements which have been effected within the last 60 years, and the feeding of our young stock in good and enclosed pastures instead of wastes and commons.

But there were many MPs who spoke only of the losses suffered as a result of enclosure as did one MP in 1797:

... the commoners and other persons entitled to the right of common, or lands intended to be enclosed, will be deprived of an inestimable privilege, which they now enjoy, of turning a certain number of their cows, calves and sheep, on and over the said land; a privilege that enables them ... to maintain themselves and their families in the depth of winter. ... In addition they can now supply the grazier with young and lean stock at reasonable price. ... A more ruinous effect of the enclosure will be the almost total depopulation of their towns, now filled with bold and hardy husbandmen ... driving them from want and necessity into the manufacturing towns, where the very nature of their employment, over the loom or the forge, soon wastes their strength. ...

The 'total depopulation' did not in fact take place. On the contrary all the evidence shows that the population of the rural areas grew almost as quickly as did the populations of the new and developing urban areas. There was a constantly high demand for labour even in the enclosed villages. Fencing, hedging and ditching had to be done, and the increasingly high price for corn tended to increase the acreage under the plough and accordingly the demand for labourers. The breaking up of the common and its conversion into arable land needed a massive labour force in an age when agriculture was a labour-intensive industry. The creation of large stocks of cattle and sheep required more stockmen and shepherds as well as labour to build the sheds and other buildings on the new and larger farms.

In 1798 John Middleton reported on the state of Middlesex after enclosure:

It may farther be observed, that commons are entirely defective in the great article of labour; but no sooner does an enclosure take place, than the scene is agreeably changed from a dreary waste to the more pleasing one, of the same spot appearing all animation, activity and bustle. Every man capable of performing such operations, is furnished with plenty of employment, in sinking ditches and drains, in making banks and hedges, and in planting quicks and trees. Nor are the wheelwright, carpenter, smith and other rural artificers under the necessity of being idle spectators of the scene, since abundance of work will be found for them in the erection of farm-houses and the necessary appendages thereto; and in the forming and making [of] roads, bridges, gates, stiles, implements of husbandry etc. Even after a few years, when these kind of temporary exertions are over, by the whole being brought into a regular system of husbandry, it will still continue to provide both food and employment for a very increased population.

4. The Changing Nature
of British Farming

Land-improvement

Land-improvement was both the cause and the result of enclosure, as Young showed by making 'inclosing' the first in his list of improving methods used in Norfolk in 1771:

Arthur ... to give a slight review of the husbandry which has rendered the name of this county so famous in the farming world. ... Great improvements have been made by means of the following:
First: By inclosing.
Second: By a spirited use of marl [powdered rock and lime] and clay.
Third: By the introduction of an excellent rotation of crops.
Fourth: By the culture of turnips well hand-hoed.
Fifth: By the culture of clover and ray-grass.
Sixth: By landlords granting long leases.
Seventh: By the county being divided chiefly into large farms.

On the question of leases – the sixth point in Young's list – there is some dispute. It seems that improvement was furthered when the landowner made a short-term lease of seven, fourteen or twenty-one years and insisted on writing 'improvement clauses' into such leases. It was essential that good tenants be found to run the tenanted land, and one benefit of the short lease was that the landowner could get rid of inefficient tenants when the lease ran out. The knowledge that failure to improve would lead to the non-renewal of a lease must have acted as a spur to other tenants, and so helped make an estate that much more efficient.

Landlords and freeholders farming for themselves had to be prepared to plough back a portion of their profits each year if they wanted to continue to raise the productivity of their land. Landed magnates had capital available from mortgages, commercial ventures, trading interests or political speculation. They could improve a large estate and benefit a number of tenants who might individually have been unwilling to undertake a particular improvement or have failed to find the capital required. Examples of such large-ranging investments are the building of a new road, the development of a system of land drainage serving a number of farms on an estate, and the enclosing of farms, which as we shall see was a costly affair. Coke of Holkham, perhaps the most famous of Norfolk's improving landlords, reckoned to plough back 20 per cent of his rent-income each year. He benefited as that income rose each year.

The 'improving' activities of the great magnates were important, although less so than the achievements of what Young called the 'great farmers' who rented farms of between 200 and 500 acres. For some magnates, the involvement in land-improvement was often merely a status-symbol, evidence of a 'contact with science'. George III's setting up of a model farm at Windsor was not the action of a landowner eager to increase his rent-income. It was rather one attempt by this Hanoverian to show his English subjects that he was determined to be English; his model farm was an outward sign of his Englishness.

But there were a number of landed noblemen who were genuinely and even passionately involved in the question of land-improvement. The example of Townshend, Coke, Rockingham, Bedford and other great landowners was put before the rest of the country by the many commentators who wrote articles and books on the new improving methods. Some of these writers were themselves bailiffs on large estates, responsible for seeing that tenants carried out the improving clauses in their leases, and for drawing up plans for further improvements on large estates. They had day-to-day experience of improving methods as well as year-by-year evidence in their accounts of the benefits to be derived from them.

The works of these commentators were read in the mansions of the improving magnates and in the homes of the 'greater tenants'. Some of the latter undertook improvement in simulation of their masters; others were forced to undertake such improvements by the clauses in their leases. While the landlord provided some of the investment-capital the tenant was obliged to provide his share – in the form of machinery, stock and labour. The higher rents demanded by the landlords proved to be a stimulus since the tenants had to produce larger cash-incomes from selling in the markets.

The magnates and the tenants of large farms led the way. Smaller freeholders, lower down in the social scale, came under great pressure particularly during the long periods of falling prices. Smaller farms became increasingly uneconomical, especially when commons were enclosed. After 1750 there was a steady decline in the number of such owners. Many sold out to the owners of the nearby large estate, sometimes using the money to establish themselves as small-scale industrialists.

For those who did not own any land but who had managed to eke out an existence by virtue of their rights on common, wastes, woods, heaths and moors, life was even worse after enclosure. It was the change in the fortunes of this class which inspired most of the complaints made about the new land-usage. These had the choice of remaining in the countryside as wage-earning labourers or leaving that countryside to seek work in the nearest developing town. Until recently it was assumed that there was a massive rural depopulation as a result of the increased introduction of the new farming methods. We now know that this was not true. Indeed some rural areas actually increased their populations – almost every parish in Holland (Lincolnshire) increased its population and this in spite of the fact that there was almost no industrial development in the region during this period. In 1797 Sir Frederick Eden wrote:

> Deserted villages in Great Britain now are only to be found in the fictions of poetry. Our agricultural parishes are better stocked now than they were one hundred years ago when industry had not purged the country of its superfluous mouths and the visionary evils ascribed to the existence of commercial and agricultural capitalists did not exist.

The flow of people from the country into the towns consisted of the surplus male population, the result of that increase in birth rate and/or decrease in death rate which we examined in Chapter 1.

There was a decline in the number of subsistence farmers in England while at the same time there was an increase in the number of wage-earning labourers. This completed the cash-nexus which enmeshed the rural economy. Farmers paid rents and wages, and received incomes from sales of produce in the market, while landowners received rents just as labourers received wages. Any change in the incomes of these three groups (landowners, farmers and labourers) had a great effect on the economy as a whole. This was not the case in Ireland where an increasing population subsisted on plots which were almost constantly being subdivided. Subsistence farmers have little if any surplus money-income. A fall in food prices in a subsistence economy means a fall in incomes for the majority of people and so leads to a fall in the demand for non-agricultural goods. In the English economy a fall in prices meant a rise in the real wages of the wage-earning population, although it meant that the incomes of the tenant-farmer and landowner fell. This only gave them even great incentive to become more efficient and innovative.

New crops and methods

Among the methods by which land might be made more pro-

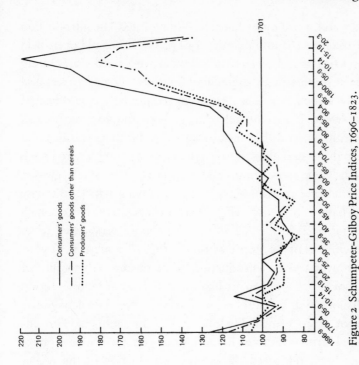

Figure 2 Schumpeter-Gilboy Price Indices, 1696–1823.
After Mitchell and Deane, 1962, pp. 468–9.

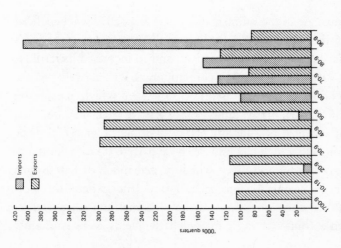

Figure 1 Wheat and Wheat Flour Trade in Great
Britain, 1700–1800 (annual average per decade).
After Mitchell and Deane, 1962, pp. 94–5.

ductive, and hence more valuable, Young listed 'the introduction of an excellent rotation of crops' (see p. 51). In the old open-field system a field was allowed to lie fallow in every third year. During the seventeenth century some English farmers learned a great deal from the Dutch experience gained in reclaiming the land behind the sea-walls. It is noticeable that in both the seventeenth and eighteenth centuries the most progressive farming was done in East Anglia, where the soil was light and sandy and where Dutch methods were more immediately applicable. Artificial grasses, clover, lucernes and sainfoin were sown in fields which otherwise would have lain fallow. These were 'recuperative' crops which 'fixed' nitrogen in the soil and made it more productive when sown with one of the more traditional crops in a subsequent year.

There was also the introduction in the seventeenth century of new root crops, swedes, mangels and the more famous turnip which along with potatoes were 'clearing' crops. The new grasses and root crops provided winter fodder for animals. This encouraged farmers to invest in more valuable stock with the object of improving the breed. Before the introduction of the winter fodder, most animals were killed off in the autumn since the only form of winter feed was the little hay that was 'saved' on the meadow and the natural pasture provided in the commons and fallow fields.

The increase in the number of animals kept alive was beneficial to the farmer: the animals, feeding on the root crops or the fields of artificial grass, manured that land and so increased its fertility. It is not surprising that many contemporary writers welcome the 'golden hoof' of the increased flocks of sheep which, feeding on root crops grown on the sandy soil of East Anglia, manured that land and made it possible for barley or some other cereal to be grown on land which had hitherto been barren. It was a combination of root crops and sheep which turned much of East Anglia from mere heathland into rich barley land where the new 'Norfolk' rotation of turnips, barley, lucernes and spring wheat provided a four-year cycle in which the fields were constantly in use and never, as in the old three-year cycle, under-used for one-third of the time.

Turnips were certainly being sown in Suffolk in the 1640s. In 1726 Defoe reported:

This part of England [Suffolk] is also remarkable for being the first where the feeding and fattening of cattle, both sheep as well as black cattle with turnips, was first practised in England, which is made a very great part of the improvement of their lands to this day; and from whence the practice is spread over most of the east and south parts of England, to the great enriching of the farmers, and increase of fat cattle. And though some have objected against the goodness of the flesh thus fed with turnips, and have fancied it would taste of the root; yet upon experience 'tis found, that at market there is no difference nor can they that buy, single out one joint of mutton from another by the taste.

There was increased interest in the question of animal-breeding and winter fodder was readily available. Robert Bakewell (1725–95) created four new breeds of sheep, the most significant of which was the Leicester breed. Realizing that there was a growing market for fresh meat he concentrated on breeding for meat rather than for wool, for which sheep had been most valued in the past. Bakewell became very wealthy as a result of his success. He was able to charge up to 6,000 guineas for a season's lettings of one of his prize rams. He was less successful in his attempts to produce new breeds of cattle. In this the Collings brothers, with their Durham shorthorn, proved to be masters. They were able to get 1,000 guineas for a prize bull and up to 500 guineas for a prize cow from farmers anxious to improve their own breeds. The vast sums charged by Bakewell, Collings and dozens of others involved in animal-breeding limited their influence. Only a small number of rich farmers would be able to afford the fees and prices charged by the breeders. However, the less well-off, while not having the money to buy in to the new breeding system, did learn from their richer fellow-farmers that care of stock was important and that better feeding would help make animals a more profitable investment.

While new methods of farming were first introduced into East Anglia, there is a good deal of evidence that the knowledge and experience of the Norfolk farmers was made available to farmers throughout the country by the many commentators on agricultural affairs. In 1748 Pehr Kalm, a visitor to this country, wrote the following description of Little Gaddesden in Hertfordshire:

It is well known that here in England it is the custom to sow turnips on the ploughed field as fodder for sheep; on which they go and bait. The turnips consequently stand in the field at this time of the year [March]. The women are in the habit of cutting off the young delicate leaves which shoot out at this season, and prepare them in the same way as we prepare Spinach in Sweden, with a little butter and eat it so with their roast meat. . . . an old farmer told me that they did not sow Rye here as food for people, but that it is sown in the autumn to be used in the following spring, in April, as food for sheep, after they have first eaten up the turnips on the turnip land. The sheep are then turned on to the rye gratten, to gratten on it, till it becomes so short they can find no more to eat. Some farmers afterwards leave the rye to stand and grow, and when it has become ripe, cut it, but most plough up the earth on which it has grown, and prepare it for wheat seed, when, the sheep's dung together with the rye gratten, becomes an excellent manure. . . . Turnips are much sown here in England, as food for the people as well as for all kinds of cattle, such as cows, swine, sheep etc. . . . The arable fields were almost everywhere divided into small inclosures always having hedges around them instead of fences, but when the hedges were cut down a dead-fence was set up. Commonly nearly all these inclosures were quadrilateral, only they sometimes resembled squares, sometimes oblongs.

Thirty years later Arthur Young undertook a tour of the North of England and reported:

> After this, it was ploughed in winter two or three times, and in the beginnings of May planted in rows three feet asunder, the plants [cabbages] two feet from each other. They were only hand hoed, but the operation repeated three or four times: they were first used at Candlemas, for some fat oxen, and they eat them very heartily. They were the Scotch cabbage. The experiment, though not conclusive, gave great hope of success on a larger scale.
>
> In 1765, two acres, a good loamy soil, were planted.... This crop was used between Christmas and Candlemas, and chiefly in a deep snow. Eighteen oxen were fatting on turnips, which being buried by the snow, the beasts were put to cabbages; they all ate them much better than the turnips.... Besides cabbages, Mr. Turner, this year, has two acres of brocoli upon a clay soil.... The design of using them was not in expectation of a great weight, but a food for sheep in the spring.

Jethro Tull (1674–1741) has an undeserved fame as a pioneer. In fact he was a crank who thought that manures were both expensive and unnecessary. He advocated ploughing and hoeing to break up the soil, arguing that this alone would be sufficient to allow good crops to be grown. His hoe resembled a plough, being designed to penetrate down to the soil around the roots of crops. His seed-drill was only one of many such drills invented during the eighteenth century, none of which were widely used until at least the 1780s. Until then seed was sown 'broadcast', the sower scattering the seed as he walked up the ridges left by the plough. Tull also advocated the use of other light iron implements – harrows and rakes – claiming that these could be drawn by a single horse. Until the late seventeenth century most of the farm work had been done by teams of oxen. The horse was more expensive to feed but was stronger and faster than the ox.

However, as a further reminder that the so-called agricultural revolution was at first a mainly East Anglian affair, we have to note that the light iron implements – ploughs, hoes, harrows, rollers and so on – were most suitable for use on the light, sandy soil of East Anglia and were almost useless on the heavy clay soils elsewhere. Not every landowner was as fortunate as was Townshend, whose estate was described by Young:

> In 1730 it was an extensive heath without tree or shrub only a sheep walk to another farm. Such a number of carriages crossed it that they would be a mile abreast in pursuit of the best track. Now in 1760 there is an excellent Turnpike road enclosed on each side with a Quicksett Headge and the whole laid out in enclosures and cultivated in the Norfolk system in superior style. The whole is let at 15 shillings an acre, ten times its original value.

Townshend was fortunate: he had enclosed his land by 1760· Many estates were not enclosed until much later, a reminder that the agricultural changes hardly deserve the description 'revolution' since some of them had been introduced in the 1640s and few of them were in wide use until the end of the eighteenth century.

Agriculture and the Industrial Revolution

We have seen that by the eighteenth century the English economy was relatively more complex and developed than, say, the economies of present-day India or Nigeria. However we have also seen that, relative to the present day, England in the eighteenth century was an undeveloped country in which the majority of people made their living in agriculture. What happened in the agricultural sector was of vital importance to the industrial sector.

English agriculture was the source of much of the investment-capital that was ploughed into industry and transport as well as into urban development. For most of the eighteenth century the industrial labour-force was one which divided its time between work on the land and work at home, in one or other of the many domestic industries. In particular this was true until the 1770s of the textile industry which, as we shall see, was the largest industry outside of agriculture. Celia Fiennes's description of Exeter in 1698 brings out some of the aspects of this industrial-cum-agricultural nexus:

Exeter is a town very well built. The streets are well pitch'd spacious noble streets and a vast trade is carryd on; as Norwitch is for coapes, callamanco and damaske so'this is for serges – there is an increadible quantety of them made and sold in the town; their market day is Fryday which supplys with all things like a faire almost; the markets for meate fowle fish garden things and the dairy produce takes up 3 whole streets, besides the large Market house set on stone pillars which runs a great length on which they lay their packs of serges, just by it is another walke within pillars which is for the yarne; the whole town and country is employ'd for at least 20 mile round in spinning, weaveing, dressing, and scouring, fulling and drying of the serges, it turns the most money in a weeke of anything in England, one weeke with another there is 10,000 pound paid in ready money, sometymes 15,000 pound; the weavers bring in their serges and must have their money which they employ to provide them yarne to goe to work againe; there is alsoe a square court with penthouses round where the malters are with mault, oat meal, but the serge is the chief manufacture; there is a prodigious quantety of their serges they never bring into the market but are in hired roomes which are noted for it, for it would be impossible to have it altogether.

The expanding industrial and urbanized areas had to depend on the native agricultural sector for food as well as for many of the raw materials used in factories and workshops. The urban population had to be fed at a low price if manufacturers were to be enabled to pay low wages which allowed them to retain a large share of the income derived from the sale of their products. Part of this share was ploughed back in investment and allowed further industrial expansion to take place. A failure on the part of the agricultural sector would have meant a slowing down in the industrializing process.

And agriculture did feed the increasing urban population, so enabling the British economy to avoid one of the pitfalls which often faces modern underdeveloped countries when they embark on industrialization and have to divert much of their scarce foreign capital to pay for food imports. The English agricultural sector was so productive that until the 1760s it was a net exporter and so earned the currency to buy foreign imports – of raw cotton, timber, iron ore and so on.

Rising prices after 1760

Low prices were the result of good harvests which led to a high demand for labour so that wages were at least regular and possibly rising. Real wages certainly rose with beneficial effects on the nation's health. These rising real wages were one explanation for the fall in the death rate and rise in the birth rate. A growing population coupled with a rise in real wages were twin forces which helped stimulate industrial expansion.

As Figure 2 on page 55 makes clear prices rose after 1760. The main beneficiaries of this rise were the very groups which had suffered most during the period of falling prices, namely the land-owners and tenant-farmers who had been obliged to pay constant or rising wages although they were receiving falling prices for their produce. The falling prices had compelled them to seek some means of making their farms and estates more efficient and pro-ductive. As prices rose so the incomes for these groups rose – and this also acted as a spur to continue trying to make land even more productive. If five bushels could be produced where previously only four had been grown then, in a period of rising prices, the increased income was more than merely 25 per cent. The increased income from the more highly priced produce itself provided the capital required for further improvement.

The increased incomes to tenants and landowners also enabled these groups to become even more frequent and larger consumers of industrial products. In the language of the economist these classes had a high propensity to consume. An increased demand for consumer goods from the better-off members of rural society encouraged manufacturers in many industries to increase their output, often by introducing new and cheaper methods of production. This in turn enabled them to sell the product at a lower price. Many of these products had in economic terms a high elasticity of demand – a slight fall in price leading to a proportionately larger increase in demand. The manufacturers, using more efficient methods of production, were able to offer their goods at reducing prices which allowed a greater number of people to buy the product. The snowballing effect of such a pattern of supply and demand encouraged other manufacturers to enter the field and so the industrial sector expanded because of the prosperity of the agricultural sector.

5. Industry on the Eve of the Industrial Revolution

Small, rural but capitalist

In Gregory King's table of population (see Table 2, pages 24–5), the total number of artisans, merchants ('by sea' and 'by land') and tradesmen was relatively small, a sign that England and Wales were underdeveloped countries in which the majority of people earned their living from agriculture. The small number of industrial workers used relatively simple and inexpensive tools and equipment. Many of them worked in their own homes for, it was said, 'every cottage had its spinning wheel and every village its loom'.

There were some larger capital investments. Merchant companies such as the East India and Hudson's Bay Companies had large amounts of capital invested in ships and warehouses in England and overseas, as well as stocks in hand. Mining also required a higher than usual capital investment to pay for the sinking of shafts, and the purchase of the winding-gear and later the steam-pump, which Dr Richard Pocock found in Cornish tin-mines in 1750:

> There are to each mine two shafts. . . . One they call the ladder-shaft in which the perpendicular ladders are fixed . . . they are about thirty feet long. . . . The other is called the wem-shaft, from the wem or windlace, turned by a horse, by the help of

which they let down the tub, called a kible, to bring up the ore.... Below the ladders, when they have come to the lode or vein, they burrow down in holes which they call gunnies.... Besides these shafts there is the fire engine shaft, by which they pump the water up by means of the engine, which was invented about forty or fifty years ago by Mr. Newcomen of Dartmouth, and Captain Savory. At the bottom is a hole, about six feet deep, to receive the water which runs from all parts; ... the water is pumped up 24 fathoms to the channel called an audit, which conveys it [away]; this audit is about thirty fathoms from the top, the whole being about 55 fathoms, or 330 feet. The lode or vein of tin (or copper) may be of a different thickness to twelve feet, and they call it a big or a small lode.... A succession of men are always in the mine, except on Sundays. They work eight hours, from six to two, and from two to ten, and from ten to six, and are out of the mine sixteen hours. When they come up, they call it coming to the grass. When the ore is brought up, women and children are employed in breaking it and separating the [waste] from the ore and the tin from the copper.... In the mines in general the lord has a fifteenth [share], and the owner, called the bounder, has a tenth.

There were a number of metal industries already well developed by the middle of the eighteenth century. Lead, tin and copper are non-ferrous metals. These could be smelted and refined in coal-fired furnaces long before this became possible in the iron industry. Because coal was cheap in South Wales, many smelting and refining works had been set up there. The copper and tin were brought from Cornish mines which had once been the sites for smelting and refining works – now rendered uneconomic as the wood-fuel for charcoal-fired furnaces became scarcer and more expensive. Many more times the weight of fuel than of ore was used in smelting. It was therefore cheaper to take the ores from Cornwall to Wales than to take the coal to Cornwall.

Anglesey copper was smelted on the Lancashire coalfields; Derbyshire lead was smelted on the Derbyshire coalfield but well over half the copper smelted in Britain in 1750 was being smelted in Swansea, near the coalfields of South Wales and the sea for import of ore and export of finished product.

The iron industry

The iron industry was to become a key industry in the nineteenth century when railways, steamships and engineering equipment, as well as engines and machines in the textile industry, would be made of iron or its offspring steel. But the iron industry was already an old one when the Industrial Revolution got under way, and as Ashton has shown had been organized on a capitalist basis for many centuries:

> From the earliest period of which we have exact information, ironmaking in this country has been conducted on capitalistic lines – capitalistic not only in that the workers are dependent upon an employer for their raw material and market, but also in that they are brought together in a 'works', are paid wages and perform their duties under conditions not dissimilar to those of any large industry of modern times. The scale of operations has increased enormously: the sapling has become an oak, deep-rooted and widespread; technique has been re-volutionized. But in structure and organization there is no fundamental change.

Before the iron appeared as a finished product it had to undergo a number of processes, all of them involving the use of furnaces requiring large quantities of fuel. The iron ore was smelted in a blast-furnace and the molten metal poured into moulds called pigs which gave the name to the pig-iron product. The pig-iron was then remelted in a small air-furnace and the refined metal used in one of two ways. Some was run off into castings – hence the name cast iron, which was brittle and hard. This was a very suitable material for the manufacture in iron foundries of domestic utensils such as pots and pans. Cast iron was also suitable for the manufacture of cannons and other weapons. The growth of the iron industry in the eighteenth century owed a great deal to the demands for such weapons by the government which was involved in long, costly but successful wars with France for a good deal of that century.

Some refined metal was taken from its air-furnace shop to a forge where it was once again reheated and hammered out by water-driven hammers. The product, known as wrought iron, was more malleable and tensile than cast iron and could stand more strain than the harder cast iron. It was taken to a slitting-mill where it was reheated and passed through grooved rollers which drew the iron out into thinner bars or rods which were then cut for the making of horseshoes, nails, picks, spades, locks, bolts and all sorts of tools.

Unlike the non-ferrous metals, it proved impossible to use coal or coke for the smelting or refining of iron before the eighteenth century. The various furnaces and works involved in the manufacture of the finished product were often widely separated from one another, since each required its own plentiful supply of charcoal which was derived from wood. The ironmasters also needed a plentiful supply of running water to drive the wheel which worked the bellows used in the furnaces and the hammers in the forges. The twin needs for water and wood ensured that ironworks were always in rural settings. When the wood in one area was used up, the ironmasters would dismantle their small furnaces and migrate to another, well-wooded, site. By the beginning of the eighteenth century the iron industry seemed to have passed its peak. Between 1625 and 1635 the output of pig-iron had been about 26,000 tons a year but in the 1720s it was down to about 20,000 tons, most of it being used to make cast-iron goods. Most of the wrought iron and steel produced in England and Wales was made from bar-iron imported from Sweden and Russia.

The centre of the industry had been the Weald with its plentiful supply of wood and running water. Defoe wrote in 1726:

All this part of the country is very agreeably pleasant, whole-some and fruitful, I mean quite from Guildford to this place [Westerham in Kent], and is accordingly overspread with good towns, gentlemen's houses, populous villages . . . and the lands well cultivated; but all on the right hand, that is to say, south, is exceedingly grown with timber, has abundance of waste, and wild grounds and forests and woods, with many large iron-works, at which they cast great quantities of iron caldrons, chimney-backs, furnaces, retorts, boiling pots, and all such necessary things of iron; besides iron cannon, and cannon ball etc., in an infinite quantity, and which turn to very great account; tho' at the same time the works are prodigiously expensive, and the quantity of wood they consume is exceeding great, which keeps up that complaint I mentioned before, that timber would grow scarce and consequently dear, from the great quantity consumed in the iron-works in Sussex.

The 'complaint . . . that timber would grow scarce, and con-sequently dear' was more than justified. Fortunately an enter-prising ironmaster, Abraham Darby, experimented with coke as a fuel in his blast-furnace. After many failures, in about 1710 he discovered how to produce good pig-iron from a coke-fired blast-furnace. This Quaker ironmaster had an ironworks at Coalbrookdale in Shropshire where the coal produced a coke which was freer from impurities than was the coke produced from coal in other areas. Pig-iron from the coke-fired furnace was suitable only for foundry work. It could not be converted into bar-iron at the forge. It was the second Abraham Darby who in 1749 discovered how to make coke-smelted pig-iron suitable for forging into bar-iron. Since the largest demand for pig-iron came from ironmasters engaged in forging, the invention made by the second Abraham Darby was even more significant for the future of the iron industry than was his father's invention.

The Darbys made no secret of their success and encouraged ironmasters to imitate them and to use coke instead of charcoal. However coke is a slow burning fuel. The coke-furnace needed more power than could be provided by the water-driven bellows. It was not until Boulton and Watt had developed an efficient steam-engine about 1775 that the coke furnaces were able to generate a sufficiently strong and continuous blast to make coke-smelting more efficient than charcoal-smelting. Charcoal was used as a fuel even by the inventive Darbys. There was also the problem of selecting the right types of iron ore and coal for use in the furnaces; some ores and some coals produced only low-quality pig-iron. Ironmasters had to experiment until they found the mixture needed to produce a high-quality iron.

The inventions made by the two Darbys were of great significance for the British iron industry. Parts of the industry were dependent on the scarcer and expensive charcoal but would increasingly be producing from blast-furnaces using the plentiful and relatively cheap fuel, coke. Iron from some coke-powered furnaces also proved to be of better quality than charcoal-smelted iron, enabling the ironmasters to produce castings of a lighter and more delicate design which had a wider variety of uses. However it has to be remembered that coke was at first used only in the blast-furnaces. Charcoal continued to be the only fuel suitable for use in the forging branch of the industry which produced bar-iron. British bar-iron continued to be a less suitable product, even when charcoal was the fuel, than bar-iron from Russia or Sweden.

The ironmasters' continued dependence on charcoal and water is shown in this letter written by a Birmingham merchant in 1759. He is writing about the setting up of the new Carron works in Scotland:

Dr. Roebuck and I think Carron Water is infinitely preferable to all others, because if the works prove prosperous as we expect, some places in the neighbourhood of the Firth of Forth will become one of the principal seats of iron works in Britain, not only for making iron from the ore into bars and slit iron, but into nails and many other manufactures; in all human probability this will be the case. Under this conviction it's undoubtedly right to begin on works in a situation that looks the most favourable for the seat of such manufacturers to settle, on account of its nearness to the Firth of Forth and its being remote from Glasgow, and where exceptionally fine coal from Acton Boughey, Toryburn and Limekiln can be had always at moderate expense; and not only charcoal be delivered cheaper from the Highlands as well as from woods that are now near it, but the land in the neighbourhood of Carron might be rented on such terms as to make it advisable to plant large woods for the supply of our works.

One furnace, three forges and a slitting mill would be a complete set of works, and the water of Carron is capable of supplying double that quantity, and it appeared to me that at a small expense we might be able to carry all our iron from one mill to another with boats, which is a very material consideration.

In that same year John Guest became manager of a new company which had been set up to develop ironworks at Dowlais in Glamorgan. The spur to the formation of this company was yet another war against the French (1756–63). This led to a great increase in the demand for cannons and other weapons. The decision to site the works at Dowlais was inspired by the presence in the valley of suitable ores and coal and, while the Carron works gave its name to the carronade, it was the Dowlais works which was to become the more significant in the long run, and was to help to make Dowlais and nearby Merthyr the iron centre of the industrial world.

The coal industry

As long ago as the thirteenth century coal had been shipped from Newcastle for sale as a domestic fuel in London where it was known as 'sea-cole'. By the beginning of the eighteenth century it was being used as fuel in a number of industries, for instance brewing and pottery-making, and in ever-increasing quantities in homes in the growing towns whose size made access to a source of wood increasingly difficult.

Coal-mining was another rural-based industry. Some owners of the land where coal was found employed people to run the mines. Others followed the example of Cornish landowners and allowed others to sink shafts and open up seams, and then collected a royalty on the output. As with tin-mining, horses were used for winding and transport, and most mine-owners had farms to provide food.

As the demand for coal increased so the problems of mining had grown. Deeper shafts had to be sunk, which increased the dangers from gas and water. Inert gas, or chokedamp, was at first brushed out of the mine with bunches of furze or gorse. Later, as in tin-mining, twin shafts were sunk. A fire was lit down one shaft, the gas-laden heavier air rose and fresh air was drawn down the second shaft. Inflammable gas, firedamp, was a greater danger, particularly since the usual method of providing light was by means of a candle attached to the miner's hat.

As mines went to greater depths they became wetter. At first the pools of water were emptied by endless chains of buckets worked by men, donkeys or sometimes windmills. The first steam-engine was invented by Thomas Savery in 1698 to provide a mechanical means of taking water out of Cornish tin-mines. Savery's engine was simply a boiler and a condenser fitted with pipes. One pipe ran down the shaft to the pool of water; the other pipe went to the surface. The vacuum created by the condensation of steam sucked the water up from the mine while an injection of fresh steam from the boiler forced it up the second pipe up to ground level. Savery's engines were fitted into a recess in the pit-shaft and he helped create a vacuum inside his condenser-cylinder by dashing cold water on its outside.

/ Savery's engine was very expensive to run. In 1708 a Dartmouth blacksmith, Thomas Newcomen, invented a different type of engine in which cold water was sprayed directly into the steam-filled cylinder to create the vacuum, so that atmospheric pressure forced a piston down. This piston was attached to one end of a great beam of timber fixed high above the mine to swing vertically through the arc of a circle. The piston's movements caused the beam to move and so activated another piston at the other end of the beam to draw the water up the mine-shaft.

Newcomen's engine was first used in a Midlands colliery and proved so successful that his engines replaced Savery's in English coalfields. By 1760 there were about 100 such engines at work along the Tyne and Wear, about 40 in use in Cornish tin-mines and about 60 in the Midlands. Abraham Darby used a Newcomen engine to pump back the water from a millpond after it had already flowed over and turned a wheel which drove the bellows for the blast-furnaces. /

After the colliers had cut the coal it had to be dragged along the mine bottom in baskets and then hauled to the surface. Men, women and children were involved in this work although as in tin-mining horse-driven windlasses were sometimes employed to bring the baskets of coal to the surface. Once at the surface the coal had to be taken away. Again the common method of transport was the horse-driven waggon. It was at coal-mines that the first experiments were made with waggon-ways or wooden rails. These were laid from the mine to the riverside and horse-drawn waggons passing along these waggon-ways were able to carry more coal more quickly than similar waggons trying to make their way through the primitive road system of the time. Inland coalfields, with no easy access to navigable rivers, had to rely on waggons moving along poor roads or more frequently on horses or donkeys with panniers slung across their backs, each carrying perhaps as little as a quarter of a ton. The full development of such coalfields depended on an improved transport system.

The coal industry by its very nature was capitalist. Someone had to pay for the sinking of the shaft, the installation of a steam-engine and the winding-gear. There was little if any chance of a workman getting together enough capital to set himself up as a mine-owner. However the amount of capital required was still fairly small, and shopkeepers, estate bailiffs, local solicitors and others who had some savings of their own were able to set up as mine-owners, sometimes borrowing additional capital from the local landowner on whose land the mine was being sunk or from a local bank.

The woollen industry

For at least four centuries before 1760 the woollen industry had been England's second most important industry, after agriculture. English sheep produced the raw material which was sorted and cleaned in the workers' cottages. It was then combed to separate the short from the long hairs, or carded to make a fleecy roll. After this it was then spun, woven, fulled, washed, tentered (or stretched), bleached, dressed and sheared.

Most of this work was done in the cottages of people whose main occupation was agriculture. Women and children did the sorting, cleaning and spinning, when the fibres were twisted (to make them stronger) on a simple spinning-wheel worked either by hand or foot, which could make only one thread at a time. Some threads were suitable for the warp, which runs the length of the roll of cloth, while others were suitable only for the weft, running across the width of the cloth.

Other tasks had to be undertaken by men. Combing was done with wire bristles which were brushed along the fibres to straighten them. Weaving – the making of cloth by interlacing the warps and the wefts – required less dexterity but more strength than spinning. Shearing, or cropping, of the finished cloth to provide a smooth surface, was done by men using huge cropping-shears with which they sheared off the nap of the cloth after it had been thoroughly brushed by teasels.

Some tasks had to be undertaken outside the cottage. There were fulling-mills where the cloth was treated with fuller's earth and beaten with heavy hammers to thicken and mat the material. These mills were driven by horses or more frequently by water-power. Dyeing was another process which required equipment which could not be housed in the cottage.

By the middle of the eighteenth century almost every county in England and Wales was producing woollen cloth. There were however some areas where the industry was particularly con-centrated and where some people thought of themselves more as workers in this industry than in agriculture. The village of Kersey in Suffolk gave its name to one type of woollen cloth; the village of Worsted in East Norfolk gave its name to another. We have seen from Celia Fiennes's account that Exeter was a centre of the West Country woollen industry (see page 61), while Norwich owed its growth to the development of the woollen industry of East Anglia.

Many of the processes needed a great deal of water – for fulling, dyeing and so on. This helps to explain the development of the Yorkshire industry described by Defoe in 1724:

Two things essential [to the cloth industry] are found here. . . . I mean Coals, and running Water upon the Tops of the highest Hills. . . . After we had mounted the third Hill, we found one continued Village . . . hardly a House standing out of speaking distance from another. . . . We could see that at almost every House there was a Tenter for stretching cloth and almost on every Tenter a Piece of Cloth . . . yet look which Way we would, high to the Tops, and low to the Bottoms, it was all the same; innumerable Houses and Tenters, and a white Piece upon every Tenter. . . . I found . . . wherever we pass'd any House we found a little Gutter of running Water. . . . At every considerable House was a Manufactory or Work-house . . . [and] the little Streams were so . . . guided by Gutters or Pipes . . . that none of those Houses were without a River . . . running into and through their Work-houses.

Having thus Fire and Water at every Dwelling, there is no need to enquire why they dwell thus dispers'd upon the highest Hills, the Convenience of the Manufactures requiring it. Among the Manufacturers Houses are likewise scattered an infinite number of Cottages or small Dwellings, in which dwell the Workmen which are employed, the Women and Children of whom are always busy Carding, Spinning, etc., so that no Hands being unemploy'd, all can gain their Bread, even from the youngest to the ancient; hardly any thing above four Years old, but its Hands are sufficient to itself.

In most counties the industry was organized by capitalist clothiers who bought the wool at a local market or directly from the farmers, gave it out to carders and spinners and then handed the spun yard to the weavers. The clothier would then give the undressed cloth to fullers, dressers and shearers working in mills under his supervision. In East Anglia the control of the industry was divided between master combers, who controlled the work of the spinners and weavers, and cloth merchants, who controlled the work of the finishers. In Yorkshire the industry was in the hands of many master clothiers, with little capital, each of whom employed a small number of weavers to work in his own home on yarn spun by women in their cottages. One weaver could use the yarn provided by many spinners and it is not surprising that the first inventions were aimed at improving the output of spinners.

Much of the finished cloth was sold to merchants engaged in the export trade. Woollen cloth provided over half the value of domestic exports in the middle of the eighteenth century. The development of this industry over many centuries had provided opportunities for the growth of a merchant class with international contacts, and experience in commercial practice. They had an eye for the varied demands of customers from different parts of the world and for opportunities for increasing trade both in the expanding empire and in neutral countries.

The cotton industry

At the beginning of the eighteenth century the British cotton industry was a small, backward industry which used a mixture of linen warp and cotton weft. This was a coarse product, unable to compete with the finer-quality printed calicoes and muslins from India. Indeed the increase in the imports of these Indian products was such that the woollen industry felt threatened, and in 1700 Parliament passed an act forbidding such imports. English businessmen then imported only white cotton cloth and had it printed and dyed in Britain. In 1721 Parliament passed an act which forbade the importing of even this cotton cloth. English merchants then had to develop the British cotton industry. Fortunately for them India – the home of the industry – underwent a series of wars during the eighteenth century when England and France sided with one Indian ruler after another in the search for empire. The political chaos almost destroyed the Indian textile industry. At the same time new supplies of raw cotton became available from Brazil, the West Indies and the southern states of what was to become the USA. The supplies of raw cotton tended to enter Britain through Liverpool with its longstanding contact with the Americas through the slave trade. Hence the manufacture of cotton cloth tended to develop in and around Liverpool.

The industry was organized on the same basis as the woollen industry, a mass of cottage workers receiving the raw cotton from a master who bought back the finished product. In 1836 Andrew Ure wrote a history of the cotton industry and described the domestic system:

The workshop of the weaver was a rural cottage, from which when he was tired of sedentary labour he could sally forth into his little garden, and with the spade or the hoe tend its ... productions. The cotton wool which was to form his weft was picked clean by the fingers of his younger children, and was carded and spun by the older girls, assisted by his wife, and the yarn was woven by himself assisted by his sons. When he could not procure within his family a supply of yarn ... he had recourse to the spinsters of the neighbourhood. One good weaver could keep three active women at work upon the wheel.

The silk industry

The woollen industry was undoubtedly very important and the clothiers and merchants very influential. As Smith noted: 'The clothiers ... succeeded in convincing the wisdom of the nation that the safety of the commonwealth depends upon the prosperity of their particular manufacture.' Smith was referring to the acts which protected the woollen industry by banning the import of Indian muslins and calicoes. The act of 1700 also forbade the import of silks, which stimulated the English silk industry. This relied on raw silk imported from China, Italy, Spain and Turkey. If cotton was too coarse a product to offer much competition to wool, silk on the other hand was too fine and expensive a product to be regarded as a real competitor for the mass market. Silk-weaving was carried on in workers' homes in Spitalfields in London, in Coventry, Norwich and Macclesfield. As with wool and cotton, so with silk; a good weaver could use the output of a number of spinners or throwers whose task was to twist the raw material into strong threads.

John and Thomas Lombe were engaged in the final stages of the silk industry, controlling the work of many weavers and spinners and selling the finished product in the London market. Competition from the finished silks manufactured in Italy and France was very strong, largely because the European goods were superior. John Lombe went to Leghorn in Italy and stole the designs of machines used in factories there and set up the first factory in Britain on an island in the River Derwent near Derby, as *The History of Derby* (1791) records:

> The Italians had the exclusive art of silk-throwing. . . . John Lombe, a man of spirit, a good draughtsman, and an excellent mechanic, travelled into Italy with a view of penetrating the secret. He staid some time; but as he knew admission was prohibited he adopted the usual mode of accomplishing his end by corrupting the servants. This gained him frequent access [to the factory] in private. Whatever part he became master of, he commited to paper before he slept. By perseverance and bribery he acquired the whole, when the plot was discovered and he fled . . . on board ship. . . . at the hazard of his life. . . . But though he judged the danger over, he was yet to become a sacrifice.
>
> Arriving safe with his acquired knowledge, he fixed upon Derby as a proper place for his purpose, because the town was likely to supply him with a sufficient number of hands, and the . . . stream with a constant supply of water. This happened about the year 1717.
>
> He agreed with the Corporation for an island or swamp in the river, five hundred feet long and fifty-two wide at eight pounds per ann. where he erected the present works, containing eight apartments, and 468 windows, at the expence of about £30,000. . . . This ponderous building stands upon huge piles of oak, from sixteen to twenty feet long. . . . Over this solid mass of timber is laid a foundation of stone. . . .
>
> Being established to his wish, he procured in 1718 a patent from the Crown, to secure the profits during fourteen years. But alas! he had not pursued his lucrative commerce more than three or four years when the Italians . . . determined his destruction. . . .

An artful woman came over ... and assisted in the business.
... Slow poison was supposed ... to have been administered
to John Lombe, who lingered two or three years in agonies,
and departed.

Clock-making

There were many smaller industries in Britain on the eve of the
Industrial Revolution, and it would not be profitable to examine
all of them since, from our point of view, they would all tell more
or less the same story of small workshops, skilled craftsmen and
small capital-equipment. However we ought to bear in mind the
industries which produced scientific instruments, watches and
clocks in the seventeenth and eighteenth centuries, and in which
the highest standards of precision and ingenuity were exercised.
After 1660 there was a great increase in the production of navigation instruments and microscopes in response to demands by
members of the new Royal Society and by the Admiralty, and
an increase in the production of watches and sophisticated
mechanical toys for the luxury market.

English workmen had a long history of mechanical ingenuity
and skill. By 1700 watch-making had become a large trade and
over 120,000 watches were produced in London with as many
more being produced in Lancashire. In this industry there was
already a division of labour and the use of highly specialized tools
and lathes.

Here then we have one basis for industrial development. It
would be foolish to exaggerate its importance. After all clock-
making and associated industries were small, and the number of
people employed was miniscule compared to the numbers
working in agriculture, wool or even cotton. The tools were also
few in number; the output was sold only in the limited luxury
market; the material used was brass and there was no evidence
that the same skills could be applied in harder metals such as iron.

For iron products people had to rely on the ingenuity and brawn of blacksmiths such as Newcomen.

But what if it were possible to marry the skills of the watch-maker to the different skills of the blacksmith? When industry created the demand for more machines, the marriage between these two sets of skills was arranged by businessmen such as Boulton, Watt and Maudslay, who taught the clock-makers and blacksmiths, the carpenters and the millwrights the new skills needed. Fitters and turners were the offspring of that marriage. These were the men who produced the lathes and engines which in turn produced the machines which made England 'the work-shop of the world'. But that did not happen until after 1830 until which time most screws, nuts and bolts were handmade, and each cylinder and piston was hand-ground. None of this would have been possible without the long-established traditions of the luxury trades with their high degree of skill. Not all underdeveloped countries have their reservoir of skilled workpeople.

6. The Government and
the Industrial Revolution

Today's underdeveloped countries

It is clear that industrialized countries offer their peoples more
opportunities than are available to the peoples of the underdeveloped countries. Regular employment at higher wages enables
people in industrialized countries to buy for themselves a wider
variety of goods and to enjoy a high standard of living. The
governments of the industrialized countries are also able to collect
high taxes needed to provide for their peoples a desirable infrastructure of e.g. transport systems and welfare schemes in which
the State provides for its citizens more or less 'from the cradle to
the grave'. Industrialized countries also have more military
'muscle' than do the underdeveloped countries, which find themselves even in post-colonial days at best the allies of, and at worst
the 'running dogs' for, the industrial giants.

It is understandable that the rulers of the underdeveloped
countries have been eager to take their countries along the road to
industrialization with its many and obvious benefits. It is also easy
to see why they have been unwilling to allow the process of
industrialization to take place at what may be described as 'a
natural pace'. This, it is argued, would be 'the pace of the tortoise'
and would mean that industrialization might take several generations to achieve. Since already industrialized countries would
advance even more quickly from their well-established base, the

relative difference between the old and newly industrialized would be even greater after a hundred years of 'tortoise' progress than it had been at the outset.

Rulers of underdeveloped countries have been 'young men in a hurry' to attain the goal of industrialization. They have used all the powers of the government to help foster that process. The tax-system has been used to encourage business-enterprise and desirable investment. The government itself may through its tax-system amass quantities of investment-capital and help provide some of the infrastructure on which industrialization depends: roads, harbours, airlines, schools and colleges, medical services are among the things which such governments seek to establish out of public funds. New and developing industries are protected from foreign competition by quotas and tariffs while the output of the new native industry may also attract further aid in the form of a bounty, or some other government grant or loan, to the industrialist.

The first Industrial Revolution

All this is at odds with the way in which the British Government behaved before and during the years of the first Industrial Revolution. That revolution was the result of the responses by many manufacturers and industrialists to market forces freely operating, with no pressure being applied by the government either on those forces or on the activities of the industrialists and manufacturers. Voltaire understood the link between commercial progress and freedom from government interference in eighteenth-century Britain: 'Commerce which has enriched the citizens of England has helped to make them free, and that liberty in turn has expanded commerce.' Indeed, as we shall see, many of the government's activities seemed designed to hinder rather than help industrial progress. What help was given by government to commerce and industry appeared for the most part to have been provided accidentally rather than of goodness aforethought.

The aims of the government in the eighteenth century

The first aim of the British Government was to provide security
for its people at home and abroad so that men were free to pursue
their interests. This *laissez-faire* attitude to industry and commerce
was not complete; we shall see that foreign trade was regulated
and aided. But the British Government did not interfere in the
lives and activities of the people to the degree that was common
throughout eighteenth-century Europe. Rulers of France, Russia,
Austria and other states, acting in the name of benevolent or
paternal despotism, tried to run their countries' economies; prices
were fixed, roads built and maintained, foreign trade and domestic
industrial development regulated by rulers who claimed also the
right to determine their people's religious beliefs, the plays they
saw, the books they read and the ideas they entertained. Given the
quite primitive forms of communication at the time, when it took
up to six days to get from York to London (when the weather
permitted), such close regulation was not possible even if it had
been desirable. It led to the creation of a vast bureaucracy more
interested in its own survival, enlargement and enrichment than
in any real furthering of the interests of the people.

Indeed the British Government seemed prepared to decrease
rather than increase the extent of its part in the nation's economic
life. Ever since Tudor times wages and prices were fixed by local
JPs. In 1738 for example the Warwickshire magistrates meeting at
quarter sessions decided:

> The particular rate of wages of all manner of artificers, labourers,
> and servants, as well by the day with meat and drink as without,
> as also by the whole year in gross or by task, made and pro-
> vided, having a special regard and consideration to the prices
> of provisions and all other circumstances necessary to be
> considered at this time. April 1738.

	£	s	d
Every servant in husbandry by the year	5	10	0
Second servant	4	0	0
Servant boy from 14 to 18 years of age	2	10	0
Servant boy from 11 to 14	1	0	0
Every head servant maid by the year	3	0	0
Second maid servant	2	10	0
Labourers from Martinmas to March 25 by the day			8
From March 25 to harvest and after harvest to Martinmas			9
Every mower of grass by the day, with drink		1	0
„ without drink		1	2
Every woman in haymaking, with drink			5
„ without drink			6
Every woman in corn harvest, with drink			6
„ without drink			7
Every carpenter by the day, March 25 to St. Michael's, with drink		1	0
„ without drink		1	2
From Michaelmas to Lady Day, with drink			10
„ without drink		1	0
Every mason by the day in summer, with drink			10
„ without drink		1	0
Every mason by the day in winter, with drink			10
„ without drink		1	0
Thatcher, by day, summer and winter		1	0
Weeders of corn by the day			4

Similar regulations were made by magistrates all over the country, acting on the Tudor principle that the labourer had to be safeguarded and guaranteed a right to the customary earnings of his trade. When most people worked in agriculture and when towns were small, such regulation was possible. As the number of people engaged in industry and the number on industrial occupations grew, the wages-system became too complex and the numbers involved too great for local magistrates to be able to impose a statutory wages-policy. In 1756 Parliament accepted the arguments of employers who wanted freedom to negotiate wages with their workpeople. Parliament abolished the fixing of wages by JPs and the role of the state was further decreased.

The government did try to protect British industries from foreign competition and England was a high-tariff country in which the woollen, silk, paper, cotton and shipbuilding industries could prosper. However, as we shall see, such intervention had its disadvantages. The government also tried to foster foreign trade during the century before the onset of the Industrial Revolution. Import duties and export bounties helped home industry and hindered attempts of the foreigner to break into the English market. Navigation Acts (see page 104) were passed to help the British shipbuilding industry as well as the carrying trade with its attendant activities of insurance, warehousing and so on which made Liverpool, Glasgow and Bristol such prosperous ports. The economic development of British colonies was regulated in the interests of British manufacturers. Wars were fought against Holland and France to exclude them from trade with British colonies. The setting up of the Board of Trade in 1696 was an indication of an early interest by government in foreign trade.

A major reason for this interest and for the protective legislation was a deep fear of unemployment in the districts which depended on the woollen industry which in turn relied so much on the export trade. There was also the 'bullion theory' which declared that it was desirable for the country to export more than it imported so that gold would flow into the country as a result of that favourable balance of trade. Bullion was in contemporary words the 'sinews of war' needed to purchase those essential imports of timber, sails, hemp, tar and the like. Bullion was also essential for some of Britain's major trading companies: the East Indian and Levant Companies had to have gold with which to purchase the goods which they brought back for sale at home or for re-export to Europe, in exchange for European gold. Adam

Smith, a critic of the bullionist theory, none the less explained it when he wrote:

> The two principles being established, however, that wealth con-
> sisted in gold and silver and that those metals could be brought
> into the country which had no mines only by the balance
> of trade, or by exporting to a greater value than it imported, it
> necessarily became the great object of political economy to
> diminish as much as possible the importation of foreign goods
> for home consumption, and to increase as much as possible the
> exportation of the produce of domestic industry. Its two great
> engines for enriching the country, therefore, were restrains
> upon importation, and encouragements to exportation.

Negative consequences of freedom

The British Government did not seek to direct the industrial growth of the country during the eighteenth century. There was little attempt to promote industrial innovation or stimulate investment by any arrangements of its tax-system. The government did not seek to develop any industrial concerns itself except for the naval dockyards and ordance works such as Woolwich Arsenal. Industrial and commercial development was left to market forces.

However there are drawbacks to such a *laissez-faire* policy. Government reluctance to involve itself in the nation's industrial development spilled over into a reluctance to concern itself with the nation's social development. It may seem legitimate to allow businessmen to build factories, harbours and other profit-making concerns. Given that they had a limited amount of capital at their disposal and that there were many competing demands for that profit-seeking capital, it now seems at least unfortunate that the freedom-seeking policies of eighteenth-century governments forced businessmen to divert part of their capital and part of their energies to urban development. They were expected to provide the houses, to lay down the water supply, to provide sanitation schemes and the like.

It was not until the Victorian period that the government began to get involved in the problem of the lack of social investment that, it may be argued, was an inevitable consequence of the government's refusal to undertake such investment at a much earlier date. Asa Briggs accuses the early industrialists of having lacked 'a social conscience . . . a civic pride'. A better view of the social problems created by early industrialization is that they were the result of too great a degree of *laissez-faire*. Bad housing, poor sanitation, a high death rate and the lack of an adequate system of education were the prices paid for industrial development. To have diverted investment to these purposes would have slowed down industrial development and hence delayed the day when Britain could become 'the workshop of the world'.

Anti-commercial legislation

Eighteenth-century governments protected and aided industries engaged in foreign trade, while passing a great deal of legislation whose unintended effects were to slow down the rate of industrial progress. After the financial disaster of the South Sea Bubble the government passed the Bubble Act of 1720 which virtually prohibited the formation of joint-stock companies and forbade the use of publicly raised capital in manufacturing concerns. If men wanted to incorporate a firm they had to apply for letters patent, a royal charter or a private act of Parliament permitting them to do so. However each such application had to pass the scrutiny of a Parliament suspicious of such enterprise and hostile to speculation.

It might then be argued that the Bubble Act was a hindrance to British industrial development since it was seemingly impossible, or at best extremely difficult, for risk capital to be raised from the wider public which might have been willing to invest. However acts of Parliament provide lawyers with opportunities to demonstrate their skills of interpretation and evasion. If Parliament would not agree to a petition for a charter, or if it insisted on writing the terms of the charter so that transference of stock was made difficult, the promoters of potential companies found able lawyers who showed them how to carry on their enterprise without breaking the law. So what appeared in law to be mere partnerships became in fact incorporation companies owing their formation to the use of a common seal and using various devices such as trusteeship. Other companies were formed with charters which specifically limited the liability of the people involved in its formation for the obligations which the company might incur.

There were a number of companies formed in this way, particularly in the metal industry and the rapidly developing insurance business. In this way the principle of limited liability was introduced by which the liability of an investor or shareholder for the debts of the company does not exceed the value of his shareholding. No one could then be brought to ruin by a small investment in what proved to be an unsound concern, as had been the case before 1720. This increased the number of investors to whom companies could appeal and so favoured the expansion of business.

However the number of such companies was small. There was no great demand by manufacturers or industrialists for amendments to the Bubble Act until the 1820s and in 1825 the Bubble Act was repealed. But even then there was no great rush to form companies. The limited amount of capital that was required in most industrial undertakings was readily available from sources closer to the industrialist than was the Stock Exchange.

In the banking field the government was influenced by its own creature, the London-based Bank of England, to limit the size of other banks in England and Wales, where they remained small and were forbidden to have more than six partners or to seek incorporation and joint-stock status. As we shall see, by 1800 there were hundreds of small banks throughout the country each free to decide the volume of its note issue and credit policy. It is hardly surprising that there was a great degree of instability in such an unhampered system and that in years of economic depression many banks were unable to repay their depositors so that the economic depression deepened. On the other hand the free-wheeling system ensured that local industrialists and manufacturers had ready access to risk capital during years of economic boom. The easy credit policies of the small banks promoted economic expansion.

Another field in which government legislation seemed designed to hinder industrial progress involved the mobility of labour. If an industrialist wished to expand an existing undertaking or start up a new one he had to obtain a workforce. Some came from the immediate locality, but more had to come from a wider area – perhaps from the county in which the development took place, perhaps from an even wider area. In any case labour was attracted from one parish to another.

But ever since 1660 legislation had aimed at preventing this sort of mobility since it was feared that the newcomers might prove to be a burden on the poor-relief system of the importing parish. It was felt that it would be unfair for one parish to be allowed to 'export' its poor to another parish. Hence a series of Settlement Acts such as the one passed in 1662:

> ... that whereas by reason of some defects in the law, poor people are not restrained from going from one parish to another and therefore do endeavour to settle themselves in those parishes, where there is the best stock, the largest commons or wastes to build cottages, and the most woods for them to burn and destroy and when they have consumed it then to another parish, and at last become rogues and vagabonds to the great discouragement of parishes to provide stocks where it is liable to be devoured by strangers ... it shall be lawful upon complaint made by the church wardens or overseers of the poor of any parish to any Justice of Peace, within forty days after any

such person or persons coming so to settle, as aforesaid in any
tenement under the yearly value of ten pounds for any two
justices of the peace whereof one to be of the Quorum of the
division where any person or persons that are likely to be
chargeable to the parish shall come to inhabit, by their warrant
to remove and convey such person or persons to such parish
where he or they were last legally settled either as a native
householder sojouner apprentice or servant for the space of
forty days at the least unless he or they give sufficient security
for the discharge of the said parish to be allowed by the said
Justices.

But the fact that there was a succession of such acts down to
1782 proved that the system was not working. People were
moving, employers were willing to take on 'immigrants' into the
parish, and, except in periods of economic hardship, parishes were
willing to allow newcomers to take up residence. And it is
difficult to see what could have been done to stem the flow of
labour into the growing industrial towns. In the small parishes of
1662 newcomers could be spotted, known and, when need be,
deported back to their original parish. But there was no way in
which the local authorities could have transported the hundreds
of thousands of people who moved into Manchester, Leeds and
dozens of other industrial centres. It is not surprising then that
government accepted the reality of the situation as they had done
in the case of wage-regulation. The Settlement Laws were increasingly ignored and industrial development furthered by the
mobility of labour.

The government's taxation system seemed designed to hinder
industrial progress. Indirect taxes, mainly imposed by customs
and excise duties, were the main forms of revenue throughout the
eighteenth century. The land-tax, fixed at a standard rate, became
an increasingly less arduous burden as land-values increased. Other
taxes on the wealthy – on playing-cards, windows, servants,
hair-powder and other luxury items – were imposed towards the

end of the century. There were no direct taxes on incomes or wealth nor was the real value of the land-tax maintained.

Indirect taxes by their very nature are regressive, since they fall equally on rich and poor, and proportionately more heavily on the poor than on the rich. King's population figures (see Table 2, pp. 24–5) show that there were very many more who qualified as less well-off than as rich. These were also the people who made up the mass of the domestic market, marginal purchasers of the products of factories and workshops. The lowering of their real incomes by taxation limited their ability to buy and was therefore a deterrent to industrial expansion. This would not have seemed so to the politicians and economists of the eighteenth century who, if they considered markets at all, thought primarily of the foreign trade and seemed to ignore the domestic market.

Taxes were imposed on beer, spirits, malt, hops, bricks, salt, glass, tea, sugar, tobacco, corn, timber, so that Sydney Smith wrote in 1820:

Taxes upon every article which enters into the mouth, or covers the back, or is placed under the foot – on everything that comes from abroad or is grown at home – taxes on the raw material – taxes on every fresh value that is added to it by the industry of man – on the ermine which decorates the judge, and the rope which hangs the criminal – on the poor man's salt and the rich man's spice – on the brass nails of the coffin, and the ribands of the bride – at bed or board, couchant or levant, we must pay: The schoolboy whips his taxed top – the beardless youth manages his taxed horse, with a taxed bridle on a taxed road – and the dying Englishman pouring his medicine, which has paid seven percent, into a spoon which has paid fifteen per cent – flings himself back upon his chintz bed which has paid twenty-two percent – makes his will on an eight pound stamp, and expires in the arms of an apothecary who has paid a licence of £100 for the privilege of putting him to death. His whole property is then immediately taxed from two to ten per cent. Besides the probate, large fees are demanded for burying him in the chancel; his virtues, are handed down to posterity on taxed marble; and is then gathered to his fathers – to be taxed no more.

But there is a corollary to this. There was little tax on profits from farming, commerce or industry. The well-off who had a high propensity to save and invest were allowed to retain their money, so that investment-capital was the more readily available. A fairer system of taxation might have proved to be a hindrance to capital accumulation and so have slowed down the rate of industrial development.

Government's unintended aid to industry

The government had not thought out its system of taxation with investment-capital in mind. The benefit described in the last paragraph was an unintended one. There were several other such unintended benefits which helped in industrial development and which were the result of government policy. There was a long period of internal peace in the eighteenth century following on the many disorders of the seventeenth century with its civil wars. There were indeed local food riots at times; the London mob was roused by cries of 'Wilkes and Liberty' in 1763 and by Lord George Gordon's campaign against Catholics in 1780; the Jacobites provided a more serious threat to internal security in 1715 and again in 1745. But such rare eruptions were small-scale. The prevailing peace made it the more likely that businessmen would put their risk-capital to work and so industrial development took place.

We have seen that these successful businessmen bought their way into the nobility. Defoe wrote about the Home Counties:

It is observable that in this part of the country there are several very considerable estates purchased and now enjoyed by citizens of London, merchants and tradesmen. I mention this to observe how the present increase of wealth in the City of London spreads itself into the country and plants families and fortunes who in another age will equal the families of the ancient gentry.

But this was not the only way in which London and its environs welcomed the new rich. The corrupt political system of the time enabled the new wealth to buy rotten boroughs and a share in the political process. There was no political hostility between old and new wealth as was the case in France and other European countries, and which led there to friction and finally revolution.

While the government played little if any part in promoting industrial schemes, the political system did enable private initiative to promote private acts of Parliament not only for enclosures but also for the building of roads and canals as well as for schemes for urban improvement. A more centrally-controlled, bureaucratic system might not have had the necessary flexibility to permit such essential legislation.

The government had fostered the growth of the British Empire, acquiring colonies either by peaceful settlement or as the results of wars. Following on the enlargement of the empire the government had helped foster colonial trade by granting to companies or individuals the monopoly of trade in certain regions. This resulted in the formation and the growth of the Levant Company, the East India Company and other companies with sole right to trade in Russia, Africa and Canada. By the middle of the eighteenth century this tightly controlled system was not only under attack from individuals eager to trade in their own right; it was in the process of being dismantled. There were now more than enough people willing to risk their capital in overseas ventures. There was no need to grant monopolies to encourage them. In part the risks had been diminished by the efficiency and strength of the Royal Navy, which had almost made Britain 'mistress of the seas' by

1800; and in part by the increase in the area of the world which now came under British dominion, so enlarging the opportunites for trade. The Africa Company lost its monopoly in 1750 when it was reorganized to include all merchants trading in Africa. In 1753 the Levant Company was similarly thrown open to any merchant. The government's willingness to abandon old practices and adopt new fashions arose from its wish to see an expansion of foreign trade, still seen as the most important outlet for British manufactures. This led to the abandonment of the bullionist concept of the favourable balance of trade.

The government which had once insisted on regulating foreign trade came under increasing pressure, from merchants and economists, to allow free trade, to dismantle the high tariffs which protected British industry and to repeal the legislation which forbade the exports of machinery, the emigration of skilled work-people and the imports of a long list of foreign goods. In 1819 David Ricardo, another leading economist wrote:

> Under a system of perfectly free commerce, each country naturally devotes its capital and labour to such employments as are most beneficial to each. This pursuit of individual advantage is admirably connected with the universal good of the whole. By stimulating industry, by rewarding ingenuity, and by using most efficaciously the peculiar powers bestowed by nature, it distributes labour most effectively and most economically: while, by increasing the general mass of productions, it diffuses general benefits, and binds together by one common tie of interest and intercourse, the universal society of nations throughout the civilised world. It is this principle which determines that wine shall be made in France and Portugal, that corn shall be grown in America and Poland, and that hardware and other goods shall be manufactured in England.

British industry may have needed protection in the sixteenth and seventeenth centuries, and in so far as government legislation

furthered such development it was to be welcomed. But the
Industrial Revolution altered the relative positions of Britain and
her competitors. Britain had nothing to fear from the foreigner,
little if anything to gain from protection but a great deal to be
derived if industry and commerce could be freed from government
regulation, as a report showed in 1806:

> The rapid and prodigious increase of late years in the manu-
> factures and commerce of this country is universally known; as
> well as the effects of that increase on our revenue and national
> strength; and in considering the immediate causes of that
> augmentation, it will appear that, under the favour of Pro-
> vidence, it is principally to be ascribed to the general spirit of
> enterprise and industry among a free and enlightened people,
> left to the unrestrained exercise of their talents in the employ-
> ment of a vast capital; pushing to the utmost the principle of
> the division of labour; calling in all the resources of scientific
> research and mechanical ingenuity; and, finally availing them-
> selves of all the benefits to be drived from visiting foreign
> countries, not only for forming new, and confirming old
> commercial connections, but for obtaining a personal know-
> ledge of the wants, the tastes, the habits, the discoveries and
> improvements, the productions and fabrics of other civilised
> nations, and, by thus bringing home facts and suggestions,
> perfecting our existing manufactures, and adding new ones to
> our domestic stock; opening at the same time new markets for
> the product of our manufacturing and commercial industry,
> and qualifying ourselves for supplying them. It is by these
> means alone, and above all, your committee must repeat it, by
> the effect of machinery in improving the quality and cheapen-
> ing the fabrication of our various articles of export, that with
> a continually accumulating weight of taxes, and with all the
> necessaries and comforts of life gradually increasing in price,
> the effects of which on the wages of labour could not but be
> very considerable, our commerce and manufactures have been

also increasing in such a degree as to surpass the most sanguine calculations of the ablest political writers who had speculated on the improvements of a future age.

During the 1820s the government passed a series of measures which started the process of dismantling the protective barriers which had once helped British industry. This new, emancipating, legislation like the older, protective, legislation, was of immediate benefit to British industry, trade and commerce, and confirmed the foreigners' opinion that the British Parliament was dominated by considerations for British business interests. It was not so in most other European countries.

There is some dispute as to whether the Patent Laws helped or hindered industrial progress. On the one hand such laws were an encouragement to the inventor who could rely on some years of monopoly for whatever he might produce and so have some measure of guarantee of an adequate return for the time and trouble spent on his work. On the other hand these laws did prevent an early, widespread application of the inventions. Watt's patent certainly held back the degree to which the steam-engine was applied throughout the industry after 1782 and the expiry of this patent in 1800 was generally welcomed. The opposition to Arkwright's attempt to renew his patent in 1781 was due to the widespread wish to use the machine without having to pay a huge royalty to the patent-holder who incidentally was probably not the inventor anyhow.

Government finance and industrialization

During the eighteenth century there was a continual increase in the size of the National Debt, the result of a gap between government revenue and government expenditure, due almost entirely to expenditure on war. The table opposite shows that the main form of revenue was indirect taxation:

Table 4 *Public Finance of Great Britain 1715–1850*

Date	Customs and Excise		Land and assessed taxes		Post Office and Stamp duties		Total	
	£m	(%)	£m	(%)	£m	(%)	£m	(%)
1715	4.0	(71)	1.1	(20)	0.4	(9)	5.5	(100)
1750	5.0	(67)	2.2	(30)	0.2	(3)	7.5	(100)
1783	8.5	(67)	2.6	(20)	1.6	(13)	12.7	(100)
1801	19.3	(58)	9.9	(30)	3.8	(12)	33.0	(100)
1820	41.4	(70)	8.0	(14)	9.6	(16)	59.0	(100)
1850	37.6	(67)	11.9	(21)	8.9	(12)	56.3	(100)

Date	Interest charges £m	(%)	Military expenditure £m	(%)	All other expenditure £m	(%)	Total expenditure £m	(%)	National Debt (cumulative total: £m)
1715	3.3	(53)	2.2	(37)	0.7	(10)	6.2	(100)	37
1750	3.2	(44)	3.0	(42)	1.0	(14)	7.2	(100)	78
1783	8.1	(34)	13.7	(58)	1.8	(8)	23.6	(100)	231.8
1801	19.9	(32)	37.2	(60)	4.2	(8)	61.3	(100)	456.1
1820	31.2	(59)	16.2	(30)	6.9	(11)	54.3	(100)	840.1
1850	28.0	(57)	14.5	(31)	7.0	(12)	49.5	(100)	793.5

Since revenue came in the main from the less well-off, and expenditure on interest payments went to the better-off, we have a shift of income from those with a high propensity to spend to those with a higher propensity to save and invest. The amounts of money involved are relatively small to modern eyes, accustomed as we are to debts totalling billions. However in eighteenth-century terms the flow of money from the poorer to the richer was relatively large-scale. In 1820 for example the amount of money sent to debt-holders was equivalent to half the total value of exports. Such a shift of resources had the effect of limiting the demand from the domestic market but of making available large sums of potential risk-capital.

During the wars against Louis XIV the government of William III had been forced to offer up to 8 per cent to people before they were willing to buy government stock. During the eighteenth century there was a steady fall in interest rates generally, and the government was able in 1757 to convert all its existing stock to one Consolidated Stock with an interest charge of 3 per cent. This was the rate of interest that prevailed throughout industry as a whole. This low rate of interest encouraged long-term investment where large sums of capital were involved, as in the construction industries where the building of docks, canals, warehouses as well as house-building, tended to lock up large amounts of capital and in a relatively unremunerative way. When the rate of interest was high there was less chance of persuading people to invest in such schemes. On the other hand when the rate of interest was as low as 3 per cent it was worth while investing in a venture even if one had to wait for thirty-three years for the return of the capital.

War and the Industrial Revolution

Only governments can wage war, and the economic effects of war have to be laid at the door of the government even though such effects were unintended. From 1700 until 1815 Britain was involved in a series of wars against France. Some were fought mainly in Europe, others were fought in Canada, India and the West Indies. During the earlier wars, military expenditure came to about £5 million a year. During the eighteenth century the cost of waging war rose, and the wars of 1793 to 1815 cost over £40 million a year on such expenditure.

One effect of victory in these wars was an increase in foreign trade and so a stimulus to industrial expansion. Even the military expenditure was a stimulus to that expansion; part of the expenditure was on loans and subsidies to allies who spent much of the money on purchasing war material in England and Wales, while a substantial part of the expenditure, on the government's own account, was on shipping and armaments which further stimulated expansion. Timber merchants, naval contractors, ironmasters and others expanded their business. It is hardly accidental that a war year, 1759, saw the development of iron-works at Dowlais in Glamorgan and Carron in Scotland. The expansion of the iron industry to meet wartime requirements left the industry with excess capacity when peace had 'broken out'. This caused manufacturers to look for new uses and new markets for their product.

Even during the long wars against France there was a steady increase in foreign trade, as a parliamentary committee heard from a London merchant in 1812 when the Napoleonic Continental system was operating to hinder British trade with Europe:

Can you inform the Committee what the state of the trade was in the years 1808, 1809, 1810 and 1811? – In 1807 we felt the whole effect of the Berlin decree, we were entirely excluded from the Continent; I speak with regard to my own transactions and those of a vast number of my friends. We had in 1807, and previous to that, trades to the South of Europe, particularly in Portugal, which were uninterrupted but which were likewise put an end to by the French invasion of that year. In 1808 the trade revived considerably: a great quantity of our goods, and of English merchandise, was introduced into the Continent through Heligoland; considerable exports were made to the Baltic; the trade in the Mediterranean increased very con-siderably; a very great trade was opened to this country in consequence of the Royal Family of Portugal removing to the Brazils, which likewise made an opening to Spanish South America. In 1809 the trade through Heligoland was most extensive; Bonaparte had his hands full with the Emperor of Germany and with the Spaniards, and had no time to attend to the coast; the trade during that year I may say was uninterrupted. The trade to the Mediterranean increased very much; the quantity of goods taken out that year greatly exceeded any previous year, for reasons that at that time we could not account for. The trade to the Brazils was equally extensive with the year before, vast exportations took place to South America, and in general, trade in the line in which I am engaged was reckoned a fair trade; the markets were never heavy.

Wartime demand for more and better cannon acted as the stimulus which led the ironmaster John Wilkinson to devise a new method of boring cannon in 1774. This was later adapted to the boring of cylinders with a new accuracy and this in turn was of great value to James Watt when he developed an improved steam-engine. However all was not gain. Wartime expansion was not always maintained by peacetime demand, more especially so because high interest payments had to be met by high and regressive taxation which lowered home demand, while for a time foreign markets might be dislocated as a result of the war. This was the case after the Napoleonic Wars as the Whig MP Henry Brougham made clear in the Commons in 1817:

It is quite true, that a transition from war to peace must always affect several branches of public wealth, some connected with foreign, but a greater proportion with domestic trade. Thus two departments of industry have suffered severely by the cessation of hostilities; the provision trade of Ireland; through it also, the cattle market of this country, and the manufacture of arms at Birmingham. The distress arising from the peace in those branches of commerce may be temporary; if all the other channels of trade unconnected with the war, were open, it certainly would be temporary. But when we find the depression general in all lines of employment, as well in those uninfluenced by war-demand, as in those wholly dependent upon it; when we see that hands thrown out of work in one quarter can no longer be absorbed into the other parts of the system, when there plainly appears to be a choking up of all the channels of industry, and an equal exhaustion in all the sources of wealth – we are driven to the conclusion that the return of peace accounts at the utmost only for a portion of the sad change we every-where witness, and that even that portion may become permanent from the prevalence of the evil in quarters not liable to be affected by the termination of the war. I have shown you that the cotton trade, wholly unconnected with the war, is more depressed than the iron trade in general, and to the full as much depressed as the very gun manufactory at Birmingham. I am entitled to conclude, first, that the transition from war to peace has not produced all the mischief; and next, that the mischief which it has produced might have been got over, as in former times, if it had been the only one which oppressed us. Sir, we must once for all look our situation in the face, and firmly take a view of the extent of our disease. It is not a partial description; it is of general prevalence.

Some historians have ascribed the economic hardships suffered by many people during these years of depression to the Industrial Revolution, ignoring the effects of the French Wars (see Chapter 14). This is to ignore a major factor in history – favourable and otherwise.

7. Commerce, Trade and the Industrial Revolution

During the seventeenth century both Royalist and Cromwellian governments had followed similar policies in two separate but linked fields, one of which has been christened the Colonial System, the other being formalized in Navigation Acts. Both of these had as their objectives the furthering of British commercial and industrial interests, and the fact that monarchist and republican governments pursued largely similar policies bears out the truth of the claim that in England commerce was master of Parliament.

The Colonial System

Under what Adam Smith called 'impertinent badges of slavery', the economies of territories in the British Empire were regulated to bring the maximum benefit to the Mother Country. Colonial states, including Ireland, were forbidden to develop their own woollen industry. The American colonies were forbidden to export beaver hats, lest this prove too great a competition for the British hatting industry. They were also forbidden to develop a steel industry, to build forges, slitting-mills or other ironworks, or to produce iron goods.

The obverse to this control of industrial expansion was that the colonies became the primary producing countries, supplying the Mother Country with the things she was unable to produce herself. They were to produce sugar, tea, rice, cotton, paper, timber and other naval materials, and pig-iron which it was hoped would drive the Russian and Swedish pig-iron imports from the English market.

The mainspring behind this development and enforcement of the system was the fear of war. Bullion was the 'sinews of war': a fall in imports from Russia and Sweden would lessen the flow of gold from Britain, while a rise in the volume of imports of primary products from the colonies would obviate the need to import such items from bullion-demanding countries such as France and Holland. It was the thought of war which inspired the demand for timber and other naval stores such as hemp, pitch, turpentine and tar. Most of these products had to be imported from the Baltic States or Russia. During a war this source of supply might be in the hands of an enemy or blockaded by an enemy fleet. The creation of a self-supplying, colonial-wide system would serve to strengthen the Mother Country.

In the 1770s the Americans finally rebelled against this system and their successful War of Independence convinced many people, including Adam Smith, that artificial interference with the free flow of commerce and trade was to be deplored. The system also required that the Mother Country guarantee a market to the colonial suppliers by imposing high tariffs on similar imports from non-colonial countries. The government welcomed the extra revenue generated by these customs duties although as Smith pointed out the customer suffered: 'Consumption is the sole end and purpose of all production . . . . But in the mercantile system the interest of the consumer is almost constantly sacrificed to that of the producer and it seems to consider production and not consumption as the ultimate end and object of all industry and commerce.'

The Americans demanded freedom to run their economies as they thought fit. When an obstinate British Government refused, they rebelled. Later on, British manufacturers, industrialist sand traders demanded an end to the system of high tariffs in which import duties on many products were as high as 30 per cent. It was a sign of British confidence and capacity that the system was dismantled by stages after the 1820s.

The Navigation Acts

During the 1650s and 1660s a number of Navigation Acts were passed, the main aim of which was to reserve trade between countries in the Empire to British and colonial merchants and ships, so that the fleets of France and Holland, our main rivals at that stage, would be underused and so go into decline. This is spelt out in the wording of the 1660 act:

> ... that from the first day of December one thousand six hundred and sixty ... no goods or commodities shall be imported into or exported out of any lands or territories to his Majesty belonging ... in Asia, Africa or America but in such ships or vessels as ... belong to the people of England or Ireland, dominion of Wales or town of Berwick-upon-Tweed, or are of the built of and belong to any of the said lands or territories, and whereof the master and three-fourths of the mariners at least are English.
>
> And it is further enacted ... that no goods or commodities that are of foreign growth or manufacture, and which are brought into England, Ireland, Wales, the islands of Guernsey and Jersey, or town of Berwick-upon-Tweed, in English-built shipping or shipping belonging to some of the aforesaid places, and navigated by English mariners, shall be shipped from any other place ... or countries, but only from those of the said growth or manufacture.

But there was a good deal more to be gained than merely the right to carry colonial produce across the Atlantic. The development of a vigorous carrying trade was of direct benefit to the shipbuilding industry. There were also a number of benefits to be derived by the inhabitants of the ports to which the imports were brought to be insured and warehoused; for example, employment for workers and profits for insurers and owners of dockside facilities. There was also an active trade in discounting the bills of exchange used to facilitate payment for the cargo. The increase in commercial activity in the docks led to the development of an active and large group of merchants connected with the financing of that activity.

Most of the imports from colonial countries had to be refined or otherwise processed, and around the ports there grew up sugar-refineries, rum-distilleries and tobacco-chopping factories as well as firms producing the packaging needed for the distribution of the processed product. Some of the colonial goods were re-exported to other countries in Europe. The profits from this re-export trade – shipping, bill-discounting and the like – further helped commercial development of the port concerned. It is not surprising that British governments were anxious that this development (the consequence of the use of the country's ships in the carrying trade) should benefit Glasgow, Liverpool, Bristol and London rather than Amsterdam.

From this controlled system of colonial trade the British gained the imports which they needed, an enlargement of the merchant navy and of that commercial class which had capital for risk-taking and which became even richer as a result of their dealings. The expertise and experience of this increasingly expanding class would prove invaluable when Britain entered on its Industrial Revolution.

British exports

The following table 5 reveals the limited volume and value of exports and imports in 1700, and reminds us again that at that time the population was small, mainly engaged in agriculture with limited economic expectations:

Table 5 *The Volume and Value of Exports and Imports 1700–1800*

	Exports £m	(Including re-exports) £m	Bullion exports £m	Imports £m
1700	6.47	(2.13)	0.83	5.97
1710	5.3	(1.57)	0.4	4.01
1720	6.91	(2.3)	1.03	6.09
1730	8.55	(3.22)	3.43	7.78
1740	8.2	(3.09)	0.67	6.70
1750	12.7	(3.23)	2.43	7.77
1760	14.7	(3.71)	0.88	9.83
1770	14.3	(4.76)	0.64	12.22
1780	12.55	(4.32)	0.9	10.76
1790	18.9	(4.83)	—	17.44
1800	40.81	(18.4)	—	28.36

Table 6 *The Main Sources of British Imports and Major Markets for British Exports 1700–98*

	Percentages of totals for England and Wales			As percentages of total for Great Britain
	1700/1	1750/1	1772/3	1797/8
Total imports from:				
Europe	66	55	45	43
North America	6	11	12	7
West Indies	14	19	25	25
East Indies and Africa	14	15	18	25
Re-exports to:				
Europe	85	79	82	88
North America	5	11	9	3
West Indies	6	4	3	4
East Indies and Africa	4	5	6	4
Domestic exports to:				
Europe	85	77	49	30
North America	6	11	25	32
West Indies	5	5	12	25
East Indies and Africa	4	7	14	13

Source: Compiled from the custom-house ledgers; PRO Customs 3 and 17. For a more detailed analysis see Deane and Cole, *British Economic Growth, 1688–1959* (1962), as also for Tables 4, 5 and 7.

Exports doubled between 1720 and 1760, and then under the impact of the American War and its immediate aftermath fell away until 1780. Then between 1780 and 1800 exports more than trebled in value. This large percentage increase was of great significance for British industry which already had the limited benefit of a domestic market which was expanding but at a relatively low rate. The great surge in the value (and volume) of exports provided the major stimulus to British manufacturers and inventors. If we are looking for major causes of the industrial take-off after 1780, one is to be found in the export market.

Table 6 opposite shows the main sources of British imports and major markets for British exports. One feature of the pattern revealed in that table is the great increase in the exports of British goods to colonial territories between 1750 (when they took only 23 per cent of such exports) and 1772/3 (when they took 51 per cent). Even after the United States of America had become independent, its share of the British export trade continued to grow, so that by 1797/8 America and the colonies were taking 70 per cent of British exports. The acquisition of colonies had paid off.

What goods were exported from Britain before and after the onset of her Industrial Revolution?

Table 7 *Goods Exported from and Imported into Britain 1700–1800*

	1700	1750	1772	1790	1800
Imports (*in £ million*)					
Groceries	16.9	27.6	35.8	28.9	34.9
Raw cotton	—	0.9	1.2	5.0	6.0
Linens	15.6	14.8	10.4	8.5	5.6
Textile materials	16.2	16.4	21.8	19.6	15.4
Exports (in £ million)					
Woollens	57.3	45.9	42.2	34.8	28.5
Cotton goods	0.5	—	2.3	10.0	24.2
Other textiles	2.4	6.2	10.6	7.4	6.1
Grain	3.7	19.6	8.0	0.8	—
Iron	1.6	4.4	8.0	6.3	6.1

There was a significant change in the type of exports. In 1700 woollen goods made up over half of all exports, a reminder that wool was Britain's second largest industry after agriculture. By 1800 wool's share of the export trade had dropped dramatically, while cotton goods were well on their way to taking the first place in the export league table. It is doubtful whether mass production would have taken place in cotton or any other industry, if the available market had been the restricted market of the 10 million or so who lived in Britain towards the end of the century. The international markets open to British trade, in colonies and elsewhere, made possible the application of mass production, factory-operated methods, particularly to cotton, a cheap yet high-quality product which could appeal even to the better-off. People in warm as well as in cold countries could be persuaded to buy cotton goods which replaced the previous British export of Indian calicoes and muslins.

This widening of the market is seen by historians as a major cause of British industrialization. As one has written:

> The inducement to invest is limited by the size of the market.
> . . . It is a matter of common observation that in the poorer
> countries the use of capital equipment in the production of
> goods and services for the domestic market is inhibited by the
> small size of that market, by the lack of domestic purchasing
> powers, not in monetary but in real terms.

The development of this mass, world-wide market was a cumulatively progressive one. British cotton-manufacturers bought vast quantities of raw cotton, which stimulated innovation in the cotton-producing countries. This was particularly true of the United States of America, where new lands were opened up for planting and Eli Whitney invented a gin which cheapened and quickened the production of raw cotton. One effect of these changes was to push down the price of the raw material, so that manufacturers were able to offer an even cheaper product, bringing it within the range of a larger section of the population.

The purchase of raw cotton by Britain put money into the pockets of thousands of workers and owners in the USA and the other cotton-producing countries. They then took advantage of the falling prices of the manufactured article to buy more cotton goods, so increasing the demand for the raw material and further stimulating manufacturers to improve their methods of production.

Re-exports

In Table 5 on page 106 it is clear that re-exporting colonial produce was an important part of British commercial effort. In Asia the East India Company bought spices, along with coffee and tea; from the West Indies came more sugar, rum or molasses than the British could consume themselves; Virginian tobacco was only one of the imports the British brought from America and then re-exported to European countries, which either did not have access to these overseas sources or else lacked the shipping to import directly to their own country.

The East India Company paid a relatively small price for the peppers, cloves and other spices which formed the bulk of its trade; these commodities were sold in Europe for as much as ten times their cost. If the bullion theory had been followed to the full the company would have been forbidden to import the spices unless they had exported a correspondingly valuable export. But the company argued that an adverse balance of trade with the East, to which gold was sent to pay for the spices, was more than compensated for by the greater inflow of bullion from Europe when the spices were sold. The significance of this trade is shown by the figures in Table 5 on page 106 which indicate that there was a very large percentage increase in the value of this re-export trade which brought all the commercial, employment and other benefits outlined on pages 105-7.

The European market

It is clear from Tables 5 and 6 on page 106 that Europe was a major market both for British domestic exports and for re-exports. This is hardly surprising; it was easily accessible to British traders and its people were likely to have tastes similar to those of the British people. Although Europeans had smaller *per capita* incomes than did the British, they were nevertheless better off than most other peoples in the world. Taken as a whole Europe was a rich market and even if it did not take as high a share of British domestic imports in 1800, because of the Continental system, it continued to take the largest share of British re-exports.

The American market

In 1750 the white population of the thirteen American colonies was about 1 million. By the time that the states had won their independence in 1783 there were over 2 million whites in a total population of about 3 million. Most of the whites were prosperous; wages were rising more rapidly than they had risen in England in the first half of the century. Adam Smith noted in his *Wealth of Nations*, first published in 1776: 'wages are much higher in North America than in any part of England. Though North America is not yet so rich as England it is much more thriving, and advancing with much greater rapidity to the further acquisition of riches.' By 1797 America was a more important market for British domestic output than was Europe, although the latter took the bulk of British re-exports. The significance of the American market was brought out in 1812 during the investigation into foreign trade by a parliamentary committee:

[Evidence of Joseph Shaw, Chairman of Birmingham Chamber of Foreign Commerce and exporter of hardwares.]

Have you had occasion to make any estimate, founded upon your own enquiries, of the number of workmen employed in the Birmingham manufactory – and the neighbouring towns?

I never particularly estimated for the whole of them, but in the year 1808 I took an estimate of the people employed in the American trade. . . . Those that could be ascertained to be (as nearly as could be) exclusively employed in the American trade, were 50,000, exclusive of the nail trade, which employed from twenty to thirty thousand [of whom two-thirds were engaged in the American trade].

Can you state to the Committee, from your observation, what proportion the foreign trade generally bears to the trade for home consumption? . . . I should think it was considerably more than one half, including the United States.

Do you think it would amount to two-thirds? I should think not far from it. . . .

[Evidence of John Bailey, exporter and home factor of Sheffield goods:]

The population of the parish of Sheffield, as returned by the overseers in the year 1811, was 53,000 odd; but including those parts of parishes in which Sheffield goods are manufactured, the population amounts to 60,000 at least.

Can you tell what proportion of hands are employed in manufacturing for the American market? – For the American market, about 4,000 male adults, and 2,000 women and children, making a total of 6,000.

How many do you estimate are employed in manufacturing for the home trade? – Six thousand male adults, and one thousand women and children.

How many do you calculate are employed in the remaining parts of the Sheffield trade, namely, manufactures for the foreign market, exclusive of the American? – Two thousand male adults, and one thousand women and children.

This last market includes Spain and Portugal? – Spain, Portugal, the West Indies, South America, and Canada, with some few other parts.

What proportion does the American market bear to the home market, as far as regards the Sheffield goods? – The American exports amount, as nearly as I have been able to ascertain, to one-third of the whole manufactures of Sheffield; the home trade to, I think, three-sixths. . . .

Commercial centres

London was the country's main port. Huge wharves and warehouses were built alongside docks old and new; London's bankers and specialist insurance brokers were well able to handle the increasing volume of business which came their way as the result of the increase in foreign trade. London became the centre of the nation's credit system and its banks and brokers played their part not only in financing British foreign trade but in channelling some of the profits made in that trade (including their own profits) into investment in domestic industrial and commercial development. Because of the great value of its re-export trade London became the centre of the European credit system, particularly when Paris and Amsterdam were adversely affected by the French Revolution and the wars which started in 1792.

The development of an active, large and experienced banking sector was of great significance for Britain's own industrial future, as we shall see in the next chapter. The same banking skills and financial resources were also responsible for providing the risk-capital needed for the development of overseas countries. In particular the economic development of the United States, Canada and the former Spanish colonies of Latin America would not have been possible but for the merchants of the City of London. In the 1820s Canning, as British Foreign Secretary, provided the diplomatic backing needed to sustain the newly won independence of the Latin American countries against the autocratic powers of Western Europe anxious to bring the former colonies back under Spanish tutelage. Canning boasted: 'I called the New World into existence to redress the balance of the Old.'

He might have paid tribute to the industrialists and merchants of Britain who had been mainly responsible for the development of this country whose power was now so great that a British Foreign Secretary was able to exercise world-wide influence. He might also have admitted that the New World might never have been in a position to come on to the world stage if it had not been for the bankers of the City who provided the capital for its development. His critics might also have pricked the bubble of his conceit, by pointing out that his determination to aid the emerging countries was dictated by the need to safeguard British financial interests in South America.

The increased foreign trade also changed the face and fortunes of Liverpool, whose population had been about 5,000 in 1700, but which grew at such a pace that Defoe declared in 1724:

> Liverpool is one of the wonders of Britain, and that more, in my opinion, than any of the wonders of the Peak. The town was, at my first visiting it about the year 1680, a large, handsome, well-built and increasing or thriving town. At my second visit, in 1690, it was much bigger than at my first seeing it, and by the report of the inhabitants, more than twice as big as it was twenty years before that; but I think I may safely say at this my third seeing of it, I was surpris'd at the view, it was more than double than what it was at the second; and I am told that it still visibly increases both in wealth, people, business and buildings. What it may grow to in time, I know not.

By 1750 its population was 30,000. Bristol, another city benefiting from foreign trade, doubled its population between 1700 and 1750, by which time there were 90,000 living in the port. The growth of these and other ports was the result of the growth in colonial trade – largely in bulky goods such as sugar and tobacco – for which shipping had to be built, maintained, insured and manned. The growth of these prosperous, urban centres led to a rise in the domestic demand for a wide variety of manufactured goods and for food, which then acted a as further spur to British manufacturers and farmers.

The take-off into industrial growth

There had been an increase in domestic real wages in the period from 1730 to 1750 and this had led to an increase in demand for manufactured goods and had quickened the pace of industrial activity. There had been a rise in the incomes of the better-off as a result of rising corn prices after 1760, and this again had stimulated industrial and commercial activity. But there seems little doubt that it was the dramatic rise in the export trades in the last quarter of the eighteenth century which provided the most important single stimulus to manufacturers and industrialists. The older methods of production would have been quite unable to meet the demand from this constantly expanding foreign market.

As we have seen this foreign trade tended to be self-reinforcing, in that payments made by Britain for increased volumes of imports tended to be spent by their foreign recipients on British goods which appear on the balance-sheet as exports. The subsequent activity at home – more employment, greater profits and so on – led at least to a maintenance of domestic demand if not always to an increase in that demand. British industrialists were then provided with many reasons for trying to exploit new methods of production to raise the total output of their plants and the productivity of each workman employed there. As we shall see in the next chapter the risk-capital for the industrial investment was provided in part at least from the profits made in foreign trade, while more capital was provided by people eager to enrich themselves from investing in the export-led, self-sustaining march towards industrialization.

8. Capital and the Industrial Revolution

Capital and caution

During the last two centuries rulers, politicians and economists of many countries have taken the British Industrial Revolution as the model for their own industrial development. Many of them have concluded that a major reason for Britain's take-off was that large amounts of capital were invested in, for example, factories, plant and transport systems. They have then sought sources from which to obtain this apparently vital capital, organized the channelling of it into – in their terms – desirable directions and sat back and waited for industrialization to happen.

The failure of many such experiments has made modern rulers and economists more cautious in their approach to the question of the significance of capital investment. We shall consider some countries which have invested heavily only to see little real evidence of take-off, and we shall consider why this was so for Russia at the end of the nineteenth century and for many under-developed countries in our own time. This is not to deny that capital formation had a part of play in British industrial development. However, capital played a limited part in that development, a part which it could not have played if there had not been a large number of other attendant factors acting as causes for change at the same time.

The demand for capital

During the early years of the Industrial Revolution the demands for industrial investment were small in absolute terms and in relation to the demands made by government for the purpose of fighting wars. By taxation and loans the government took about £1,000 million from the British people between 1793 and 1815. Even when railway-building was at its height – between 1830 and 1850 – this largest user of capital only required about £250 million. In the pre-railway era, in the early days of industrialization, the economy was relatively small, as we can see from population figures and statistics on the value of exports (see Table 5, page 106). A small-scale economy had no need of large-scale technology even if such had been available. And the fact is that it was not available; the first machines were small and cheap. Modern underdeveloped countries have less good fortune in that, if they want to buy into the industrial race, they have to lay out vast sums of capital on steelworks, oil-refineries and other large-scale technology even if such had been available. And the fact is mantle their furnaces and move them around the country in search of fuel and water; their need for investment-capital was in proportion to the modesty of their plant.

There were of course other competing demands for capital during the period from 1760 to 1830 by which time about £32 million had been invested in turnpike trusts for the building of new roads and about £20 million in canal companies. Landowners invested heavily in enclosure, spending their capital on getting bills through Parliament and on the process of enclosure itself. There was also the demand of the government, whose borrowing increased from £46 million in 1738 to £244 million in 1793, when the wars against France began, which led to a further increase in government borrowing.

Capital investment in productive industry was relatively small. It has been estimated that between 1783 and 1802 investment in fixed capital in the cotton industry totalled only £8 million, while the total fixed capital investment in the iron industry in 1806 was about £11 million. While there was also a good deal of short-term, variable capital invested in each of these industries – to cover stocks, goods in the process of manufacture, raw materials and so on – it is clear that capital formation and its provision was on a limited scale compared to other demands for capital.

Availability of capital

Of course even such modest demands would have been beyond the reach of a really underdeveloped country. But by 1760 Britain had an already well-developed economy, able to provide the large loans to successive governments engaged in wars against France. The conspicuous consumption by many members of the richer classes is commemorated in the splendid and costly buildings still surviving, and in the diaries and memoirs of those who travelled widely in great luxury, spending ostentatiously and bringing back the cultural artefacts of Europe as memorials of their visits.

The rising middle classes also had large sums of money surplus to their normal requirements. Some of this, as we have seen, they poured into the acquisition of large estates and the building of grand houses – the outward sign of their commercial success. And having acquired estates they joined with many of the established landowners to invest heavily in land-improvement schemes which often provided them with even higher incomes and a greater surplus of money.

We have seen that towards the middle of the eighteenth century the land-market was drying up so that the now successful merchant was unable to gratify his social ambitions by investment in land and building. This meant that there was a great deal of potential investment-capital looking for new channels down which to flow.

Capital-owners

King's table (see Table pp. 24–5) shows clearly that at the beginning of the eighteenth century the majority of the wealth-owners
were, not surprisingly, to be found in the countryside. The landowners, smaller freeholders and prosperous tenants were more
numerous and collectively wealthier, than the merchants and
others in the middling classes. As we have seen these were joined
during the eighteenth century by an increasing number of people
who had become richer because of the growth in foreign trade.
There was a more than average growth in mercantile profit,
particularly towards the end of the century, and a good deal of
capital was accumulated in the ports associated with this trade –
Glasgow, Liverpool, Bristol and London. There is plenty of
evidence that there was a direct link between these mercantile
profits and the industrial development which took place in the
hinterlands around Liverpool, Bristol and Glasgow for example.

But linking up those who had capital available for investment
and those who needed such capital was not always or indeed
often as simple as that. Since most of the available capital was in
the countryside (East Anglia for example), while the demand
from capital came from industrialists in another part of the
country (Lancashire for example), some means had to be devised
for getting the capital from one to another.

Capital structure

Before considering the mechanism by which the nation's capital
was transferred from its holders to the borrowers, some consideration has to be given to the nature of the capital structure of
industry during the first years of the Industrial Revolution. We
have already seen that the amount of technology was small and the
amount of fixed capital investment modest. Indeed as a rule-of-
thumb we may take it that fixed or long-term capital represented

only about one-seventh of the capital of a firm. Movable or circulating short-term capital represented the bulk of investment. The industrialist spent more on raw materials, goods in the process of being manufactured and goods sold but not yet paid for than he did on buildings, machines and other forms of fixed investment.

This 6:1 division of capital would not have been true of all industrial concerns. Iron and coal were industries in which fixed capital represented as much as half the total capital investment of a firm. But these heavily capitalized industries were in a minority. In the early days of the textile revolution, when work was done by people in their own cottages, the capitalist clothier had almost all his investment in circulating capital with little in the form of buildings or machinery.

The majority of the early entrepreneurs had relatively little need for capital for long-term investment, but they had a continual and growing need for capital to finance their dealings in the short term. They needed money to buy the raw materials and some means of discounting the bills of exchange received from customers, to provide them with cash in hand before the period of customer-credit expired.

Sources of long-term capital

The Stock Exchange had existed in at least an embryonic form since the 1690s when jobbers and stockbrokers used to meet in Jonathan's Coffee House in 'Change Alley', not far from the Bank of England. This was burnt down in 1748 and replaced by New Jonathan's and it was this building which was officially entitled the Stock Exchange in 1773, although members in referring to 'the House' still recall the coffee-house origin. By the end of the eighteenth century almost all the work done on the exchange involved the issuing of new government stock and the buying and selling of old stock. Industrial development made few demands on the skill, expertise and efficiency of this highly developed capital market, partly because few industries needed very large amounts of capital investment, and partly because the Bubble Act of 1720 made it a less than simple matter to raise public money for speculative ventures. The canal companies were among the largest users of the Stock Exchange, and by 1830 they had borrowed only about £20 million.

A good deal of the capital required for the building of canals and the local turnpike came from landowners, some of whom mortgaged their estate to provide themselves with the capital for investment. Many landowners also provided part of the long-term capital requirements for other local undertakings; there were close links between the agricultural wealth of the Earls of Durham and the Marquesses of Londonderry and Bute, and the development of the coal and iron industries on or near their estates.

The successful industrialist ploughed back a portion of his profits, and so provided some of his own long-term capital investment. Successful industrialists invested part of their profits in the acquisition of landed estates, and the profits from the estate later provided a source for investment in the industrial concern, which had originally provided the capital for the purchase of the estate.

Since the amount of capital required was small, an industrialist might raise what he needed by a mortgage on his own land, as did Robert Peel, grandfather of the Prime Minister of that name (see page 196). The money for the mortgage might be provided by the local solicitor acting for a London-based firm which had access to the London financial market with its country-wide contacts. But the money might also be raised locally if the sum involved were not too large. The enterprising industrialist might also tap his own circle of acquaintances when looking for capital. Membership of a religious sect often provided the key to the door marked 'capital'. There were many such examples of what may be termed intra-religious investment and in Chapter 9 we will consider the reasons for and implications of this link between religion and industrial investment.

As an illustration of a good deal of what has been said there is the journal of David Whitehead of Rawtenstall in Lancashire. He was born in 1790. His father died leaving the widow with seven young children, whom she maintained by taking up work as a weaver, sending the children into apprenticeship as soon as possible. David Whitehead became a weaver, and in 1817 he and two brothers decided to set up as cotton-manufacturers in their own right. As we can see from the journal, they rented a mill and borrowed £100 from another, older, Quaker manufacturer; the later expansion of the business owed a great deal to the ploughing back of profits:

My brothers and I agreed that the firm should be called Thomas Whitehead and Brothers. . . . Brother Peter attended to his warping and at nights assisted me in planning. He was very diligent and persevering.

We had not been brought up mechanics but had good ideas of mechanism and we soon made a great improvement in our machinery. . . . We had got a large stock of weft on hand which did not sell well. I bought some warps and began to manufacture. I got a few weavers in the neighbourhood of Balladenbrook. I got my mother who lived at Newchurch to weave for us, and a few weavers more at Newchurch. I took in pieces at my mother's house, and made them up there, ready for the market. My mother was one of the best weavers I had, and when I had any cloths more difficult than the rest, I gave them to her to weave. . . .

Balladenbrook was a small place and had no shop to sell any food. The workpeople complained of having so far to go to buy their food. So I began to sell meal and flour, and other grocery. . . .

Warbourton, who had the mill of whom we took the room, had a woollen engine and carded woollen for country people.

His business was not doing well for him. He said if we had no objections he would deliver the mill up to us. We went with him to Mr. Hargreaves, of whom he rented the mill, but did not agree with Mr. Hargreaves about the mill at that time. We found that with all the money we could collect together we had little enough. We got mother to go and see if she could prevail of old Mr. Thomas Hoyle of Manchester (Printer) to lend us a hundred pounds. My grandfather Lionel Blakey was one of the 'Friends' (called Quakers), as was also Thomas Hoyle. They were relations and fellow playboys. . . .

On Monday I went to Manchester to see Mr. Thomas Hoyle. . . . He made particular enquiry of me, what we were doing and what we intended to do. I answered every question (which were not a few) as positively as I could. . . . His conversation was very encouraging and instructive to me. I mentioned the sum of money we wanted to borrow of him. He said, 'Our Lord says: From him that would borrow of thee, turn not thou away. I have been thinking about it and who knows but I may make thee ride in thy carriage? I have made some ride in their carriages by helping them into business. I will lend thee and thy brothers one hundred pounds, but thou must take care to pay me the interest punctually. . . .'

After we had made an agreement for the mill with Mr. Hargreaves for a term of seven years, he also agreed to build us a spinning shop, and we got a new weft engine upon the most improved plan, on which we carded Bengal cotton, and turned off 1,000lb per week and sometimes more. . . .

The new improved engine did its work so well, we got another of the same kind; and the old engine which we had had for a companion all night so often, we now turned adrift. . . . Our business continued to increase and we took care to be punctual in all our engagements and never to break a promise of payment. . . .

When we began business in 1817, trade was very bad; so much so that some of our friends who knew we had saved a

little money said to us, 'There will never be a good trade in
the cotton again, it is quite overdone.' Some said, 'There are
goods enough made to fill the sea.' I said little to them but I
thought, I understood the business, and I am not afraid to work;
and it will be bad indeed if I cannot get as much or more than
any wages any other manufacturer can afford to pay me. If I
can do that I shall be satisfied. . . . These clouds of darkness had
now passed away and we had now a good trade I took in
pieces at Haslingden one day in the week, and also one day in
Newchurch and one day at Balladenbrook. For some time
brother Peter, when he had done his warping at Longholme,
joined brother Thomas and I every Friday night, and we hooked
up all the pieces, loaded the cart, and sent them off to
Manchester. Sometimes it was as far as four o'clock on a
Saturday morning before we had done; and for perhaps
twelve months or more we generally received a letter back per
cart on Saturday night, that the goods were sold.

Short-term capital

David Whitehead had little need to look for a long-term capital
investment, and his experience was typical of most of the early
industrialists. It was far more important to him to get short-term
finance to pay for the raw materials and for labour while the goods
were being manufactured. Some of this financing was provided
by merchants who allowed their customer-industrialists up to
three months' credit, and were often prepared to extend that
period, sometimes almost endlessly so that some bills remained
unpaid for years.

But the main source for short-term capital for the majority of
industrialists was the well-established banking system which had
grown very rapidly since the establishment of the Bank of England
in 1694. There were before that date a number of small banks,
most of them run by goldsmiths with whom wealthier people

had deposited their gold and plate for safekeeping and who had become used to lending some of that gold to businessmen and merchants against bills of exchange or mortgages. In London and other important towns the goldsmiths led the way. But they were not alone. There were a number of other people who were prepared to give up being merchants or craftsmen to become bankers. For instance wine-merchants, who had safe cellars and well-guarded warehouses, were well able to take on the task of financing other people's trade. They had always had either to give credit (to the merchants who bought their wine for sale throughout the country), or ask credit (from the vineyard-owners from whom they bought the wine). Now they used their knowledge of this credit-giving to good effect by offering to finance other people's trading ventures. Wool merchants were also accustomed to asking for, and granting, credit.

In the 1650s and 1660s Britain had fought a series of wars against Holland which had to be financed. One of the reasons for the fall of the Stuart monarchy was that these wars cost more than the king could afford out of his ordinary revenue. And when the Stuarts asked Parliament to approve new taxes to meet the cost of the wars, their requests were refused until they agreed to change their system of government and give Parliament more power.

So to meet the cost of the wars the Stuarts went to the goldsmiths and borrowed gold – at an agreed rate of interest. However Charles II announced that he would not pay the interest due on loans he had received from the goldsmiths. James II continued this 'stop on the Exchequer'; some goldsmiths were ruined and by 1692 the debt owing to them, including the arrears of interest, amounted to £2 million.

In 1688 the Stuart king James II was driven from the throne of Britain by his numerous opponents. Political enemies – the Whigs and the Tories – united in common opposition to the king's attempts to gain greater power. They sent an invitation to William of Orange and his wife Mary (daughter of James II) to become joint rulers of Britain. William of Orange was willing to accept the invitation, hoping that this would enable him to provide stronger resistance to the ambitions of his neighbour Louis xiv of France.

When the political situation had become calmer and William and Mary were firmly settled on the throne, the London gold-smiths and their friends, the London merchants, proposed that the financing of wars should be taken out of the king's hands and that his revenue – from his estates and from parliamentary grants – should be spent only on his own living expenses, the upkeep of his palaces, the paying of his staff and so on. William, anxious to wage a war against Louis of France, wanted £1,200,000 im-mediately and feared that if the war was a long drawn-out affair, he would need more. But he appreciated that the goldsmiths, having suffered at the hands of Charles ii and James ii, would be shy of advancing such a large sum to another king. His need for money to finance a war and the demands of the London merchants coincided, and the result was an act which established the Bank of England.

In 1694 Parliament passed an act which allowed a small number of merchants to collect for the king the sum of £1,200,000. The king promised to pay an interest of 8 per cent to those who subscribed the money. To ensure that this interest would be paid, the act imposed taxes on beer, ale and vinegar, and from these taxes a sum of £100,000 was to be kept back to pay the interest:

XIX. And it shall be lawful for their Majesties to authorize and appoint any number of persons to receive all such voluntary subscriptions as shall be made on or before the first day of August, 1694, by any person or persons.

XX. And it shall be lawful for their Majesties to direct how the said sum of twelve hundred thousand pounds, and the said yearly sum of one hundred thousand pounds, may be assigned to such persons as shall freely and voluntarily accept the same;

and to incorporate all subscribers to be one body corporate, by the name of the governor and company of the bank of England.

XXVIII. Nothing shall hinder the said corporation from dealing in bills of exchange or in buying or selling bullion, or in selling any goods, wares, or merchandise whatsoever, which shall be left with the said corportion for money lent and which shall not be redeemed at the time agreed on.

The Governor and the Company

There was no difficulty in raising the £1,200,000. Some came from goldsmiths, more came from merchants and the amount was made up by six important Whigs in the City of London – three brothers named Houblon, with Sir Michael Godfrey, T. Papilloon and Sir Gilbert Heathcote. These six became the directors of the bank. The act allowed the bank to issue notes to the value of £1,200,000 – the value of the loan made to the king. The bank, like all banks, handed out these notes to people who wished to borrow money and made a profit from the interest which it charged on such loans. The first years of the bank's existence were quite precarious since it had no gold to back its note-issue, apart from the £100,000 which the government paid each year in interest. Fortunately the bank's directors were prepared, when required, to hand over their own gold to help it; more fortunately still the public readily accepted the Bank of England notes and rarely wanted to exchange them for gold.

The six directors were responsible for supervising the day-to-day work of the bank's staff. They had to give an account of their work to the others who had subscribed towards the £1,200,000. These shareholders owned the Bank of England, a joint-stock company drawing its subscriptions from a number of shareholders, unlike the goldsmith banks usually owned by one man or occasionally by partnerships of two or three.

The Bank of England was a joint-stock bank. It enjoyed two main advantages – the support of the government and great public trust because of its connection with the government, so that 'as safe as the Bank of England' soon became a byword. The bank had the right to carry on all the business of a normal bank. It was allowed to make loans, issue notes and accept deposits of gold from merchants, which enabled it to make more profitable loans. Because it had more funds than most of the other smaller banks, it soon became the bank to which large firms and companies went when they wanted a loan. In this way the Bank of England became involved in financing the East India Company and the Hudson Bay Company. Because of its apparent strength it soon began to attract deposits from overseas merchants, especially from Holland. This was a sign that the great money market of Europe and the financial capital of the world had passed from Antwerp to London.

Not everyone welcomed the setting up and growth of this new company. The goldsmiths and the other bankers resented its size, feared its rivalry and foresaw the decline of their own profitable, but much smaller, businesses. Some tried to set up rival institutions. In 1708 the government passed an act which said that if a partnership of more than six decided to open a bank, such a bank would not be allowed to print and issue its own notes. This did not stop individuals or firms with two, three, four or five partners from opening note-issuing banks. The act was designed to limit the size of note-issuing banks, since banks owned by individuals or a small number of partners would have only a limited amount of gold backing – unlike the Bank of England which had the support of the owners of its joint-stock.

During the eighteenth century the existing banks continued to issue their notes and some new note-issuing banks were formed. But these banks were small and unable to provide the volume of credit or cash which the new industrialists of a developing Britain required. Their needs were satisfied by the increasing number of larger banks, with their many partners, and the joint-stock banks in which a wider public were the 'partners'. These larger banks were allowed to accept deposits of gold, advance loans to clients and discount bills of exchange – to do everything that people expected a bank to do – but they were not allowed to print and issue their own notes. To satisfy the needs of their clients, who preferred to have notes than large sums in gold, the banks bought or borrowed the notes they needed from the Bank of England in return for a deposit of some securities.

One of the privileges of the Bank of England was that it became the government's bank. When the government needed to raise new loans from the public it asked the bank to act as its agent. And in the course of the eighteenth century the government was constantly asking the public to lend it money to finance new and more costly wars. It was the Bank of England which raised these loans; it was the bank which issued the advertisements, printed the shares which subscribers received, collected the money, handed it over to the government and arranged the payment of interest each year. For each of these activities the bank charged the government a fee, and as the amount of government borrowing rose, so too did the bank's income, and its ability to issue notes and engage in the normal working of a bank.

London Private Banks

Some of the older London banks founded by the goldsmiths tended to have a clientele drawn from the wealthy landowners and to have little to do with commerce and industry. They acted as agents for their clients, buying government stock, arranging for the transfer of money from the estate perhaps to a foreign bank to finance a Grand Tour or to a country bank to pay for the purchase of land in another part of the country.

There were other London banks whose clients were traders and merchants. These banks had their offices in the City of London. As Britain took off into her Industrial Revolution there was a growth in the number of such banks from about 30 in 1750 to 50 in 1770 and 70 in 1800. They provided a good deal of short-term capital for their clients, discounting bills of exchange and making short-term loans which had to be repaid usually in twelve months. The maxim of 'borrowing long and lending short' was standard English banking practice.

These City banks acted as agents for the increasing number of private banks set up in the provinces. The City bank would send down supplies of gold, silver or Bank of England notes, handle the country banks' surplus cash or provide an overdraft if this were needed. A major function of the City banks was to act as intermediaries for the country banks in the matter of discounting bills of exchange. The country banks in East Anglia tended to have a surplus of cash, deposited by prosperous landowners and farmers; the banks in the industrial areas tended to be the banks which were discounting merchants' and industrialists' bills and so needed more cash than they had on hand. The City banks provided the conduit through which the money flowed from the one area to the other. A portion of this work was taken over after 1800 by specialist bill-brokers, and after 1826 the Bank of England set up its own provincial offices which took away a good deal of the agency work from the City banks.

There were no banks outside London until 1716 when the first provincial or country bank was set up in Bristol. It is not sur-prising that this first venture should be Bristol, the leading commercial centre outside London. The link between the development of commerce and industry on the one hand and country banking on the other is also reflected in the steady increase in the number of such banks during the eighteenth century. There were about 10 founded by 1750, 120 by 1784, 290 by 1797, 370 by 1800 and about 700 by 1810.

Once a man had set up as a banker – often only as a side-line to his main undertaking – he issued his own bank notes which were normally accepted in the local community and which he under-took to change into gold or into Bank of England notes if asked to do so. He was therefore obliged to keep a certain amount of gold in reserve to cover his note-issue and he could usually call on a London agent to advance extra gold should his own stock seem in danger of running out. However there was a great danger that the unregulated, free-running banker might issue more notes than he could possibly cover. While this helped promote economic activity in the area, and perhaps over a wider field, it was all too easy for financial panic to set in if customers found that they were unable to get their notes converted into cash.

Such panics were frequent and the failure of one country bank often had the cumulative effect of driving customers of other soundly-based banks to rush off to get what notes they had converted into gold. Even the soundest bank was unable to meet the demand when a majority of its customers demanded gold for their notes. The news of the failure of one local bank would quickly spread in the small towns of the eighteenth century and cause a local panic, news of which would be carried by the drivers and passengers of stage-coaches so that the panic might spread throughout the country and finally affect the London banks, and agents for the over-committed country banks, who were maybe themselves over-issuing in their own right. During the great panic of 1825 over eighty country banks failed and several City banks were ruined as a result.

The country banks started business as credit-creators, discounting bills and making loans to customers. As they became more trusted some of them became deposit-bankers, customers being prepared to lend their money to the banker for safekeeping. This enabled him to enlarge his credit-creating business and also forced him to look for an outlet for these deposits. If he were fortunate he would find local industrialists or merchants with bills to be discounted. The less fortunate would send his surplus cash to his London agent so that some other investment might be made which would be profit-making for the banker and the depositor-client.

There slowly but surely developed a nationally linked financial system, which was sometimes thrown into panic, but normally acted as a good method of finding a safe investment for creditors' money and a sure source for that short-term capital so badly needed by the industrialists and merchants seeking finance for their purchases of raw materials, wages and other short-term costs.

Short-term capital becomes long-term

The fact that the industrialist had ready access to sources of short-term capital was a great benefit. He did not have to provide the money for the purchase of raw materials, for wage-bills and other running expenses, or for the servicing of the goods on their way from factory to point of sale. All this could be done with the short-term capital from one or other of the many people seeking an outlet for their investment-capital. The industrialist was then free to use his own money for long-term, fixed-capital investment. There is then a close link between the provision of the short-term capital and the development of long-term capital.

The banks developed the myth that they borrowed long but lent short, boasting that they always knew the difference between a bill (which was realizable in at most a year) and a mortgage (which in the prevailing custom of the time might never be realizable). But the distinction between the short- and the long-term was not always easy to define. There were those short-term loans which were continually renewed so that in effect they became long-term loans, repayable only by forcing the debtor into bankruptcy, which would profit no one. Even merchants' bills, which banks readily discounted, provided indirectly much long-term investment, since the merchants often used the money to provide the financial cushioning they needed to be able to extend their credit to industrialist-customers.

Money and wages

The industrialists were often short of ready money, either because they were overspending on fixed investment or because they had to use what ready cash they had on paying off bills which had fallen due. They were reluctant to borrow more than they needed urgently because the interest on borrowing increased the cost of running their business. A major part of the money spent by industrial firms went on wages, and there were a number of ways in which enterprising industrialists lessened their need for 'real' money in this respect, and so lessened their need to borrow. Some, notably in mining areas, paid the men only once each quarter, at the end of which time, hopefully, the output had been sold and money was available for paying the wages. Meanwhile the men's families ran up bills at the local shops – often owned by the mine-owner. The quarterly pay-day would see the men's wives paying off their bills, purchasing whatever extra they felt they could afford and the money making its way from the owner's shop back into the overall financial system of the mine. The men were forced to buy their beer in ale-houses operated by the owner so that their expenditure was also helping to finance the development of the mine.

Company shops were to be found in many centres other than in the mining valleys. Sometimes the men would not be paid in cash but would receive tickets which were exchangeable for goods at the owner's shop, nicknamed 'tommy' shop. This saved the owner having to find ready money each week and also enabled him to make extra profit from running the 'tommy' shop, of which a common complaint was that prices were high and quality low.

Many industrialists coined their own 'money' usually in the form of metal tokens carrying the name, perhaps the figure, of the owner and the value which he wished the coin to represent. Normally such tokens were only exchangeable at an owner-operated 'tommy' shop. In the case of a respected industrialist, such as ironmaster John Wilkinson, a company's tokens might be accepted in other shops in a neighbourhood.

Payments in kind were forbidden by several acts of Parliament long before the Industrial Revolution had got under way. An act passed in 1701 declared:

> That all payments and satisfactions hereafter to be made to any of the same labourers and workmen, for any work by them done in the same manufacture, shall be by the lawful coin of this realm, and not by any cloth, victuals, or commodities, in lieu thereof; and all wool delivered out to be wrought up, shall be so delivered, with declaration of the true weight thereof, on pain that every offender, in either of the said cases, shall forfeit and pay to such labourer or worker, double the value of what shall be due for such work by him, her or them done; and if any such labourer or worker shall be guilty of any such fraud or default in the work by him, her, or them done, then such labourer or worker shall allow and answer to the owner of such work double the damages thereby sustained.

In 1726 another act declared:

> ... every clothier, sergemaker or woollen or worsted stuff-maker, or person concerned in making any woollen clothes, serges or stuffs, or any labourers in the woollen manufactory, shall ... pay unto all persons by them employed ... the full wages or other price agreed on in good and lawful money of this kingdom; and shall not pay the said wages ... or any part thereof, in goods or by way of truck.

But the new energetic and ambitious industrialists were not altogether free agents in this matter of paying wages in 'coin of the realm'. Sometimes there just was not enough money available, particularly in remote mining districts where there were no banks. And even in districts where there were banks there was not always a sufficient amount of the small coins needed for wage payments when wages were small, as can be seen from this extract from the *History of Cotton Manufacture in Great Britain* written in 1835:

Table 8 *Wages of Operatives in the Cotton-mills of Lancashire Specifying their Different Ages*

Age	Number Employed	Males Average Weekly Wage		Number Employed	Female Average Weekly Wage	
		s	d		s	d
11	246	2	$3\frac{1}{2}$	155	2	$4\frac{3}{4}$
11–16	1,169	4	$1\frac{3}{4}$	1,123	4	3
16–21	736	10	$2\frac{1}{2}$	1,240	7	$3\frac{1}{2}$
21–26	612	17	$2\frac{1}{2}$	780	8	5
26–31	355	20	$4\frac{1}{2}$	295	8	$7\frac{3}{4}$
31–36	215	22	$8\frac{1}{2}$	100	8	$9\frac{1}{2}$
36–41	168	21	$7\frac{1}{4}$	81	9	$8\frac{3}{4}$
41–46	98	20	$3\frac{1}{2}$	38	9	$3\frac{1}{2}$
46–51	88	16	$7\frac{1}{4}$	23	8	10
51–56	41	16	4	4	8	$4\frac{1}{2}$
56–61	28	13	$6\frac{1}{2}$	3	6	4
61–66	8	13	7	1	6	0
66–71	4	10	10	1	6	0
71–76	1	18	0	—		—
76–81	1	8	8	—		—

The user of capital

What sort of men were they who borrowed the capital, used other people's inventions to produce goods for sale to a mass market? They were certainly a new breed of men, different from the producers of goods in the pre-industrial era when the greatest profit had been made from the production of a small number of luxury items for sale to the limited market of the better-off. But in the industrialized world, where a mass market exists waiting to be satisfied, it is otherwise; here mass production on machines lowered the cost of the individual items and created its own markets by making goods available to an increasing number of customers able to pay the lower prices.

The job of the capitalist entrepreneur was to see what market existed, ways in which that market might be extended and satisfied, and to bring together the various agents of production so that the demand might be met by an increased supply. Such a man did not have to be an inventor, although he had to be aware of the technical problems facing the people who worked in the factory and had to be able to perform most of the functions himself if need be. He had to make the day-to-day as well as the long-term decisions as regards volume and type of output, whether or not to invest or retract, whether to buy from this one or that one. He purchased the raw materials, fuels, machines and whatever else had to be bought; he had to enforce the standard of production that his customers expected; he had to teach the industrial workforce, accustomed to setting its own pace in the cottage industries, to follow the pace of the machine; he had to organize the sale of goods, send the invoices and see that bills were paid and customers satisfied.

Perhaps it is easiest to overlook a major problem facing the new industrialists in the matter of controlling the workforce, which had grown accustomed over the years to a self-imposed family discipline which aimed to finish whatever piece of work was being done by the Saturday, when the clothier came to collect it. It was quite common for the family to take the weekend off and to bless 'St Monday' for the extra day. In the factory the discipline had to be different, the pace set by the machine, each workman doing his bit constantly and well. Factory-owners imposed their own forms of discipline, fining latecomers, careless workers and idlers, as can be seen from the list of fines imposed in one Lancashire mill:

	s.	d.
Any Spinner found with his window open	1	0
dirty at his work	1	0
washing himself	1	0
leaving his Oil Can out of its place		6
spinning with Gas light too long in the morning	2	0

	s.	d.
heard whistling	1	0
being Five Minutes after the last Bell rings	2	0
being Sick, and cannot find another Spinner		
to give satisfaction, must pay for steam, per day	6	0
Two Spinners found together in Necessary		
[lavatory] each	1	0

Since women and children tended on the whole to be more easily disciplined and also cheaper to employ it is not surprising that many mill-owners preferred to employ them rather than men.

The industrialist was often the creator of a new community as were the Crawshays and Guests who turned Merthyr and Dowlais from being mere villages into the largest centres of population in South Wales and the iron capital of the world. Such men had not merely to run a business, they had also to build homes, shops, schools and churches; if the community were to have any sort of cultural life they would have to help get it established and provide reading-rooms, concert halls and in very many cases minor but significant items such as the uniforms and instruments for the local brass or silver band.

Who were these employers? As with bankers they came from a number of varied sources. Some like David Whitehead were workmen who had saved a little money; others were merchants like the Crawshays who, having sold iron products from London warehouses, went to South Wales to become great ironmasters. If there is any distinction to be drawn between one sort of capitalist entrepreneur and another it is that when the scale of the business was relatively small the field was open for almost anyone to enter, whereas when the technology was greater and more costly, or the scale of the enterprise much larger, then the entrepreneurs tended to be drawn from already well-to-do families who had access to more capital, were probably a little better educated and maybe had a greater degree of confidence in their own abilities. There is some evidence that many of the early

entrepreneurs were members of one or other of the many
Nonconformist sects and that there was to be found among them
a disproportionately high number of Quakers. We shall see more
of this in Chapter 9.

9. The Social and Intellectual Framework

'Heroic' reasons for the Industrial Revolution

Earlier histories of the British Industrial Revolution tended to place great emphasis on the extent and importance of the great technological changes. Modern historians do not give technological change such a central and dominant position in their accounts. They are aware that today the most advanced technologies are available to countries which may wish to adopt them. Even underdeveloped countries can be provided, through international aid agencies, with the finance to acquire these technologies. But the modern historian knows that the results of buying into technological process has often been disastrous. We have come to realize that it is not enough to ship machinery to this country or a modern steelworks to another: great industrial or agricultural change has not always followed the acquisition of the instruments of change.

It is now clear that the technology will not be productive if there is not a large number of people with a variety of skills and qualifications to carry out the hundreds of different tasks involved in running a large industrial concern. There has also to be, as part of the national infrastructure, a section of the community which is able to use the products of the new plant. There is little use in having a large output if this cannot be used for the production of other goods. The infrastructure has also to contain an adequate system of transport, a developed system of basic education for the mass of the population and of higher education to provide the more highly qualified personnel required. But even more significantly there has to be permeating the whole society the intangible quality of a readiness to welcome the innovation, to accept the social changes which industrialization brings and to respect and reward the entrepreneurs whose drive and skill is an essential part of the industrial system.

In the 1890s, a decade or so after the publication of Tonybee's classical account of the British Industrial Revolution, a Russian minister, de Witte, set about the task of industrializing Russia. He borrowed money overseas, bought a great deal of capital equipment from the already industrialized countries, imported the managers and technicians needed to run the coal-mines, steelworks and other industrial plants he hoped to develop. Yet Russia remained hopelessly backward. There was great opposition to de Witte's ideas from various sections of society. Many of his fellow-politicians, more conservative than he, disliked this 'Westernization' of Russia; some feared the political consequences of herding together masses of industrial workers; others feared the emergence in Russia of a profit-seeking, ambitious and driving middle class whose attitudes would be at odds with the traditional habits of the agricultural society which the politicians understood; there were religious leaders, always influential in less developed countries, who feared the consequences of mass education and saw in industrialization a disrupting force which would turn the pious peasant into a godless, grasping urban worker.

A number of modern underdeveloped countries have had similar experiences: in some, religious attitudes have presented an obstacle; in almost all there has been the lack of that skill, those attitudes and that framework which have either to be the consequences of long practice or to be imposed, sometimes brutally as in Stalinist Russia, by an autocratic government.

Modern economists and historians know that before technological changes are widely and readily adopted, there has to be a pre-existing favourable infrastructure. They do not believe that the British Industrial Revolution was the work of a small number of great men. A modern scientist, Michael Polanyi, is quoted by Ashton as remarking, 'Invention is a drama enacted on a crowded stage', and as Ashton pointed out the success of a dramatic performance does not depend only on the work of the few stars who happen to be on the stage at the end of the performance. Success depends on the co-operation of many bit-players, and on the work of many behind-the-scenes operators.

It was neither individual genius nor chance that were responsible for the industrialization of eighteenth-century Britain. If it were, we would have to look for some divine intervention to explain why it was that England was so specially blessed in the eighteenth century and we might wonder at the malevolence of the divinity that has seemed to have withdrawn its favour in more recent times.

Ashton quotes a modern master cotton-spinner's version of the men who created the technologies of the first Industrial Revolution:

> Being neither demigods nor heroes,
> But ingenious, hard-working descendants of homo sapiens,
> Who had the luck to plant their seedlings in fine weather,
> Not in the frost or storm, but when the slow ripening of
> Time, the felicitous crossing of circumstance
> Presented unimagined opportunities,
> Which they seized. . . .

The 'fine weather' to which Armitage refers, and the 'slow ripening of time ... unimagined opportunities', are the spinner-poet's way of summarizing the great social changes which over many centuries had created the infrastructure on which further industrial progress could grow.

Welcome to innovation

The list of the great inventions which transformed British industry in the last quarter of the eighteenth century is impressively
long. But it does not tell the whole story of the inventiveness of
the British people at this time, as the records of the Patent Office
show. Before 1760 there had been about ten patents granted each
year; the change after that date is revealed by the figures in the
following table:

Table 9 *Patents Granted 1760-92*

Year	Number of Patents granted	Year	Number of Patents granted
1760	31	1802	107
1769	36	1824	180
1783	64	1825	250
1792	83		

Part of the increase may be explained by the fact that more
inventors were applying for patents; earlier inventors did not
always do so and the Darby family's unselfishness in this regard
was not uncommon. But the table does show that Englishmen
were increasingly aware of the possibilities of innovation.

The interest in science

The development of a steady stream of scientific thought in
seventeenth-century England was so great and marked that
historians rightly describe it as the 'Scientific Revolution'. The
teaching of Francis Bacon was furthered by the work of geniuses
such as Boyle and Newton who taught the educated world that
observation and experiment were the pathways to scientific and
industrial progress. In 1660 this interest in science had received the
royal accolade with the foundation of the Royal Society which
at least in its early years directed its efforts to applied sciences.

Many of the inventions of the eighteenth century had no link with scientific experiment. Newcomen was a blacksmith, and Darby was an ironmaster. They worked without any of the theoretical knowledge that was available in the laboratories of the chemists. They were empiricists, not scientists. However, many engineers, ironmasters, instrument-makers and industrial chemists were members of the Royal Society and many pure scientists such as Priestley, Dalton and Davy spent at least part of their time in foundries and workshops, forming links between the work of the pure scientists and industrialists.

Growing accustomed to some change

It is not difficult to sympathize with those Russians who vigorously opposed de Witte's proposals for Russian industrialization. After all, the ways of life had run relatively unchangingly in Russia for many centuries. In Britain there had been perceptible changes in the way of life since the beginning of the Tudor period. During the first half of the sixteenth century there were a number of changes – in religion, and in agriculture, where sheep-farming became more profitable so that there was an enclosure movement which altered the pattern of life in many villages.

The changes in industry in this period were such that one historian, J. U. Nef, writes of 'The Industrial Revolution, 1549–1640'. Certainly there was a shift in attitudes from the sixteenth century onwards and an increasing number of people had rising expectations based on the slow but almost continual expansion in the economy which provided greater opportunities for economic advance and also made available an increasingly greater and more varied volume of goods.

It would be wrong to exaggerate the degree of change in the sixteenth century. The rate of growth was slow, but still there was growth and change. The English were not surprised by a slight increase in the rate of change at the beginning of the eighteenth century nor by the even greater degree of change which took place at the end of the century.

The entrepreneurs

It was not enough that there were scientists and others who were able to produce the new technology; there had also to be people who would put the new techniques to work in industry. Someone had to bring together capital and labour on an industrial site, buy the raw materials and fuels and sell the product. Some of the inventors (e.g. Darby and Watt) were also business organizers. But most of the entrepreneurs were not inventors but organizers of the factors of production who applied other people's inventions.

The very large degree of change in the economy at the end of the eighteenth century was the work of a considerable number of such entrepreneurs in British society at the time. Like inventors, entrepreneurs are different from the ordinary run of men. Like Whitehead, they are more ambitious, more willing to work hard, can see possibilities of success where others see only the dangers of failure and have a highly motivating drive for success and achievement. We know that they came from all sections of society and included aristocrats such as Bridgewater, industrialists such as Darby and newcomers to industry such as the wig-maker Arkwright.

What many of the early businessmen had in common was membership of one or other of the many Nonconformist sects. There was a disproportionately larger number of Quakers, Congregationalists, Baptists, Presbyterians and Unitarians among the entrepreneurial class. Nonconformists made up only about 3 per cent of the population of England and Wales in the 1770s, yet about 50 per cent of the early inventors and main entrepreneurs of the Industrial Revolution were Nonconformists.

There have been many and varied explanations for the Nonconformist domination of the capitalist scene. Professor Tawney in his *Religion and the Rise of Capitalism* claimed that the doctrines of Nonconformity were favourable to the development of capitalist enterprises:

> In their emphasis on the moral duty of untiring activity, on work as an end in itself, on the evils of luxury and extravagance, on foresight and thrift, on moderation and self-discipline and rational calculation, they had created an ideal of Christian conduct, which canonized as an ethical principle the efficiency which economic theorists were preaching as a specific for social disorders. It was as captivating as it was novel. . . .
>
> The idea of economic progress as an end to be consciously sought, while ever receding, had been unfamiliar to most earlier generations of Englishmen, in which the theme of moralists had been the danger of unbridled cupidity, and the main aim of public policy had been the stability of traditional relationships. It found a new sanction in the identification of labour enterprise with the service of God. The magnificent energy which changed in a century the face of material civilization was to draw nourishment from that temper. The worship of production and ever greater production – the slavish drudgery of the millionaire and his unhappy servants – was to be hallowed by the precepts of the same compelling creed.

The extract from David Whitehead's journal on pages 121–3 bears out some at least of Tawney's argument with its emphasis on hard work, thrift, frugality, punctuality and attention to detail. The Puritan or Protestant ethic of hard work seemed, in Whitehead's case at least, to have borne fruit. But not all historians accept what they see as a simplistic attempt to explain the emergence of such a large number of Nonconformists capitalists. The American economist K. Samuelson declares:

> It needs no very advanced mathematics to demonstrate that thrift cannot have been the explanation of the wealth of such as

Carnegie or Rockefeller. . . . Genius, sheer luck, a clear eye for market opportunities, a flair for publicity, hard work, low cunning, vast capital gains on natural assets – all these are possible and plausible factors. But to speak of thrift as a decisive or even substantial factor where large fortunes are concerned is utter nonsense.

Indeed there seem to be more practical reasons for the development of capitalism among Nonconformists who were not allowed to hold any civil or military office, or to go to the only two English universities, Oxford and Cambridge. They were in a sense aliens in an Anglican world. There were a number of pro-Anglican and anti-Nonconformist acts of Parliament such as this Test Act of 1673:

> For preventing dangers which may happen from [Roman Catholics] and quieting the minds of his Majesty's good subjects: Be it enacted That all and every person or persons, as well peers as commoners, that shall bear any office or offices military or civil, or shall receive any pay, salary, fees or wages, by reason of any patent or grant from his Majesty, or shall have command or place of trust from or under his Majesty . . . shall . . . in public and open court . . . take the several Oaths of Supremacy and Allegiance . . . and shall also receive the Sacrament of the Lord's Supper according to the usage of the Church of England.

Ambitions and energies which might have been spent on one or other of the careers now closed to them were directed into the economic field where there was no legal restraint on their activities. Capital which might otherwise have been spent on the buying of an estate or the building of a large mansion was available for industrial investment. Some made this investment in their own businesses; others provided the capital needed by other fellow-religionists. The minority group of alienated Nonconformists tended to intermarry, so that ties of kinship were developed and provided other channels down which investment-capital might be drawn.

Some Nonconformists had more confidence in the honesty of fellow-members than in government. One Quaker lady sent a loan of £6,000 to a fellow-Quaker and wrote: 'I had rather it lay in your House than in the Stocks, for I may then have it when I please without difficulty. . . . you will give me better interest and it may be convenient to both you and myself.'

Education and economic progress

One of the ways in which Anglican politicians tried to keep the Nonconformists in their place was by excluding them from the universities; another was to permit only communicant members of the Anglican Church to teach in the ancient grammar schools. Excluded from secondary and university education the Non-conformists set up their own institutes or academies for higher learning. There were a number of these dissenting academies scattered throughout England; some provided a university-type education, others were of a lower standard. One of the aims of these academies was to train ministers for the Nonconformist sects. Another was to provide pupils with an education that was more relevant to the needs of their time and their place in society. For many boys from the Anglican upper classes, education at one of the nine great schools (Eton, Harrow, Winchester, Shrewsbury, Rugby, St Paul's, Westminster, Merchant Taylor's and Charter-house) was a matter of learning Greek, Latin and ancient history, as this extract from Coleridge's diary reveals:

Wednesday at 7 – Translation of English theme looked over. Repeat Tuesday's Poetoe Groeci.
At 10 – Thirty-five lines of Scriptores Groeci.
At 3 and 5 – The same as Monday; but a selection ex Cicerone, or his letters (at the end of the book), were construed on

Monday, and Selecta e Livio, Tacito (you may leave out perhaps e Paterculo) were construed on a Wednesday Exercise Latin Verses – Lowest number of lowest fifth is sixteen. Note – Tully repeated for themes and Ovid for Verses is good but sometimes Greek grammar must be said, instead of these lessons – at least the principal parts of it. Thursday, at 7 – Latin verses looked over. Thirty lines of Selecta ex Ovidio repeated, or Greek grammar.

At 10 – as on Monday.

Half-Holiday – In honour of one or even two (perhaps one of these from the fifth form) of the best praepostor's exercise.

Thursday's exercise – Lyrics of various sorts: Iambics, Sapphies, Asclep., Alc., Trochaics. Two upper praepostors make Greek.

The universities and the ancient grammar schools were directed by their foundation charters and/or the wills of benefactors to teach these subjects. When the parents of boys at Leeds Grammar School tried to get the master to introduce new subjects into the curriculum – mathematics, a modern language, geography, commercial practice, mechanical drawing and the like – he refused and his decision was supported by the Lord Chancellor, Lord Eldon, in a famous decision which affected the development of grammar-school education for a long time after that date.

The dissenting academies were free to teach whatever the masters were qualified to teach and, whenever possible, what the parents of the pupils desired them to teach. Among the more famous of the pupils of the academies were Defoe, Malthus, Hazlitt the essayist and Howard the penal reformer, Roebuck the ironmaster, Boulton and Wilkinson, some of whom were taught by men of the calibre of Priestley and Dalton, eminent scientists as well as distinguished Nonconformists.

The two English universities, Oxford and Cambridge, made little if any contribution to the Industrial Revolution. Ashton in his classical study, *The Industrial Revolution, 1760–1830*, puts it kindly when he says of these that 'the torch burnt dim'. The two

Scottish universities, Glasgow and Edinburgh, had a broader-based curriculum, included theoretical and practical sciences among the subjects offered and trained a large number of graduates, many of whom took the high road to England, and played their part in British industrial development. The habits of thoughtful experiment learned at the Scottish universities were applied to the industrial and technological problems of expanding industries. Some graduates remained in Scotland and helped to develop Scottish industry. In both Scotland and England they helped form learned societies where scientists and industrialists met to discuss a wide variety of topics.

But the take-off needed a much deeper infrastructure than could be provided by the highly educated scientists from universities or academies. There was the demand for a large number of people in different sectors of industry and commerce, educated in different ways and to different levels. There was the need for managers and accounts clerks, for people to write the letters to foreign customers and suppliers, arrange shipping of exports and imports and the discounting of bills of exchange. At the lower level there was the demand for an ever increasing number of skilled workmen, some at least of whom could read blueprints and plans, make calculations and carry out work calling for a high degree of accuracy and manual skill.

The British Industrial Revolution did provide the opportunity for many uneducated people to make their marks. Neither Stephenson the famous railway engineer nor Brindley the great canal-builder had any schooling. The fact that these succeeded without formal education encouraged a later generation of English industrialists to put little store by formal education, even when the new and important industries were science-based and needed a more qualified workforce. In 1911 John Wigham Richardson wrote in his *Memoirs:*

Much has been said in recent years about technical education. The expression has been much abused, for technical education

A Newcastle chaldron, 1764, being drawn along wooden rails.

Harvesting, a detail from a painting by G. Stubbs (1724–1806). Even this idealized picture shows that harvesting was a slow, dirty and laborious task.

A drawing from *The Farmer's Companion*, September 1748, which gives us an idea of the various ploughs, horse-drawn hoes and waggons then in use.

James Gillray (1757–1815) did not approve of the ways in which some prosperous farmers spent their money.

A view of the work in progress at the site of St Katharine's Dock, London, in January 1828, a sign of the increase in foreign trade and a symbol of 'booming Britain'.

A Dame School, painted by T. Webster.

Stone breakers on a road in Yorkshire, 1813. Macadam and the other road engineers had to rely on the work of men such as these.

LEFT The 3rd Duke of Bridgewater (1736–1803) with the aqueduct over the River Irwell in the background.

BELOW A view of East India Wharf, London, by Monamy.

ABOVE TOP The Sankey Valley Viaduct on the Liverpool–Manchester Railway, 1831, a tribute to the engineering skills of the new breed of civil engineers and a reminder of the pastoral nature of England even as late as 1831.

ABOVE Crossing the bog of Chat Moss, 1831.

BELOW Charcoal burners, painted by W. H. Pyne in 1807, by which time there was a diminishing demand for their product in the new ironworks.

Iron puddlers at work in one of the new furnaces c. 1800, using Cort's method to stir the molten ore.

A Sheffield cutler finishing off a knife, 1803.

Inside the smelting house at the ironworks, Broseley, Coalbrookdale, 1788.

Mathew Boulton's works at Soho, Birmingham, before Watt joined him in 1774. Notice the rural setting in which the works were set.

An improved spinning jenny with its cogs made by clockmakers and its cumbersome timber frame.

A Newcomen steam engine. A Boulton and Watt beam engine, 1788.

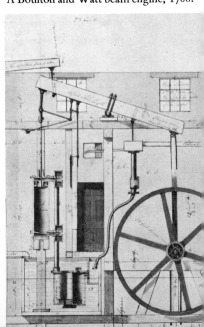

can surely only mean the teaching of an art. In our own arts I can conceive of no better school than the workshop. You have there the experience and skill of the best artisans, you have the feeling of being engaged in serious construction, you are in the very atmosphere of your craft.

More than this, you are learning by doing. There is the learning by committing to memory, and there is the learning of doing, and of the two perhaps the latter is the better education. Some of the most successful men whom I know in other walks of life have been educated in the workshop. The workshop will develop some faculties in a way that Cambridge or Oxford cannot touch. But when your years of apprenticeship are over, or during them, you will do well to add to your practical knowledge all that you can cull from the schools of science. Nor should you neglect the study of modern languages, which are not difficult to acquire if you have a hearty will to do so, and if you learn by the ear rather than or as well as by, the eye.

It was fortunate that the industrial changes of the eighteenth century were not, in general, science-based and did not require a very large number of highly qualified workpeople. But there was still in Polanyi's phrase the 'crowded stage' of workpeople who had to be something more than the illiterate peasants of a really underdeveloped country. England was fortunate in that from about 1700 onwards there had been a move to set up a school alongside every Anglican church where 'the poor' could receive some sort of formal teaching.

It is a matter for debate among historians of British education whether the provision of education for the poor was inspired by fear or by philanthropy. At the beginning of the nineteenth century Robert Owen founded schools for infants as well as for older children who lived in the village around his cotton-mills in New Lanark. Owen also insisted that the curriculum had to be attractive, broadly based and such that the children would grow up with enquiring minds. But Owen was a latecomer into the field; he was also a *rara avis* who had the good of the children at heart. The majority of those who promoted the founding of schools for the poor did so because they were afraid that the increased number of children (resulting from a fall in the death rate and a rise in the birth rate) might turn into a horde of ill-disciplined savages. It was a Christian duty to 'tame' these children. That this would ensure the continuation of the *status quo* in the economic and social sphere was a welcome by-product of the religious aim of helping to save the children's souls. Hannah More helped found many schools in the West Country. After she had been attacked for promoting 'schools for Jacobinism' she wrote to the Bishop of Bath and Wells in 1801:

> My plan of instruction is extremely simple and limited. They learn on weekdays such coarse work as may fit them for servants. I allow of no writing for the poor. My object is not to make fanatics, but to train up the lower classes in habits of industry and piety. I know of no way of teaching morals but by teaching principles; or of inculcating Christian principles without imparting a good knowledge of Scripture. I own I have laboured this point diligently. My sisters and I always teach them ourselves every Sunday, except during our absence in winter. By being out about thirteen hours, we have generally contrived to visit two schools the same day, and to carry them to their respective churches. The only books we use in teaching are two little tracts called 'Questions for the Mendip Schools', The Catechism, broken into short sentences, Spelling Books, Psalter, Common Prayer, Testament, Bible. The little ones repeat 'Watts' Hymns'. The collect is learned every Sunday. They generally learn the Sermon on the Mount, with many other chapters and psalms.

In 1821 she explained how she provided a better education for the slightly better-off, but as this extract shows had no sympathy with Robert Owen's views:

Not the very poor only are deplorably ignorant. The common farmers are as illiterate as their workmen. It therefore occurred to me to employ schoolmasters, who to sound piety added good sense and competent knowledge. In addition to instructing all the poor children in the parish on Sundays at my expense, I directed him to take the farmers' sons on weekdays at a low figure, to be paid by them, and to add writing and arithmetic to reading, which was all I thought necessary for labourers' children. The master carefully instructed these higher boys also in religious principles, which the fathers did not object to when they got it gratuitously. I had long thought that the knowledge necessary for persons of this class, was such as would qualify them for constables, overseers, churchwardens, jurymen and especially tend to impress on them the awful nature of an oath; which I feel is too commonly taken without any sense of its sanctity. Further than this I have never gone.

Now I know the ultra-educationist would despise these limits. Truth compels me to have seen a book on popular education, written by a man of great talents. Truth compels me to bear my public testimony against his extravagant plans, which is that there is nothing which the poor ought not to be taught; they must not stop short of science. They must learn history in its widest extent: Goldsmith's Greece is nothing – he recommends Mitford, etc. Now the absurdity of the thing is most obvious; supposing they had money to buy such books, where would they find time to read them, without the neglect of all business, and the violation of all duty?

Many of the children of the skilled workers and better-off farmers did not go to these 'schools for the poor'. Some went to a dame school where for a weekly fee of about 2p the clergyman's wife or sister or some other 'respectable' female more or less kept order among a dozen or so children who were fortunate if they acquired any real learning. Other children may have been fortunate enough to live within reach of the local grammar school where a graduate schoolmaster, licensed by the local bishop, taught Latin, Greek and ancient history. Samuel Bamford remembered his days at Manchester Grammar School around 1800:

> The school was a large room of an oblong form, extending north and south, and well lighted by large windows. At the northern end was a fireplace, with a red cheerful fire glowing in the grate. The master's custom was to sit in an armed chair with his right side towards the fire and his left arm resting on a square oaken table, on which lay a newspaper or two, a magazine or other publication, a couple of canes with the ends split, and a medley of boys' playthings, such as tops, whips, marbles, apple-scrapers, nutcrackers, dragon-binding, and such like articles. The scholars were divided into six classes, namely, accidence, or introduction to Latin, higher Bible, middle Bible, lower Bible, Testament, and spelling class: the accidence class sat opposite the master's face, and the higher Bible one was at his back. Each class sat on a strong oaken bench, backed by a panel of the same, placed against the wall, with a narrow desk in front so that all sat around the school in regular gradation. The spellers only had not a desk, they sat on forms outside the desk of the higher Bible class, they being considered as children among boys. The boys of each class were placed according to their proficiency, and the first and second boys of the class exercised considerable authority over the others. The school hours were from 7 to 8.30 at morning, from 9.30 to 12 noon and from 2 till 5 afternoon.

But the majority of the nation's children had the sort of schooling described by Joseph Lawson. He wrote *Progress in Pudsey* in 1887 and recalled his schooldays of the 1820s:

> There were very few schools, and many of the teachers could not have passed our present Board Schools' sixth standard. Some taught nothing but reading and spelling, or knitting and sewing; others only reading and writing from printed copies

(not being able to write themselves so well). A few taught arithmetic as well, but a grammar, geography or history were scarcely ever seen in a school in those days. A few of the sons of the middle class learnt writing and arithmetic, but very few others learnt anything but reading. Large numbers never entered the door of a schoolhouse – having to work at something when they arrived at school age, or were allowed to run about all day, as if they were mere animals, and not capable of cultivation, or did not possess faculties waiting for, and needing, development. Writing was looked upon by many parents as a mere luxury for the rich only, and never likely to be wanted by their sons and daughters. A person who was a good reader of the newspaper, and could talk about various wars, battles, and sieges, was looked up to by the people, and said to be a 'great scholar' and 'a far-learned man'. There were few school books, and those were of a poor kind – the tax or duty on paper, and the small demand, causing them to be very high in price. Sunday schools were in their infancy, and there was considerable prejudice against them at first, especially if writing was taught. Many of the teachers were very unfit for their position, and knew less than some of their pupils and were appointed as teachers because older than the rest. Besides, the great or prime object of Sunday schools with many was not so much to teach children to read, as to make the school a kind of nursery which should supply the church or chapel with adherents to its particular faith or creed, and thus replenish it by adding to the church membership. It was quite common for some of the little ones when they returned from Sunday school to talk to their parents about the many errors of the teachers; but even that state of things was better than having no school. Very few attempted to teach writing in a Sunday school – that being looked upon as a desecration of the Sabbath.

The general education of the mass of the people was of a low standard but it did make the majority literate; it did provide a basis however flimsy on which those who wanted to could construct some further building. The establishment of mechanics' institutes and other clubs for working-class adult education indicate both that there was a widespread thirst for learning and the existence of a base on which this 'secondary' education could be constructed. British industry benefited from the existence of this large if shallow pool of general education. The children from the dame schools, charity schools and Sunday schools provided some of the crowd on the stage on which the principal actors played their part.

10. The Transport Revolution

English roads 1700

The Romans had withdrawn from Britain in the fourth century, leaving behind a network of fine roads, but little had been done since then to even maintain it. In medieval times lords of manors were supposed to maintain the roads near their estates; road-making and maintenance was one of the feudal duties imposed on the peasantry. The small medieval towns imposed a toll at the entrance gates set in the walls around the town; part of this toll was supposed to be spent on repairing the roads leading to the town. In fact little was done either by lords or by town corporations.

During the sixteenth century Tudor monarchs had ruled that each parish had to appoint a road-surveyor. He was empowered to recruit parishioners to work for a stated number of days each year on road-repairs. In some parts of the country this system operated as late as 1798. We may not be surprised to read in *A Survey of Somerset, 1798*:

> Whenever a farmer is called forth to perform statute labour, he goes to it with reluctance and considers it a legal burden from which he derives no benefit. His servants and his horses seem to partake of the torpor of the master. The utmost exertion of the surveyor cannot rouse them, and the labour performed is scarcely half what it ought to be.

In 1691 Parliament passed an act which declared that all main roads had to be widened to eight feet. Few parishes took any notice of this act, which the central government was incapable of enforcing. In 1721 Parliament accepted the fact that little was being done by way of road-maintenance. It passed an act which banned the use of more than six horses to a waggon or cart. Again in 1733 Parliament ruled that wheels on carts or wagons had to be of a certain width. There were several later 'Broadwheel Acts', passed by Parliaments which hoped that the use of such wheels would lessen the degree to which road surfaces were being cut up. Parliament tried by such acts to limit the extent of road-ruination, accepting the impossibility of doing much about road-repair or maintenance.

The government and the nation's roads

We have already seen that the government played little direct part in promoting economic development. This is further illustrated by the history of road-improvement. Other European countries had better road systems – and interfering governments. These compelled people to work for so many days each year on building and repairing roads. The *corvée*, or forced labour system, was a symbol of autocracy and bureaucracy, which no English government tried to introduce into England. English governments relied on the parish authorities to administer the law – on the relief of the poor for example, as well as on road-maintenance. If this system broke down there seemed to be little the central government could do about it.

The Jacobite Rising of 1715 did cause the government to take some interest in the building of roads which might have some military significance. General Wade was ordered to build new roads in Scotland so that English troops might be more easily deployed in the event of a further uprising by the Scottish clans. Between 1726 and 1737 Wade built about 200 miles of roads and some 40 stone bridges. However these seem to have facilitated the second Jacobite Rising in 1745 when Bonnie Prince Charlie invaded England and managed to get as far as Derby before a frightened government recovered its wits sufficiently to send troops against him. After this rebellion had been bloodily ended at Culloden and the Highlands subsequently harried, the government decided that the Great North Road from London to Edinburgh should be rebuilt. Once this great work had been set in hand the government then turned to its administrative arms – the magistrates and the parochial authorities – and urged them to add to the network of roads.

The road-users

In 1724 Defoe described the condition of the roads in the Midlands:

> ... the soil of all the midland part of England, even from sea to sea, is of a deep stiff clay ... and it carries a breadth of near 50 miles at least, in some places much more; nor is it possible to go from London to any part of Britain, north, without crossing this clayey dirty part. ... these are counties which drive a very great trade with the city of London, and with one another ... and that, by consequence, the carriage is exceeding great, and also that all the land carriage of the northern counties necessarily goes through these counties, so the roads had been plow'd so deep, and materials have been in some places so difficult to be had for repair of roads, that all the surveyors rates have been able to do nothing; nay, the very whole country has not been able to repair them.

Everywhere the story was the same. Unmade roads became deeply rutted, muddy in winter and dusty in summer. It is not surprising that the few people who could afford to travel did so on horseback, rather than face the battering they would have

received in the unsprung coaches of the time. In 1670 the journey
from London to Oxford – about forty miles – took twelve hours,
and this along one of the more important highways which was
maintained so that Charles II might make his way safely to the
university city. Journeys north of Oxford took much longer
because the roads were worse. Every coach carried a set of wheelwright's tools in case of accident and even as late as 1760 the
Ipswich Journal reported: 'This Day an inquest was taken at
Ingatestone on the body of Richard Aimes when it appeared that
the deceased was thrown from his horse, a little on this side of
Ingatestone, into a ditch, and was suffocated by mud and filth.'

In 1736 the gossip-politician Lord Hervey was living in
Kensington. He wrote: 'The road is grown so infamously bad
that we live here in the same solitude as we should do if cast on a
rock in the middle of the ocean, and all the Londoners tell me that
there is between them and us a great impassable gulf of mud.' It
was not only the waggons and carts which churned up the roads.
There were also the armies of animals making their almost
constant way to markets and fairs; 40,000 Highland cattle and
30,000 Welsh cattle were driven along the roads each year to be
slaughtered at Smithfield in London. Other livestock also had to
walk to market – geese, pigs, chickens and sheep – and while
London's markets were larger there were similar if smaller
markets in every town. An eighteenth-century nursery rhyme
makes it all sound so gay:

> As I was going to Banbury,
> Upon a summer's day,
> My dame had butter, eggs and fruit,
> And I had corn and hay;
> Joe drive the ox, and Tom the swine,
> Dick took the foal and mare.

In fact the approach roads to London and other towns were
made even more disgustingly dangerous because of the hordes of
animals. All the people in the nursery rhyme would have walked

except the carter taking the corn and hay. He, and thousands of his fellows, used clumsy waggons to carry merchandise These with their iron-shod wheels made between ten and fifteen miles a day. Their heavy loads of hay, grain, clay, iron, coal or whatever ensured that the roads became even more rutted and dangerous than they had been before. It is not surprising that merchants who had fragile goods – pottery for example – preferred to use pack-animals rather than the waggons, which easily overturned. Horses, donkeys or mules were roped together in a line, the leader having a bell attached to its saddle. Each animal carried two pannier baskets each holding about one hundredweight of goods. In hilly districts and in remote areas where there was not even the beginnings of a road system bulky goods such as coal, stone, corn and hay also had to be carried in this fashion. In the 1750s there were 500 pack-animals at a time taking coal from the Cornish port of Hayle for use in the steam-engines in the nearby Cornish tin-mines. This was a slow and costly business, particularly after 1760 when the price of animal-feed was rising.

Transport and industrial change

Much of the raw material needed for industrialization and for urban development was very bulky, relative to its value. Transport costs played an important part in determining the market for iron, stone, timber, clay and similarly heavy items. Coal, cheap in the neighbourhood of a mine, became expensive even in a nearby town, when the cost of transport was added. It was difficult to extend the market for coal until transport costs were reduced. And if the market for coal, iron and clay remained local and small, the industrialist would not be tempted into innovation and the introduction of cost-cutting systems. Producers of lighter but fragile goods were unwilling to seek a wider market until there was a transport system to ensure that most of their product got to market safely.

Another effect of an improved transport system would be to lessen the time taken to get goods from mine to factory or from factory to market place. This would lower overall costs, since the animals and their attendants would have to be fed or paid for a shorter time. It might then be worth while developing a region or a raw material which had hitherto remained undeveloped.

These were the backward linkages between the development of a good transport system and the rest of the economy. There were also forward linkages. The development of a good transport system would of itself stimulate economic activity. Road- and canal-building led to a high demand for stone, timber, iron and above all for bricks. Some of the capital invested in transport development put money into the pockets of the suppliers of these goods. Some of it went to pay wages to the thousands of people engaged in making roads and canals and so played a part in increasing the domestic demand for a wider variety of goods which helped stimulate the economy as a whole.

Turnpike trusts

We have seen that the government allowed a free hand to private enterprise and to the promotion of private acts of Parliament for social and economic purposes. In the matter of road-improvement the government permitted the creation of local companies or trusts which had as their aim the improvement of the roads in a particular locality. A trust began with a group of merchants, landowners and others interested in having a good road in their neighbourhood. The trustees applied to Parliament for permission to take over responsibility for building and repairing the road between two named places. After the act was passed the trustees were allowed to set up toll-gates at each end of their stretch of road. The charges to be levied at the gates were laid down in the act.

In 1663 the JPs in Hertfordshire, Cambridgeshire and Huntingdonshire got permission to set up toll-gates at Wadesmill in Hertfordshire, Caxton in Cambridgeshire and Stilton in Huntingdonshire. Passengers along this Great North Road paid their tolls, and the money was used to maintain this important highway. Writing in 1727 Defoe used sixteen pages to list all the turnpike trusts that had been set up between 1663 and 1726. He noted:

> This [the condition of the roads] necessarily brought the country to bring these things before the Parliament: and the consequence has been that turnpikes or toll-bars have been set up on the several great roads of England, beginning at London, and proceeding through almost all those dirty, deep roads in the midland counties especially; at which turnpikes all carriages, droves of cattle and travellers on horseback, are oblig'd to pay an easy toll; that is to say, a horse a penny, a coach three pence, a cart four pence, at some six pence to eight pence, a waggon six pence. In some a shilling and the like; cattle pay by the score or by the head, in some places more, in some places less; but in no place is it thought a burthen that I ever met with, the benefit of a good road abundantly making amends for that little charge the travellers are put to at the turnpikes.

The money collected by the trustees was partly a profit for the investors who had spent their own money on making or repairing the road, setting up gates and providing homes for gate-keepers. Part of the toll-money was then re-invested in maintaining the road for the period for which the trust was allowed to collect tolls, usually twenty-one years. The enthusiastic Defoe outlined the economic benefits of the new and better roads:

> ... travelling and carriage of goods will be much more easy both to man and horse than ever it was since the Romans lost this island ... as for trade it will be encouraged by it every way; for carriage of all kinds of heavy goods will be much

easier; the waggoners will either perform in less time, or draw heavier loads, or the same load with fewer horses; the packhorse will carry heavier burthens, or travel farther in a day, and so perform their journey in less time; all of which will tend to lessen the rate of carriage and so bring goods cheaper to market. The fat cattle will drive lighter and come to market with less toil, and consequently both go farther in one day and not waste their flesh ... in wallowing through the mud and sloughs as is now the case. The sheep will be able to travel in the winter and the city not be obliged to give great prizes to the butchers for mutton because it cannot be brought up out of Leicestershire and Lincolnshire, the sheep not being able to travel.

Landowners were equally enthusiastic supporters of the new roads, which enabled corn to be taken more quickly and so more cheaply from their estates to markets. This increased the value of the land on the estate and so helped push up landlords' rent-rolls. It is not surprising that there was a 'turnpike trust revolution' during the eighteenth century. Between 1700 and 1750 there were on average about 8 acts passed each year; between 1750 and 1770 the annual average shot up to about 40, a sign of increased local initiative and a reminder of the low rate of interest prevailing in that period. There was a slight fall in the number of acts passed between 1770 and 1790, but from 1790 to 1810 the annual average increased again to about 55.

Few trusts built long stretches of road. The average length of the fourteen turnpikes in the East Riding of Yorkshire was $17\frac{1}{2}$ miles. The length varied from a link road of $5\frac{1}{2}$ miles to the 52-mile turnpike from York to Scarborough. Each trust built as it pleased. On a long journey a traveller passed over a number of roads of different widths and surfaces, maintained in varying degrees depending on the honesty, efficiency and activity of the trustees in each case.

Not everyone share Defoe's enthusiasm for the new system. Some opposed the building of a new road merely because they were against change of any sort. Others complained of the toll-charges, alleging that these pushed up prices. There were many anti-turnpike riots, notably in 1726, 1732, 1749 and 1753. In 1749 the *Gentleman's Magazine* reported:

Bristol 29 July. On Monday the 24th at night great numbers of Somerset people, having demolished the turnpike gates near Bedminster on the Ashton road, the commissioners offered a reward of £100 to the discovery of any persons concerned therein. On the 25th at night, a body of Gloucestershire people . . . destroyed a second time the turnpike gates and house at Don John's cross, about a mile from this city; they bored holes in the large posts and blew them up with gunpowder. Cross bars and posts were again erected and chains put across the roads, and men placed to assist the tollmen, and the commissioners took it by turns about a dozen in a body, to stand at the gates also, to awe the people and oblige them to pay the toll. On the 26th between ten and eleven at night a prodigious body of Somersetshire people came with drums beating and loud shouts, armed with cutting instruments fixed in long staves etc., and some disguised in women's apparel, and demolished the turnpike erections newly fixed. . . . On 29th the turnpike gate was again erected on the Ashton road, and guarded with a body of seamen, well armed with muskets, pistols and cutlasses.

Bristol 7 August – on Tuesday the 1st at 8 o'clock in the morning, about 400 Somersetshire people cut down a third time the turnpike gates on the Ashton road and burnt the timber; then afterwards destroyed the Dundry turnpike and thence went to Bedminster, headed by two chiefs on horseback, one with his face blacked. . . . the rest were on foot, armed with rusty swords, pitchforks, axes, guns, pistols, clubs, etc.

Friday the 4th – about 12 at night, the colliers, as they had threatened the day before came to Stokes-cross . . . and partly cut down that turnpike. Notice being given by signals and the clanging of fire bells a large body of gentlemen and citizens well armed, with some soldiers and seamen, marched to attack the colliers, who did not stay to receive them. . . . By the arrival of six troops of dragoon guards on the 5th we are secured from all insults of the country people, who immediately dispersed, and posts and chains are again erected, but the turnpikes are fixed nearer the city.

The road-engineers

Some of the turnpike trusts employed specialist road-engineers, some of whom have earned a well-deserved reputation. There was John Metcalfe (1717–1810), who had been blind since he was six years old. He had earned his living in various ways, as fiddler, horse-dealer, timber-merchant and stage-coach proprietor, before he was appointed surveyor of a three-mile stretch along the Harrogate-Boroughbridge Road. He went on to build many roads for a number of trusts, using techniques which had been employed by the Romans. He began with a firm foundation of stone blocks, covered these with layers of stone chippings, rammed these down hard into the cracks and then formed a convex surface to enable the water to drain off into ditches dug at the roadside.

A second great road engineer was John MacAdam (1756–1836), who insisted on the need for a dry, firm foundation. He wrote:

The first operation in making a road should be the reverse of digging a trench. The roads should not be sunk below, but rather raised above the ordinary level of the adjacent ground; care should at any rate be taken that there be a sufficient fall to take off the water, so that it should always be some inches below the level of the ground upon which the road is intended to be placed. . . .

Having secured the soil from under water, the road maker is next to secure it from rain water, by a solid road, made of clean, dry stone or flint, so selected, prepared, and laid as to be perfectly impervious to water; and this cannot be effected, unless the greatest care be taken, that no earth, clay, chalk or other matter that will hold or conduct water, be mixed with the broken stone, which must be so prepared and laid as to unite by its own angles into a firm, compact, impenetrable body.

In 1815 MacAdam was appointed surveyor-general of all British roads. His supporters claimed that he made a major contribution to road-building. In 1851 G. R. Porter wrote:

The chief improvement made of late years in England in regard to turnpike roads, has consisted in reconstructing them upon more scientific principles than were previously employed, an advantage which is mainly owing to the exertions of the late Mr. M'Adam, whose plans have been adopted generally throughout the kingdom, as well as in several foreign countries. England had long been provided with roads in every quarter; yet we find, from Parliamentary returns, that, between 1818 and 1829, the length of turnpike-roads in England and Wales was increased by more than one thousand miles ... but this increase is of little importance if viewed comparatively with the improvements introduced in their construction and management.

The third great road-engineer was Thomas Telford (1757–1834), who was responsible for the strategically important London–Holyhead road and the bridge across the Menai Straits. Like Metcalfe he had little schooling, but had the same tenacity as his fellow-Scot. He built tunnels, canals, harbours and aqueducts, as well as roads and bridges, and became the acknowledged leader of a new profession. Telford's work as bridge-builder was helped by Cort's work in the iron industry which allowed the production of cheap wrought iron, which was three times as strong as cast iron yet less brittle. It was this material which allowed Telford to give wide spans to his bridges.

The effects of the new road-system

Defoe had pointed out some of the benefits of the improved roads (see pages 161–2). Travel was much easier; coach-builders were encouraged to build well-sprung and lighter coaches to take advantage of the new roads. After 1784 the time taken on journeys along trunk roads to Scotland and the North of England was halved; in 1754 it had taken '10 days in summer, 12 days in winter' to go from London to Edinburgh; in 1830 the journey was advertised as taking 42 hours and 33 minutes.

Adam Smith saw the economic benefits of the new roads which opened up new markets and put producers in closer touch with consumers:

> Good roads, by diminishing the expense of carriage, put the remote parts of the country more nearly upon a level with those in the neighbourhood of the town. They are upon that account the greatest of all improvements. They encourage the cultivation of the remote which must always be the most extensive circle of the country. They are advantageous to the town, by breaking down the monopoly of the country in its neighbourhood. They are advantageous even to that part of the country. Though they introduce some rival commodities into the old market, they open many new markets to its produce. Monopoly, besides, is a great enemy to good management, which can never be universally established but in consequence of that free and universal competition which forces everybody to have recourse to it for the sake of self-defence.

But even good roads were incapable of coping with the increased volume of bulky traffic which resulted from the first stirrings of industrial change. As a Mr Philips noted in 1828:

About half a century ago, the heavy goods passing through Leicester for London to the South, and on the great northern lines to Leeds and Manchester did not require more than about one daily broad-wheeled waggon each way. These were fully adequate for the supply and transit of goods for all the intermediate towns, of course including Leicester. One weekly waggon to and fro, served Coventry, Warwick, Birmingham, and so on to Bristol and the West of England; the return waggon being capable of bringing all from that quarter that was directed to Leicester, and all the northern and north-eastern districts beyond. At present, there are about two waggons, two caravans, and two fly-boats, daily passing or starting from Leicester for London and its intermediate towns; the same number ... extend the connection not only to Leeds and Manchester, but by means of canal conveyance to the ports of Liverpool and Hull. There are at least six weekly waggons to Birmingham, independent of those to Bristol three times a week and the same to Stamford, Wisbech, and the eastern counties: to Nottingham to the same extent, exclusive of carts.

Water-borne transport

It is not surprising that English industrialists and merchants had always made good use of the sea and navigable rivers. As Smith pointed out:

... by means of water carriage a more extensive market is opened to every sort of industry than what land carriage alone can afford it, so it is upon the sea coast and along the banks of navigable rivers that industry of every kind naturally begins to subdivide and improve itself, and it is frequently not till a long time after that those improvements extend themselves to the inland parts of the country.

London's growth would have been impossible if it had not been for the fleets of ships bringing coal, stone, clay and grain needed for the housing, warming and feeding of the population of the ever-growing city. No point in England is further than 70 miles from the sea and few are more than 30 miles from a navigable river. The coalfields of Durham and Northumberland were on the coast, and 'sea-cole' had been carried from Newcastle around the coast to London since the thirteenth century. The river-systems of the Severn and Trent enabled water-borne traffic to get into the industrial Midlands where coal was close to the rivers, and the roads were in poor condition. The river-systems of the Thames and Wash provided highways for the produce of the main agricultural regions of the country. As Defoe noted: 'In a word, all the water of the middle part of England which does not run into the Thames or the Trent comes down into these Fenns.'

As early as 1564 the Exeter canal had been cut as an artificial channel to by-pass the river where it was unnavigable. During the century from 1650 to 1750 there were many schemes for improving river-navigation. In the 1720s Liverpool merchants financed a scheme which lowered the cost of transporting coal from Wigan along the River Ribble, and another which linked the Irwell with the Mersey. Other schemes using the River Weaver opened up the saltfields around Winsford in Cheshire.

The first English canal proper was cut in 1757 and linked the Mersey to St Helens and the Cheshire saltfields to the Lancashire coalfields. But the canal age is usually dated from 1761 and the opening of the Duke of Bridgewater's canal built by Brindley. This ran from the Duke's collieries at Worsley almost into Manchester. A contemporary noted how an underdeveloped area became developed: 'This mine had lain dormant in the bowels of the earth from time immemorial without the least profit to the noble owner, on account of the price of land carriage which was so excessive that they could not be sold at a reasonable price.'

This canal was built at the instigation of the duke, a colliery-owner, a reminder of the close link that existed in England between landowning and industrial enterprise. It was financed by the duke himself. He had sufficient investment-capital to lay out the large sum required – a reminder of the importance of agricultural income as a source of industrial investment-capital. When the rate of interest fell in 1763 with the end of the Seven Years War against France, the duke extended his canal down to Runcorn at the mouth of the Mersey and provided the first efficient communication between the growing textile region of south-east Lancashire and the port of Liverpool. Finally we ought to note that the canal was designed and its building supervised by Brindley, who had never been to school, a reminder that illiteracy was not the handicap that it became in a more technologically advanced age.

Brindley was unable to write and had to do all his calculations in his head. Before embarking on the project he went to bed for a few days to think it out. This meant preparing schemes for cutting tunnels through hillsides, building bridges across footpaths and most notably building the Barton Bridge Aqueduct, which was 36 feet wide and ran 38 feet above the River Irwell. Arthur Young wrote:

> The effect of coming at once on to Barton Bridge, and looking down upon a large river, with barges of great burthen sailing on it; and up to another river, hung in the air, with barges towing along it, form altogether a scenery somewhat like enchantment, and exhibit at once a view that must give you an idea of prodigious labour . . . and I should remark that it is a maxim throughout this whole navigation, to keep the canal of an equal depth everywhere: I believe it scarce ever varies above six inches, from four feet, to four feet six inches.

A contemporary watched Brindley at work and marvelled at the organization that was involved:

> The smiths' forges, the carpenters' and masons' workshops, were covered workshops, which floated on the canal and

followed the work from place to place. The Duke made the rubbish of one work help to build another. Thus the stones which were dug up to form the basin for the boats (near the coal mine at Worsley) were cut into different shapes to build the bridges over the rivers, brooks or highways, or the arches of the aqueduct. The clay, gravel and other earths taken up to preserve the level at one place were carried down the canal to raise the land in another or reserved to make bricks for other uses.

Ships were hauled along the Bridgewater canal by horses although they also used sails when the weather was favourable. They carried coal from Worsley to Manchester where the price of coal was halved, to the delight of industrial and domestic consumers. The duke also benefited. His income rose by half as much again as it had been when he already had enough to finance the building of the canal. The evident success of this venture encouraged him to undertake an extension to Runcorn which linked Manchester to Liverpool and the sea. He financed this venture which brought him great financial rewards. It also cut the cost of transport from the £2 a ton charged by road-hauliers to 6 shillings (30p) a ton. The effect was to attract a good deal of business to the canal and to lower the price of goods in Manchester and Liverpool.

Canal mania

While Bridgewater was building his extension, he and Josiah Wedgwood had the idea for building a canal to pass through the salt-mining areas of Cheshire and the pottery areas of Staffordshire. This would link the Mersey with the Trent and the Humber. This Grand Trunk Canal was Brindley's greatest engineering feat and its cost was so great that Bridgewater was forced to look for partners. There were enough people willing to

lay out large sums of investment-capital in this scheme. Bridgewater's brother-in-law the Earl of Gower, the explorer-naval
officer Lord Anson, Wedgwood the pottery-king and many
others joined Bridgewater to finance this scheme. Brindley died
in 1772, five years before the scheme was completed, a very poor
man, the duke not having paid his wages for over two years – a
reminder of one of the ways in which industrialists overcame their
shortage of ready cash. In 1774 Bridgewater gave Brindley's
widow £100, a poor reward for the widow of the man who had
helped double then treble Bridgewater's own income, which was
further increased after the opening of the Grand Trunk in 1777.

Many canals were cut in the 1760s and 1770s but the fall in the
interest rates in the late 1780s after the American War led to the
canal mania of the period from 1790 to 1794. Canals were cut to
link all the main ports – London, Liverpool, Hull and Bristol
were all linked by the end of the 1770s and there was a series of
canals linking the Midlands and Lancashire. In 1789 the Thames
and Severn Canal was opened and the *Annual Register* for 1790
reported:

This day was effected the greatest object of internal navigation
in this kingdom. The Severn was united to the Thames, by an
intermediate canal ascending by Stroud, through the vale of
Chalford to the height of 343 feet, by 28 locks; there entering a
tunnel through the hill of Saperton, for the length of two miles
and three furlongs, and descending 134 feet by 14 locks, it
joined the Thames near Lechlade. With respect to the internal
commerce of the kingdom, and the security of communication
in time of war, this junction of the Thames and Severn must be
attended with the most beneficial consequences, as even stores
from the Baltic, and provisions from Ireland, may reach the
capital, and the ports of the mouth of the Thames, in safety.
And all the heavy articles from the mines and foundries in the
heart of Wales, and the counties contiguous to the Severn,
may find a secure and certain conveyance to the capital.

In short, this undertaking is worthy of a great commercial nation, and does great credit to the exertions of the individuals, who have promoted and completed a work of such magnitude at an expense of near two hundred thousand pounds.

Few individuals could afford to finance their own schemes as Bridgewater had done in 1760/1. A wider public was invited to subscribe for shares in the many canal companies formed after 1765. Joint-stock companies were forbidden under the terms of the Bubble Act (see pages 87–8) but there were means of getting around this prohibition. Most canal companies were joint-stock companies, the investor's liability restricted to the amount he decided to put into the company. Local newspapers carried advertisements such as the one which appeared in a Bradford newspaper in 1766:

... whereas such a navigation would be of great utility to trade, especially in time of war, and more particularly to the counties of York and Lancaster, a meeting would be held at the house of Mr. John Day, known by the Sign of the Sun in Bradford aforesaid, on Wednesday, the 2nd day of July 1766, at 10 of the clock in the forenoon ... at which meeting the nobility, gentry and clergy of the said several counties, and all others who think it their duty to interest themselves in a matter of so great importance are requested to attend.

By the 1790s the investing public was in the grip of a speculative mania illustrated by this extract from an old history of Bristol:

... On the 20th of November 1792 a meeting to promote the construction of a canal from Bristol to Gloucester was held in the Guildhall, when the scheme was enthusiastically supported by influential persons, and a very large sum was subscribed by those present, who struggled violently with each other in their rush to the subscription book. A few days later, a Somerset paper announced that a meeting would be held at Wells to promote a canal from Bristol to Taunton. The design had been formed in this city (Bristol) but the promoters strove to keep it a secret, and bought up all the newspapers containing the advertisement. The news nevertheless leaked out in the evening before the intended gathering, and a host of speculators set off to secure shares in the undertaking, some arriving only to find that the subscription list was full. The third meeting was at Devizes, on the 12 December. Only one day's notice was given of this movement, which was to promote a canal from Bristol to Southampton and London but the news rapidly spread and thousands of intending subscribers rushed to the little town, where the proposed capital was offered several times over. The 'race to Devizes' on the part of Bristolians who had hired or bought up at absurd prices all the old hacks that could be found, and plunged along the miry roads through a long wintry night, was attended with many comic incidents. A legion of schemes followed, Bristol being the proposed terminus of canals to all parts of the country, and some of the projected waterways running in close proximity to each other. A pamphlet published in 1795, narrating the story of the mania, states that the passion of speculation spread like an epidemical disease throughout the city, every man believing that he would gain thousands by his adventures.

The availability of capital and the willingness of its owners to invest it in long-term schemes was vital to the furthering of industrialization.

The navvies

The unlettered Brindley employed huge gangs of labourers to dig the ditches, blast the tunnels and construct the aqueducts. These men, engaged in the construction of navigable ways, were formally termed 'navigators', which was quickly shortened to 'navvies'. Southey watched the building of one of Telford's greatest undertakings, the Caledonian Canal, and wrote:

The earth is removed by horses walking along the bench of the Canal, and drawing the laden cartlets up one inclined plane, while the emptied ones, which are connected with them by a chain passing over pullies, are let down another. This was going on in numberless places, and such a mass of earth had been thrown up on both sides along the whole line, that the men appeared in the proportion of emmets to an anthill amid their own work. The hour of rest for men and horses is announced by blowing a horn; and so well have the horses learnt to measure time by their own exertions and sense of fatigue that if the signal be delayed five minutes, they stop of their own accord without it. . . .

Such an extent of masonry, upon such a scale, I had never before beheld, each of these locks being 180 feet in length. It was a most impressive, rememberable scene. Men, horses and machines at work, digging, walling and puddling going on, men wheeling barrows, horses drawing stones along the railways. The great steam-engine was at rest, having done its work; but the dredging machine was in action, revolving round and round, and bringing up at every turn matter which had never before been brought to the air and light. Iron for a pair of lock-gates was lying on the ground, having just arrived from Derbyshire.

These men were paid about 1s 6d per day (about $7\frac{1}{2}$p). Most of this money went on gambling and drinking in the shanty towns which sprang up alongside the huge ditch as it was being dug. They terrorized the people of the neighbourhood through which they moved, fought with them and among themselves. They deserve however to be remembered as part of the 'crowded stage' on which the major stars played their larger roles.

Economic effects of canal-building

By the end of the eighteenth century the canal-engineers had provided about 600 miles of new inland waterways, in addition

to the older river-improvement schemes and the navigation provided by naturally navigable rivers. The main motive behind
canal-building was to provide cheap transport for the coal needed
in the growing urban areas by brewers, smiths, tanners, sugar-
refiners, bakers and millers, as well as by the newer industries in
which the steam-engine was being used in mills and engineering
shops. The Duke of Bridgewater appreciated the importance of
the coal trade for canal-owners. He declared that 'a navigation
should have coals at the heel of it.'

Whenever coal was 'at the heel of it' a canal paid a handsome
profit. Everywhere the story was the same; the price of coal fell,
the market expanded, output increased and mine-owner, canal
company and coal-consumers all benefited. But where coal was
not at the heel of it the fortunes of a canal company were less
happy. Most of the canals of southern England were cut to serve
only agricultural areas and interests. While farmers and consumers
benefited, canal-owners rarely made much profit from these
non-coal-carrying canals.

The Duke of Bridgewater gave it as a rule of thumb that the
cost of canal-building was '10,000 guineas a mile'. The capital
outlay on a single canal was by eighteenth-century standards very
large. Such a scheme could not be undertaken piecemeal as could
other forms of industrial development. A man could start with a
small blast-furnace and plough back his profits to buy a second.
Textile-manufacturers often began in a small way as did Whitehead and slowly built up their business. This was not possible
with a canal. A stretch had to be built and a large sum of
investment-capital found. By 1820 canal companies had capital of
about £13 million which was small compared to the amount of
money taken from the investing public by a voracious government, but was still very large relative to the demands from other
sectors and to the prevailing real value of money when wages
averaged about 1s or 5p per day.

However all this was worth while, as Telford pointed out in
1804:

It will be found that canals are chiefly useful for the following purposes: first, for conveying the produce of mines to the Sea-Shore; second, conveying fuel and raw materials to some Manufacturing Towns and Districts and exporting the manufactured goods; third, conveying groceries and Merchant goods for the Consumption of the District through which the Canal passes; fourth, conveying fuel for domestic purposes: Manure for the purposes of Agriculture; Transporting the produce of the Districts through which the Canal passes, to the different Markets; and promoting Agricultural purposes in general.

The widening of the market and the lowering of costs had beneficial social effects, as Thomas Pennant realized as early as 1782:

The cottage, instead of being half-covered with miserable thatch, is now covered with a substantial covering of tiles or slates, brought from the distant hills of Wales or Cumberland. The fields, which before were barren, are now drained, and, by the assistance of manure, conveyed on the canal toll-free, are cloathed with a beautiful verdure. Places which rarely knew the use of coal, are plentifully supplied with that essential article, upon reasonable terms; and, what is of still greater public utility, the monopolizers of corn are prevented from exercising their infamous trade; for, the communication being opened between Liverpool, Bristol and Hull, and the line of canal being through countries abundant in grain, it affords a conveyance of corn unknown to past ages. At present, nothing but a general dearth can create a scarcity in any part adjacent to this extensive work.

Others benefited from the very high profits earned by some companies and from the high prices they were able to get for their shares. The original shares in the Birmingham Canal Company had cost £140 each; by 1792 they were selling for £900 and by 1825 for £2,880. Some companies paid a 30-per-cent profit in some years, although the average was 8 per cent, a very high return in an age when the government stock paid only 3 per cent. Profits from canal shares provided yet another source of investment-capital for the later stages of the Industrial Revolution.

The canal companies broke through the barrier erected against joint-stock companies and so paved the way for the formation of the railway companies which would require much greater capital-investment and so had to call on a wider investing public. The navvies were the forerunners of the men who built the railway network in the 1830s and 1840s, and so laid the foundation for a second stage of industrial change. Perhaps most significantly of all, the canal movement provided an opportunity for Brindley, Telford and others to learn the skills of engineering and so helped produce a new breed of men who called themselves civil engineers. In 1820 they formed themselves into the Institution of Civil Engineers and invited Telford to become their first president:

The Institution of Civil Engineers
Gilham's Coffee House
3rd February 1820

To Thomas Telford, Esq., F.R.S.E.
Dear Sir,

The cultivation of the profession of Civil Engineer is a subject which does not appear to have met with that attention in this country which its importance deserves.

Until lately there does not appear to have been any attempt towards establishing a common centre of information for that profession, although its practical nature would suggest the necessity of it.

A conviction of the advantages of an Institution of Civil Engineers has however now induced a few young men of the profession to come forward with their endeavours to obtain that object, and they are now desirous to acquaint you with a description of their design, and the principles on which they have proceeded. . . .

To facilitate the acquirement of knowledge in engineering; to circumscribe the profession; to establish in it the respectability which it merits and to increase the indispensable public confidence, are the objects of the Institution, the members of which now have the honour of addressing you.

During the nineteenth century Britain would come to depend on the skills, ability and capacity for work of these people and their successors. If there had been no canal movement Britain's march along the road to take-off would have been the slower.

11. The Revolution in the Textile Industry

Early signs of change

In Chapter 5 we saw that the woollen industry was the most important sector of the textile industry, that the cotton industry was growing rapidly while the first factory had been built by the Lombes who were silk-manufacturers. We also saw that the textile industry was basically a cottage industry in which all the members of the family played some part in the production process.

In 1733 John Kay, a Lancashire clock-maker, made a simple improvement to the existing weaving-loom. He put the shuttle on wheels and had a hammer to strike the shuttle to drive it through the warp. Previously the weaver had to push the shuttle by hand. This had limited the width of the cloth that could be woven. Kay's invention enabled the weaver, sitting at his loom and pulling strings attached to the hammers, to make a cloth of a width that had previously required the work of two weavers.

However Kay's shuttle was not brought into use until after the 1760s, partly because of opposition from most of the handloom-weavers, partly because of the difficulty of making and repairing even this simple wooden device, but largely because there was little call for improvements in the weaving sector since a single weaver could use up the yarn provided by a number of spinners.

What was potentially a significant invention was made in 1738 when a doctor's son, Lewis Paul, invented a carding-machine. The carded wool or cotton was passed through two sets of rollers which revolved at different speeds. This drew the material out before passing it to the spindle where it was given its twist. In 1740 Paul and his partner Wyatt opened a small mill employing ten women to work the machines, driven by donkeys. Other factories were opened in London, Northampton and Leominster. All of them failed, their owners driven into bankruptcy. Paul claimed that the failure was due to the workers' unwillingness to work at the regular pace required by machines.

Hargreaves and the spinning jenny

James Hargreaves was a weaver-carpenter from Blackburn. At some time between 1764 and 1767 he made a simple, wooden, hand-driven machine on which a number of threads could be spun at the same time. His first machine had 8 spindles; when he patented it in 1770 the machine had 16 spindles. By 1784 there were jennies with 80 spindles and by 1800 large jennies held 120 spindles. Unlike the flying shuttle, the jenny was quickly and widely adopted. Hargreaves did not get the full financial benefit from his machine since he sold many before applying for the patent.

The first jennies were small enough to be used in the cottage. It was cheap to make and did not require much strength to operate the handle. By 1788 there were about 20,000 in use throughout the country, producing a soft yarn, suitable for weft but unsuitable for use as the warp, the thread for which had still to be produced on the spinning-wheel. The jenny went a long way to solving the problem facing the weavers who had previously to depend on the work of a number of spinners. With even the simplest jenny one spinner could produce all the weft thread needed by a weaver. As the jennies became larger the spinner's output increased and a new bottleneck appeared. It was the weavers who were holding up production.

The jenny, like most other new machines in the textile industry, proved more suitable for use with cotton than with wool. It was eagerly adopted by workpeople who saw in it a way of increasing their incomes. As William Radcliffe noted: 'From the year 1770 to 1788 a complete change had gradually been effected in the spinning of yarns. That of wool had disappeared altogether and that of linen was also nearly gone; cotton, cotton, cotton was becoming the almost universal material for employment.'

A cotton revolution

Why this change to cotton? Factory production had first appeared in the silk industry and one might have thought that this industry might have continued to be the technological leader. But the silk industry suffered a number of handicaps. The supply of raw material was relatively inelastic. An extra supply would not be forthcoming without a great increase in price. The demand for silk products was also inelastic. A slight fall in price would not lead to a large increase in demand. There was no market force impelling the manufacturers to increase their output which went to the small, luxury market.

Why did the well-established woollen industry not lead the way and adopt the new machines? Again it is a question of supply and demand as well as suitability of material. The supply of wool varied with the number of sheep in English and European flocks. Australian sheep-farming did not develop until after 1793 when MacArthur, the father of the Australian wool-growing trade, left the army and began experimenting in sheep-breeding in the convict settlement around Botany Bay. Given that Bakewell and other breeders went in for breeding for meat rather than wool, the supply of wool from British farms remained fairly static as can be seen from Figure 4 on page 183. There was also little change in the demand for woollen goods even when the British economy got under way and the demand for many other products began to rise. There was little demand-stimulus driving clothiers to seek new methods of production. Even if there had been, it is likely that the adoption of new methods would have been resisted by the many guilds which controlled large sections of the industry. These tended to restrict the number of apprentices that a skilled workman could employ and the amount that a guild-member could produce.

Cotton suffered none of these disadvantages. A small fall in price led to a large increase in demand for cotton goods. British families preferred cotton goods to woollen; they were lighter, more easily washable and cheaper. Domestic demand was reinforced and quickly outstripped by the demand from exporters who found that they could sell cotton goods in almost every part of the enlarged empire as well as in Europe. Cotton-manufacturers were under great pressure to increase their output.

It was easy to get increased supplies of the raw material, even though the East India Company was unwilling to increase the volume of imports of raw Indian cotton for fear that the development of a British industry would harm its own trade in Indian muslins. West Indian planters made some effort to increase their output in response to the increased demand from British manufacturers. But the best response came from the owners of estates in the southern states of what became the USA in 1783. Here land was cheap and after the Louisiana Purchase of 1801 almost unlimited. It was relatively simple to extend the acreage under cotton and even to grow two crops in one year. The supply of slave labour was cheap and plentiful, and a potential bottleneck was cleared in the 1790s when Eli Whitney invented the gin. In 1791 the US cotton crop was 2 million pounds. By 1821 this had risen to 182 million pounds in spite of a sharp fall in prices.

The cotton industry was relatively a new industry and suffered none of the hampering restrictions which affected the woollen industry. It also tended to grow in the hinterland of Liverpool, the port through which came most of the raw cotton imports. Here there were few old towns. The industry created its own

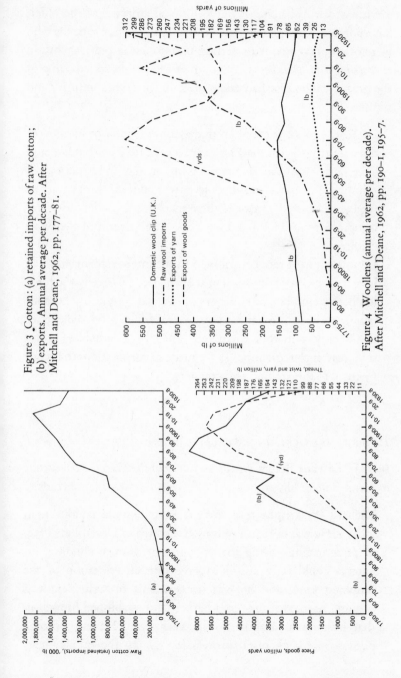

Figure 3. Cotton: (a) retained imports of raw cotton; (b) exports. Annual average per decade. After Mitchell and Deane, 1962, pp. 177–81.

Figure 4 Woollens (annual average per decade). After Mitchell and Deane, 1962, pp. 190–1, 195–7.

towns, which had none of the traditional attitudes of the older, incorporated boroughs towards 'foreigners', the non-citizens who were often prevented from setting up business in older towns. In *A description of Manchester, 1783* James Ogden described some of the great changes that had taken place in the cotton industry and wrote:

> ... large exports for foreign trade [and] the interior business of the country is [such that] no exertion ... [by] workmen could have answered the demands without the introduction of spinning machines. ... People saw children from nine to twelve years of age manage these machines with dexterity and bring plenty into families that were before overburdened with children.
>
> Nothing has more contributed to the improvements in trade here than the free admission of workmen ... whereby the trade has been kept open to strangers of every description who contribute to its improvement by their ingenuity; for Manchester being only a market town, governed by Constables, is not subject to such regulations as are made in corporations to favour freemen to the exclusion of strangers.

Richard Arkwright, *the father of the factory-system*

In 1835 Edward Baines wrote a *History of the Cotton Manufacture in Great Britain*. His account of Arkwright's rise to fame reads:

Richard Arkwright rose from a very humble condition in society. He was born at Preston on the 23rd of December, 1732, of poor parents; being the youngest of thirteen children, his parents could only afford to give him an education of the humblest kind, and he was scarcely able to write. He was brought up to the trade of a barber, and established himself in that business at Bolton in the year 1760. Having become possessed of a chemical process for dyeing the human hair,

which in that day (when wigs were universal) was of considerable value, he travelled about collecting hair, and again
disposing of it when dyed. In 1761 he married a wife from
Leigh, and the connexion he thus formed in that town are
supposed to have afterwards brought him acquainted with
Highs's experiments in making spinning machines. He himself
manifested a strong bent for experiments in mechanics, which
he is stated to have followed with so much devotedness as to
have neglected his business and injured his circumstances. His
natural disposition was ardent, enterprising and stubbornly
persevering.

In 1767 Arkwright fell in with Kay, the clockmaker, at
Warrington, whom he employed to bend him some wires, and
turn him some pieces of brass. He entered into conversation
with the clockmaker, and called upon him repeatedly; and at
length Kay, according to his own account, told him of Highs's
scheme of spinning by rollers. Kay adds that Arkwright induced
him to make a model of Highs's machine, and took it away. It
is certain that from this period Arkwright abandoned his
former business, and devoted himself to the construction of the
spinning machine.

The statement of Arkwright was, that 'after many years of
intense and painful application he invented, about the year
1768, his present method of spinning cotton...' Being altogether
destitute of pecuniary means for prosecuting his invention,
Arkwright repaired to his native place, Preston, and applied to a
friend, Mr. John Smalley, a liquor merchant and painter, for
assistance. . . . His spinning machine was fitted up in the parlour
of the house belonging to the Free Grammar School, which was
lent by the headmaster to Mr. Smalley for the purpose. The
latter was so well convinced of the utility of the machine, that
he joined Arkwright with heart and purse.

In consequence of the riots which had taken place in the
neighbourhood of Blackburn, on the invention of Hargreave's
spinning jenny in 1767, by which many of the machines were

destroyed, and the inventor was driven from his native county to Nottingham, Arkwright and Smalley, fearing similar outrages directed against their machine, went also to Nottingham, accompanied by Kay. This town, therefore, became the cradle of two of the greatest inventions in cotton spinning.

Here the adventurers applied for pecuniary aid to Messrs. Wright, bankers, who made advances on condition of sharing in the profits of the invention. But as the machine was not perfected so soon as they had anticipated, the bankers requested Arkwright to obtain other assistance, and recommended him to Mr. Samuel Need, of Nottingham. This gentleman was the partner of Mr. Jedediah Strutt, of Derby, the ingenious improver and patentee of the stocking-frame; and Mr. Strutt having seen Arkwright's machine, and declared it to be an admirable invention . . . both Mr. Need and Mr. Strutt entered into partnership with Arkwright.

Thus the pecuniary difficulties of this enterprising and persevering man were terminated. He soon made his machine practicable, and in 1769 he took out a patent. . . . It is remarkable that the inventor, in his application for a patent, described himself as 'Richard Arkwright, of Nottingham, clockmaker'. He and his partners erected a mill at Nottingham, which was driven by horses; but this mode of turning the machinery being found too expensive, they built another mill on a much larger scale at Cromford, in Derbyshire, which was turned by a water-wheel, and from this circumstance the spinning machine was called the water-frame.

This frame enabled the spinner to produce his thread by a combination of rollers and spindles. It produced a coarse thread, suitable for the warp, for which linen thread had been used previously. Arkwright's product was cheaper than linen thread. The cheap, coarse calicoes which he produced were the first all-cotton goods; and their appearance marked a major step along the road to industrialization.

The frame was too large to be housed in the cottage, too expensive for cottage workers to buy and was designed to be driven by horse-power, although it was quickly adapted to be driven by water-power. After Watt had invented a rotary-motion engine in 1782 the frame was further adapted to be driven by steam-power. But even when driven by water-power this was the machine which required factories to be erected near constantly flowing water.

Baines's account goes on:

On the 16th December 1775 Mr. Arkwright took out a second patent, for a series of machines, comprising the carding, drawing and roving machines, all used in preparing silk, cotton, flax, and wool for spinning. When this admirable series of machines was made known, and by their means yarns were produced far superior in quality to any spun before in England, as well as lower in price, a mighty impulse was communicated to the cotton manufacture. . . . Cotton fabrics could be sold lower than had ever before been known. The demand for them consequently increased. The shuttle flew with fresh energy, and the weavers earned immoderately high wages. The fame of Arkwright resounded through the land; and capitalists flocked to him, to buy his patent machines, or permission to use them. . . . Mr. Arkwright and his partners expended, in large buildings in Derbyshire and elsewhere, upwards of £30,000, and Mr. Arkwright also erected a very large and extensive building in Manchester, at the expense of upwards of £4,000. Thus a business was formed, which already, i.e. in 1782 (he calculated) employed upwards of five thousand persons, and a capital of not less than £200,000. . . .

The factory system in England takes its rise from this period. Hitherto the cotton manufacture had been carried on almost entirely in the houses of the workmen; the hand or stock cards, the spinning wheel, and the loom, required no larger apartment than that of a cottage. A spinning jenny of small size might also be used in a cottage, and in many instances was so used. But the water-frame, the carding engine, and the other machines which Arkwright brought out in a finished state, required both more space than could be found in a cottage, and more power than could be applied by the human arm. Their weight also rendered it necessary to place them in strongly-built mills, and they could not be advantageously turned by any power then known but that of water.

Arkwright had factories at Cromford, Belper and Milford where carding-machines and water-frames were under one roof. The first water-driven factory in Lancashire was put up in 1777 at Chorley. In 1781 the patent for the carding-machine was revoked. A large number of new factories were built throughout Lancashire, Cheshire, Derbyshire and Nottinghamshire.

Arkwright may have had no inventive genius. He did have a great drive, an ambition to be a success. He also wanted that success to be recognized by others and to be reflected by possession of the status-symbols of the time – estates, carriages and titles. Baines goes on:

> Arkwright commonly laboured in his multifarious concerns from five o'clock in the morning till nine at night; and when considerably more than fifty years of age – feeling that the defects of his education placed him under great difficulty and inconvenience in conducting his correspondence, and in the general management of his business, he encroached upon his sleep, in order to gain an hour each day to learn English grammar, and another hour to improve his writing and orthography! He was impatient of whatever interfered with his favourite pursuits; and the fact is too strikingly characteristic not to be mentioned, that he separated from his wife not many years after their marriage, because she, convinced that he would starve his family by scheming when he should have been saving, broke some of his experimental models of machines.

Arkwright was a severe economist of time; and, that he

might not waste a moment, he generally travelled with four horses, and at a very rapid speed. His concerns in Derbyshire, Lancashire and Scotland were so extensive and numberous, as to show at once his astonishing power of transacting business and his all-grasping spirit. In many of these he had partners, but he generally managed in such a way, that, whoever lost, he himself was a gainer. . . .

In 1785 Arkwright's patent was finally set aside; and those most useful machines, which though invented by others, owed their perfection to his finishing hand, were thrown open to the public. The astonishing extension of the manufactures which immediately followed, shewed that the nullification of the patent was a great national advantage.

Arkwright continued, notwithstanding, his prosperous career. Wealth flowed in upon him with a full stream from his skilfully managed concerns. . . . In 1786 he was appointed high sheriff of Derbyshire; and having presented an address of congratulation from that county to the King on his escape from the attempt of Margaret Nicholson on his life, he received the honour of knighthood. Sir Richard was troubled for many years with a severe asthmatic affection; he sunk at length under a complication of disorders, and died at his house at Cromford on the 3rd of August, 1792, in the sixtieth year of his age.

Samuel Crompton (1753–1827)

Arkwright obtained a large income from his patents on the carding-machine (until 1781) and on the frame (until 1785). He earned an even larger income from the profits made in his own cotton business. Samuel Crompton had less good fortune even though he made a truly original contribution to the development of the cotton industry. He was a Bolton weaver who spent many years experimenting in his own home. A contemporary recalled his method of working:

'My mind,' he relates, 'was in a continual endeavour to realise a more perfect principle of spinning; and, though often baffled, I as often renewed the attempt, and at last succeeded in my utmost desire, at the expense of every shilling I had in the world.' He was, of course, only able to work at the mule in the leisure left after each day's task of spinning, and often in hours stolen from sleep. The purchase of tools and materials absorbed all his spare cash; and when the Bolton theatre was open, he was glad to earn eighteen-pence a night by playing the violin in the orchestra. The first mule was made, for the most part, of wood, and to a small roadside smithy he used to resort 'to file his bits o' things.'

Crompton proceeded very silently with his invention. Even the family at Hall-in-the-Wood knew little of what he was about, until his lights and noise, while at work in the nightime, excited their curiosity.

By 1799 he had devised a machine which could produce a yarn which was strong, fine and even – suitable for both warp and weft. It could be used in the manufacture of every kind of cotton product, even for the production of fine muslins such as had previously been imported from India. His contemporary recalled:

Meanwhile, he created much surprise in the market by the production of yarn, which, alike in fineness and firmness, surpassed any that had ever been seen. It immediately became the universal question in the trade, 'How does Crompton make the yarn?' . . .

Hall-in-the-Wood became besieged with manufacturers praying for supplies of the precious yarn, and burning with desire to penetrate the secret of its production. All kinds of stratagems were practised to gain admission to the house. Some climbed up to the windows of the workroom and peeped in. Crompton set up a screen to hide himself, but even that was not sufficient. One inquisitive adventurer is said to have hid himself for some days in the loft, and to have watched Crompton at work through a gimlet hole in the ceiling.

Crompton's machine was named the 'mule' because it incorporated features of both the spinning-jenny and the water-frame. Crompton, unlike Arkwright, was a better inventor than he was a businessman. He did not take out a patent: some claim that this was because he could not afford the expense of so doing; others argue that he knew that the Patent Office would not have allowed him to have a patent because of Arkwright's patent on the water-frame. In 1812 he petitioned Parliament:

> A Petition of Samuel Crompton, of Bolton-le-le Moors, in the county of Lancaster, cotton spinner, was brought up and read, setting forth:
>
> That in the year, 1769, Sir Richard Arkwright obtained a patent for the use of a machine ... for spinning cotton, commonly called a water-frame, the benefit of which invention he exclusively enjoyed during the full period of fourteen years, and derived great advantage therefrom; and that the above machine ... was exceedingly limited in its application, being utterly incapable of spinning weft of any kind, or of producing twist of very fine texture; and that to remedy this defect the petitioner in the year 1779 completed a machine now called a mule ... being capable of producing every then known description of weft, as well as twist of a very superior quality, but gave birth to a new manufacture in this country of fine cambrics and muslins, by producing yarns of treble fineness, and of a much more soft and pleasant texture, than any which had ever before been spun in Great Britain; and that the merit of the petitioner's machine soon brought it into general use, and has been the means of extending the cotton manufacture to more than double the amount to which it was before carried, whereby all persons employed in the cotton manufactory and the public in general, have been greatly benefited; and that notwithstanding the great and numerous advantages derived by

this country from the petitioner's labours, the petitioner has hitherto received no adequate reward for his discovery.

Parliament granted him only £5,000, a reward out of keeping with the value of his work and so much less than the rewards obtained by the more astute Arkwright.

Steam-power

In 1785 Arkwright's patent on the frame expired. In the same year a Boulton and Watt steam-machine was used to operate a spinning-mill and the industrialization of the textile industry entered on a new phase. Steam-driven spinning-machines produced as much yarn as weavers could use. The way was open to the development of cheaper and better-quality products. Spinning became concentrated in factories, although weaving remained unmechanized for some time to come. Handloom-weavers, using the plentiful supply of factory-spun yarn, were kept so busy that many gave up their work in agriculture to concentrate on weaving. Some moved into towns to be nearer the spinning-mills and the clothiers who bought the woven cloth.

A spinning firm

The expiration of Arkwright's patents opened the way for other enterprising men to open their own factories. We have seen how David Whitehead became a factory-owner with little capital at his disposal. Most of the early factories were small affairs. An early biographer of the unfortunate Crompton noted:

During this year [1792] also the word 'factory' occurs almost for the first time in the rate books of the township [of Bolton]; but these buildings were invariably assessed at a lower rate than the public-houses and inns, which were still the most important business buildings in the town. In 1792 the Swan Inn was rated at £26, and the Horse Shoe Inn and Assembly Room at £33 7s; while the new factory erected by Mr. Thomas Fogg was rated at £22, the new factory of Mr. Nathaniel Bolling at £15, the new factory of Mr. John Rushton £20, the new factory and fire-engine of Messrs. Carlile at £12, and the new factory and fire-engine of Mr. George Grime, £25.

The system spread to many other towns. In 1856 G. J. French, the author of *Historical Sketches of Oldham*, noted:

It was at this period, 1794, that what may truly be called the present system of the cotton manufacturer commenced. Previously the manufactories were comparatively small, and in many instances the processes were conducted in large two storeyed and three storeyed dwelling houses. . . . A few edifices had certainly been erected for the sole purposes of manufacture, of which I have already noticed several instances in Oldham and neighbourhood; but the introduction of the steam engine led to the building of spacious mills devoted to all the processes of the spinning department of the trade. . . .

The great consumption of coal which ensued as the inevitable consequence of the introduction of the steam engine as the moving power of cotton mills, served to develop the mineral resources of the district, and stimulated the colliery proprietors to extraordinary activity.

Even as late as 1822 the typical Manchester mill employed only about 150 people. Mills in neighbouring towns were even smaller. In the 1770s Arkwright's mill at Cromford employed about 300 men and by 1816 there were just over 700 on the workforce there. There were indeed some very large establishments employing even as early as 1816 over 1,500 people. But the typical factory even as late as 1835, was described by Baines when he wrote:

A cotton-spinning establishment offers a remarkable example of how, by the use of very great power, an enormous quantity of the easiest work can be accomplished. Often we may see in a single building a 100 horse-power steam-engine which has the strength of 880 men, set in motion 50,000 spindles, besides all the auxiliary machines. The whole requires the service of but 750 workers. But these machines, with the assistance of that mighty power, can produce as much yarn as formerly could hardly have been spun by 200,000 men, so that one man can now produce as much as formerly required 266! Each spindle produces daily from $2\frac{1}{2}$ to 3 hanks of yarn, and thus the 50,000 together will furnish in 12 hours a thread 62,000 English miles in length – that is to say which would encircle the whole earth $2\frac{1}{2}$ times.

The handloom-weavers

With the vast increase in demand for cloth and in the supply of spun yarn, the handloom-weavers enjoyed a golden age. Samuel Bamford recalled his uncle's home:

My uncle's domicile, like all the others, consisted of one principal room called 'the house'; on the same floor with this was a loom-shop containing four looms, and in the rear of the house on the same floor, were a small kitchen and scullery and a buttery. Over the house and loom-shop were chambers; and over the kitchen and buttery was another small apartment and a flight of stairs. The whole of the rooms were lighted by windows of small square panes, framed in lead, in good condition; those in the front being protected by shutters. The interior of this dwelling showed that cleanly and comfortable appearance which is always to be seen where a managing Englishwoman is present. There were a dozen good rush-bottomed chairs, the backs and rails bright with wax and rubbing; a handsome clock in mahogany case; a good chest of oaken drawers; a mahogany snap-table; a mahogany corner cupboard, all well polished; besides tables, weather-glass, cornice and ornaments.

In his *Life and Times of Samuel Crompton* Gilbert French recalled that weaving was a trade for gentlemen:

> They brought home their work in top boots and ruffled shirts, carried a cane, and in some instances took a coach. Many weavers at that time used to walk about the streets with a five pound Bank of England note spread out under their hat-bands; they would smoke none but long 'churchwarden' pipes, and objected to the intrusion of any other handicraftsmen into the particular rooms in the public-houses which they frequented.

The higher wages earned by this prosperous section of the working class enabled them to buy themselves a greater and more varied supply of household goods and so to provide a stimulus to manufacturers in many other sectors.

Weaving-machines

Edmund Cartwright (1743–1823) was a clergyman-poet. In 1787 he devised a loom which could be operated by horses, water-power or steam-engine. But his attempt to run a power-loom factory in Doncaster proved a dismal failure. Within two years he was driven into bankruptcy. A number of other industrialists improved on his power-loom during the first years of the nineteenth century. But the introduction of power-weaving was slow and it was not generally adopted until the 1820s. A combination of falling prices and a post-war fall in trade had led to some fall in their earnings before 1820. But as Gilbert French pointed out it was after this that handloom weavers fell on really hard times:

> This prosperity did not continue, and few operatives endured greater privations than the hand-loom weavers of Bolton for the succeeding fifty years. In 1797 the price for weaving twenty

four yards of cambric muslin fell to twenty-nine shillings, in 1807 to eighteen shillings, in 1817 to nine shillings, and in 1827 . . . to six shillings and sixpence.

The weavers who had once marched through towns with the £5 notes stuck in their hats became the subject of a parliamentary committee which reported in 1835:

A very great number of the weavers are unable to provide for themselves and their families a sufficiency of food of the plainest and cheapest kind; that they are clothed in rags . . . that they have scarcely anything like furniture in their houses; that their beds and bedding are of the most wretched description, and that many of them sleep upon straw; that notwithstanding their want, they have full employment; that their labour is excessive, not infrequently 16 hours a day.

A textile-owning family

We have seen that social mobility was one of the features of preindustrial Britain. A short history of three generations of the Peel family shows that success in business continued to win both economic and social rewards. The first Robert Peel (1723–95) was a prosperous farmer who like many of his neighbours in the Lancashire hills combined farming with domestic textile production. In the 1760s he moved into Blackburn, mortgaging his land for about £3,000 to provide his share of the capital needed to form a calico-printing firm. His partners were his brother-in-law and a man called Yates whose capital came from money earned in his family's innkeeping business. By 1772 this firm had prospered into a cloth-making firm with the partners looking for ways of expanding even further. Two of them moved to Bury to open another business while Peel remained in Blackburn.

The second Robert Peel (1750–1830) went to Bury to join the other two partners. By 1790 this Peel had become an MP and a baronet and was widely accepted as a leading representative of the new class of cotton-manufacturers. In 1852 W. A. Abram in his *History of Blackburn* noted:

> He was a favourable specimen of a class of men, who, availing themselves in Lancashire of the discoveries of other heads and of their own, and profiting by the peculiar local facilities for making and printing cotton goods as well as the wants and demands ... for the articles manufactured, succeeded in realizing great opulence, without possessing either refinement of manners, culture of intellect or more than commonplace knowledge.

He could afford to give his son (1788–1850) the education that had previously only been given to sons of the aristocratic upper class. He went to Harrow and Christ Church, Oxford, became an MP and by 1820 was a leading member of the Tory Party. In 1830 on the death of his father he inherited $£1\frac{1}{2}$ million. Some idea of the relative value of Peel's inheritance can be gained from the thought that in 1830 the members of the Metropolitan Police which he had founded in 1829 were receiving 12s 6d per week (about $62\frac{1}{2}$p).

This third Robert Peel was to become Prime Minister in 1834 and again in 1841. Between 1841 and 1846 he took England a long way along the road to Free Trade as demanded by manufacturers from his native Lancashire. From Lancashire farmhouse to Number 10 Downing Street in three generations: such mobility would have gratified even Defoe. From a mortgage of $£3,000$ to an inheritance of $£1\frac{1}{2}$ million: this progression must have gratified even the most eager seeker for financial rewards for investment and endeavour.

Urbanization, the result of mechanization

With the introduction of water-power as a driving force for the frame, factories had to be built on the hills of Lancashire, Yorkshire, Derbyshire and other counties where the flow of the streams would be strong enough to drive the water-wheels. There were disadvantages in this location. The factories were sited away from the ports from which they obtained their raw materials and through which they sent out their exports. They were also at a distance from their domestic markets, the bankers who discounted their bills and the other businessmen with whom they had to deal – weavers, dyers and so on.

After 1785 steam-power was introduced and the location of the industry changed once again. The industrialist now had to consider the cost of transporting coal when deciding on locating his factory. Industry came down from the hills, back to the more populated plains, within easier reach of ports, domestic markets and other businessmen. One of the most important considerations that industrialists had to bear in mind was the need for simple access to someone who could maintain and if need be repair the new machinery and engines. Such engineers were to be found in the urban areas. The external economy which brought the factory-owner to site his plant in an urban area also brought other people and firms to the area. The first Peel had come down from the Lancashire hills at a time when the majority of people lived in small towns and villages. By the time of the death of the third Peel in 1850 the face of England had changed. The census of 1851 was to show that for the first time over half the population of England and Wales lived in urban areas with populations of over 50,000 people.

Labour and the new machinery

There was relatively little difficulty in recruiting the labour force required to work in the mills and factories. Most of the machines could be worked by women and children. With a fall in the death rate and a rise in the birth rate there was enough local labour to man the first machines. When the demand for labour exceeded the local supply, there were enough people from the neighbouring countryside willing to leave the farm, even perhaps compelled to do so after enclosure. If industrialists were still short of labour they wrote to the Poor Law authorities in London and elsewhere, offering to employ the pauper children. Hundreds of these were sent off by authorities anxious to lower the burden of the Poor Rate and to find work for the children in their care.

Although there were local riots when Hargreaves's jenny was first introduced, there was relatively little opposition to the introduction of machinery in the cotton industry. There was no traditional workforce with long memories of domestic work, guild-membership and other inhibiting traditions. But there was a great deal of opposition from workers in other sectors of the textile industry. On 13 June 1786 a petition appeared in the *Leeds Intelligencer*:

To the Merchants, Clothiers and all such as wish well to Staple Manufactory of this Nation.

The Humble Address and Petition of Thousands, who labour in the Cloth Manufactory.

Sheweth, That the Scribbling-Machines have thrown thousands of your petitioners out of employ, whereby they are brought into great distress, and are not able to procure a maintenance for their families, and deprived them of the opportunity of bringing up their children to labour. . . .

The number of Scribbling-Machines extending about seventeen miles south-west of Leeds, exceed all belief, being no less than one hundred and seventy! and as each machine will do as much work in twelve hours, as ten men can in that time do by hand, (speaking within bounds) and they working night and day, one machine will do as much work in one day as would otherwise employ twenty men.

How are those men, thus thrown out of employ to provide for their families; – and what are they to put their children apprentice to, that the rising generation may have something to

keep them at work, in order that they may not be like vaga-
bonds strolling about in idleness?

During the long wars against Napoleon trade was often
depressed and unemployment frequently at a high level. This
increased the hostility felt by workpeople towards the new
machines and their owners. During 1811/12 the machine
smashing took on some of the signs of being organized, with the
legendary Ned Ludd appearing as a leader of the wreckers. In
Nottingham the framework-knitters in the lace industry quoted
an ancient law in appealing against the act of 1788 which was
aimed at punishing machine-wreckers. They wrote:

By the charter granted by our late sovereign Lord, Charles II,
the framework knitters are empowered to break and destroy
all frames and engines that fabricate articles in a fraudulent and
deceitful manner, and to destroy all framework knitters' goods
whatsoever that are so made. An Act passed in the 28th year of
our present sovereign Lord George III enacted that persons
entering by force into any house, shop or place to break or
destroy frames should be adjudged guilty of felony.

We are fully convinced that such Act was obtained in the
most fraudulent manner; we therefore, the framework knitters,
do hereby declare the aforesaid Act to be null and void. And we
do hereby declare to all hosiers, lace manufacturers and proprietors of frames that we will break and destroy all manner of
frames whatsoever that make the following spurious articles
and all frames whatsoever that do not pay the regular prices
heretofore agreed to [by] the masters and workmen . . . and all
frames of whatsoever description the workmen of whom are
not paid in the current coin of the realm will invariably be
destroyed. . . .

Given under my hand this first day of January, 1812 at Ned
Lud's Office, Sherwood Forest.

In Yorkshire there were many riots and attacks on factories and
the houses of factory-owners. Among the leaders of the Luddite

movement in that county were the croppers, who finished off the woven cloth with the aid of giant shears. They resented the introduction of power-driven shearing-frames. Among their songs was one which went:

> Come all ye croppers stout and bold,
> Let your faith grow stronger still,
> Oh, the cropper lads in the county of York
> Broke the shears at Forster's mill.
>> The wind it blew
>> The sparks they flew
> Which alarmed the town full soon.
>
> Around and around we all will stand,
> And sternly swear we will,
> We'll break the shears and windows too,
> And set fire to the Tazzling mill.

Ludd also sent a letter on behalf of the croppers:

Sir,

Information has just been given in, that you are a holder of those detestable Shearing Frames, and I was desired by my men to write to you and to give you fair warning to pull them down. . . . If they are not taken down by the end of next week, I shall detach one of my lieutenants with at least 300 men to destroy them and further more take notice that if you give us the trouble of coming far, we will increase your misfortune by burning your buildings down to ashes, and if you have the impudence to fire at any of my men, they have orders to murder you and burn all your Housing. You will have the goodness to go to your neighbours to inform them that the same Fate awaits them if their Frames are not taken down. . . . We will never lay down our arms till the House of Commons passes an act to put down all the machinery hurtful to the

Commonalty and repeal that to the Frame Breakers – but we petition no more, that wont do, fighting must,

Signed by the General of the Army of Redressers,

NED LUDD, Clerk.

[Letter sent to a Huddersfield manufacturer (1812)]

In 1812 Parliament passed a Framework Act which increased the existing penalties on people found guilty of machine-wrecking. Many thousands were punished in 1811/12. At the end of our period, 1830, there was an outbreak of machine-wrecking in the agricultural districts of southern England where new, power-driven threshing-machines had been introduced. The legendary leader of this outbreak was Captain Swing. On 8 December 1830 the Whig Home Secretary Lord Melbourne urged magistrates to deal harshly with the rioters:

> These machines are as much entitled to the Protection of the Law as any other Description of Property.... It is my duty therefore to recommend in the strongest Manner, that for the future all Justices of Peace, and other Magistrates, will oppose a firm Resistance to all demands of the Nature above described, more especially when accompanied with Violence and Menace; and that they will deem it their Duty to maintain and uphold the Rights of Property of every Description against Violence and Aggression.

On 2 January 1831 Mr Justice Alderson sentenced machine-breakers to transportation to Botany Bay. After passing sentence he said:

> I hope that your fate will be a warning to others. You will leave the country, all of you; you will see your friends and relatives no more; for though you will be transported for seven years only, it is not likely that at the expiration of that term you will find yourselves in a situation to return. You will be in a distant land at the expiration of your sentence. The land which you have disgraced will see you no more; the friends with whom

you are connected will be parted from you for ever in this world.

Child labour

Children had always played a part in the cottage industries and in farm work. Under the direction of parents, even the younger children had a part to play in carding, sorting, spinning and so on. It was not surprising that many parents sent their children to work in factories when these were set up. However there was a great difference between the conditions of work in the cottage and in the factory, where the pace was set by the machine, discipline imposed by a master or his foreman, hours regular and longer than was customary in the cottage.

Few people, not even Owen the leading Radical, thought that government had a right to interfere in the relationship between parents and children. However Owen had the support of many leading industrialists when he waged a campaign against the employment of pauper children who had no parents to defend them. The second Robert Peel became a leader of this campaign. In 1802 and again in 1819 Parliament passed acts aimed at limiting the employment of these children. In the act of 1802 the working day for pauper children was limited to twelve hours and they were not to do any nightwork. All factories employing such children had to register with the local magistrates who were empowered to see that the terms of the act were carried out. The majority of factory-owners did not employ pauper children and were eager to see the imposition of some control on the activities of the less scrupulous. Unfortunately the magistrates were reluctant to move against offenders.

In 1819 a second act extended the terms of the 1802 act to all children. It said that no children under nine years of age were to be employed and that children between the ages of nine and thirteen were not to work more than twelve hours a day. This act failed to appoint any inspectors to see that its terms were carried out and by 1829 there had been only two prosecutions.

Not until 1833 did the government appoint factory inspectors to travel the country to see that the terms of the 1833 Factory Act were carried out. Even then only four were appointed and their activities confined to textile-mills. The law was not yet concerned about conditions in mines, engineering shops, iron foundries, brickyards and other places where children continued to work at dangerous, dirty and ill-paid jobs until well into the 1860s.

It is easy to see why the government was slow to take action in this matter of working conditions. To have done so would have been to run counter to the whole idea of that freedom which as we have seen was one of the hallmarks of the eighteenth century. This freedom from government regulation had allowed free rein to enterprise, commerce, industry and trade. At a more practical level it would have been almost impossible for central government to operate effectively until a new, quick method of communication had been set up. The building of the railway network after 1830 provided this. Again at a practical level, there was no administrative machine – at central or local level – to supervise the implementing of whatever laws a central government might have passed. The history of the nineteenth century may be seen as the continued attempt by central government to create the administrative framework and bodies to supervise the implementing of legislation. During the nineteenth century the civil service was enlarged and reformed to become an efficient machine. After a tentative beginning in 1835 there was a gradualist approach to the creation of democratically elected local councils which as the century went on became responsible for administering laws on housing, health, and education. All this lies outside the scope of this story of the Industrial Revolution from 1760 to 1830. It is necessary to refer to it so that we may have a better understanding of the government's failure to play an active role in the economic and social life of the country before 1830.

12. Iron and Coal and the Industrial Revolution

Small but growing

By 1760 a small number of ironmasters were using the Darby method to produce pig-iron from coke-fired blast-furnaces. For some purposes this iron proved a suitable substitute for wrought iron produced at the charcoal-fired forge. Sometimes the iron was cast direct from the blast-furnace into moulds. Some ironmasters became producers of finished products, whereas in the past they had normally produced bar-iron for sale to manufacturers of finished products. Most of the ironmasters, e.g. Darby, Crawshay and the owners of the Carron works, had their own warehouses in London, Bristol and elsewhere. Here they sold their cast-iron products; cooking pots for the home, bushes for cart-wheel axles, parts for steam-engines as well as larger items such as pillars and beams for warehouses.

However no one had yet solved the problem of producing suitable wrought iron from coke or coal-fired furnaces. In forge, rolling-mill and slitting-mill, charcoal seemed to be the only suitable fuel. This meant that the larger part of the iron industry was still dependent on a good supply of wood. Hence it continued to be rural and migratory in character with this latter section of the industry in the hands of many small manufacturers. Even the seemingly liberated sector which produced the pig- and cast iron was a rural-based industry. Until Watt developed an improved steam-engine in the 1770s the ironmasters were dependent on constant supplies of running water to work their bellows, forge-hammers and mills.

Ironmasters had a twin problem: to find a source of *charcoal* near a *stream* which could provide a constant flow. During the winter the flow of water was normally satisfactory. But even during modest summers the flow might fall below what was required, while a drought could force a master to close his works. Darby had a Newcomen engine to raise the water again after it had once passed over the wheel. But even this did not always prove successful and the production of iron at Coalbrookdale was held up for weeks on end. Ashton quotes a letter written in June 1786 in which Watt complained that he could not get the parts he needed because the supplier was unable to get his forges to work: 'I know not where to get plates. Parson's forge will have no water at present and we may be long enough before we can get them from him.'

The coke-fired blast-furnace required a much greater draught than did the charcoal-fired furnaces. Hence the ironmasters' need for stronger bellows at their blast-furnaces. In 1761 at the Carron works air-cylinders provided this draught. A French visitor described the Carron bellows:

Four blast furnaces, forty-five feet high, devour day and night immense quantities of coal and ore. We can therefore realize the amount of air needed to keep alive these fiery furnaces which, every six hours, pour forth streams of liquid iron. Each furnace is kept going by four air-pumps of the largest size, in which the air, compressed into iron cylinders, and driven on to the flame through a single tube, produces such a piercing whistle and such a violent disturbance, that anyone who did not know what was coming would certainly feel terrified. These wind machines, a kind of huge bellows, are set in motion by the action of water. A considerable volume of air is indispensable in order to keep a column of coal and ore forty-five feet high in the most intense state of cadescence. The current of air is so rapid and strong that it produces a live and bright flame ten feet above the top of the furnace.

One result of this improved draught was that the furnace which had produced only 12 tons of pig-iron a week could now produce over 40 tons. However most ironmasters continued to rely on a water-wheel to drive the bellows and provide the draught.

The rural setting of the industry caused a major transport problem. Iron was a heavy product and transport costs were high relative to the value of the product. British iron was a high cost industry in the eighteenth century. It was as expensive to haul iron twenty miles along the poor roads of the time (see Chapter 10) as it was to bring iron from Sweden. And Swedish iron was of a better quality and was cheaper in spite of the Swedish export duty and British import duty.

The consumers

Cast iron from the coke-fired furnaces was cheaper than wrought iron and proved to be a suitable substitute for many purposes; gates, gun-carriages, cannons, nails, joists, pipes and bridges were increasingly made from the cheaper product. However the cast iron was brittle and so wrought iron was still required for such items as ploughshares, hoes, tools of all kinds, locks and bolts.

The ironmasters sold a good deal of their cast iron to other manufacturers in the Black Country, Birmingham, Sheffield and Lancashire. Here, in small workshops, masters and men worked in small cottage workshops and at small forges to produce consumer goods. Iron was in this sense a producer's good. It is worth while noting here that as the output grew and the price fell there was pressure on ironmasters and other producers to devise new ways of using this more plentiful and cheaper product. The first machines in the textile industry – frame, jenny and the rest (see Chapter 11) – were made of wood. Later machines were made of iron which proved to be a better medium than wood for the manufacture of larger machines. There was a limit to the size of a wooden machine, but almost no limit to the size of an iron machine. The iron machines also allowed manufacturers to use the steam-engine as a motive power; the wooden machines were shaken to pieces by this new form of power.

The demand for iron was limited; even as late as 1788 less than 100,000 tons was being used. However this was a great increase on what had once been. In 1720 the total British consumption of iron was less than 50,000 tons, most of it imported from Sweden or Russia. The prosperous domestic market provided the iron industry with a steadily increasing demand. This encouraged manufacturers to invest in new plants and to seek ways of improving their methods of production and the quality of their product.

But until the coming of the railway age after 1830 the major contributor to innovation and development in this industry was war. The eighteenth century saw Britain engaged in almost constant wars against France, during which the demand for weapons of all kinds increased dramatically. The Carron works owed their growth to the demand for cannon; the ironmasters of South Wales were also proud of the great guns they turned out. When Nelson visited the Crawshay works at Merthyr, he did so in order to see the place where the men produced the guns which enabled him to win his victories over the French. Henry Cort, whose work we will examine later in the chapter, started out as a navy agent anxious – as he explained – to improve the quality of British iron 'in connexion with the supply of iron to the navy'. Henry Maudslay, the pioneer of the lathe and of machine tools, began his career at the Woolwich Arsenal and his aim was to find a means of fulfilling the naval contracts into which he had entered.

Growth after 1770

The demands made on the iron industry during the Seven Years War (1756–63) had led to the opening of several new works and the enlargement of some existing works. In addition to the founding of the Carron works and the enlarging of the works in Merthyr and Dowlais there was the opening of John Wilkinson's new works at Broseley. In all of these new works the masters used coke-fired furnaces. In 1760 there were only 17 such furnaces in Britain; 14 more were opened in the 1760s and by 1790 there were over 80. Meanwhile there was a decline in the charcoal iron industry. No new charcoal-fired blast-furnaces were built after 1775 and by 1790 the number of such furnaces had fallen to 25.

Most of the new furnaces were built on the coalfields. Of the 81 at work in 1790, 35 were in the Midlands, 24 in Shropshire and 11 in Staffordshire. By 1806 almost 90 per cent of the pig-iron furnaces were on coalfields. This is not surprising since it took 10 tons of coal to produce 1 ton of pig-iron. The new furnaces were larger than the older charcoal-furnaces and this trend was increased after Watt had developed a steam-engine to provide the required blast. The first such engine was installed in 1776 at John Wilkinson's Broseley works.

The development of the coke-using iron industry had its effects on the demand for coal. The mine-owners had to dig deeper to get their coal and this in turn meant that there had to be even stronger pumps to take away the water from the mine. The development of the steam-engine for this purpose was Watt's first contribution to industrial development, and the refinement of his first engines proved of major significance in the iron industry. The interdependence of industries is also shown by the relationship between the building of better engines and two developments in the iron industry. John Wilkinson's success with a new method of boring cannon provided Watt with the high-quality cylinders and pistons he needed for his engine. The better-quality cast iron from the coke-fired furnaces provided him with many parts for his engines.

The forge-masters

The ironfounders prospered, using the cheaper, high-quality cast iron from coke-fired blast-furnaces. They did so at the expense of the owners of the forges whose more expensive wrought iron was displaced in some markets at least by cast iron. This forced the forge-owners to look for some way of reducing their costs of production so as to become more competitive. Thus did improvements in one field lead to a search for improvements in others.

Many forge-masters tried to use cheap and plentiful coal instead of the more expensive and increasingly scarcer charcoal at their forges. The problem was that if coal or coke came directly into contact with the pig-iron being reheated in the forge, impurities passed from the fuel into the molten metal and rendered it useless. Some masters tried using a mixture of coal and charcoal; others used coal in the early stages of the process of forging, then used a charcoal-fired furnace in the later stage in the hope that at that stage they could extract the impurities resulting from using coal earlier on.

It is difficult to say which forge-master succeeded in producing good wrought iron from a coal-fired furnace. In 1760 John Wood took out a patent for doing so but there is no evidence that he actually succeeded. In 1762 Roebuck of the Carron works obtained a patent which seemed to have anticipated most of the ideas involved in Cort's puddling process. But Roebuck failed to produce a pure enough iron. In 1766 two brothers, Thomas and George Cranage, were employed at Coalbrookdale. Their employer was Richard Reynolds, son-in-law to the second Abraham Darby. The Cranages seem to have hit on the idea of the reverberatory furnace.

Thomas Cranage was in charge of the company's forge at

Bridgenorth and the other brother was a founder at the Dale works. They took out a patent in 1766 which showed that the hearth containing the pig-iron was separated from the grate holding the coal-fire by a bridge of bricks. As the flame passed over the bricks it was deflected so that it played on the metal. But the metal and the coal did not come into contact. Once the metal had reached a molten state it was then 'puddled' in much the same way as was done by Cort. The Cranages had some success and their method was widely adopted. However iron produced in this way was not suitable for every purpose, so that there was still pressure on masters to try to devise even better methods of production.

One part of the industry which found Cranage iron particularly suitable was nail-making. This was a major user of iron and the fact that cheaper iron was now available was of great importance for the nail-makers and their customers. Ashton quotes a nail-maker:

> The nail trade would have been lost to this country had it not been found practicable to make nails with iron made with pit coal. We have now another process to attempt, and that is to make bar iron with pit coal; and it is for that purpose we have made, or rather are making, the alterations at Donnington Wood, Ketley, etc.

In 1782 John Payne took out a patent for the use of rollers in the refining process. Passing the cooling metal through huge iron rollers would, it was hoped, help to press out whatever impurities remained in the wrought iron produced in the coal-fired forges. There is no evidence that Payne actually tried out his method. There is evidence that in 1783 Peter Onions, a foreman at the Crawshay ironworks at Merthyr, hit on a new method. In May of that year he took out a patent for a method of puddling the molten metal in almost exactly the same way that Cort described in his patent of February 1784.

There is no evidence that either was aware of the existence of the other or that either of them copied the other's methods. They, like many other forge-masters and workers, were empirical experimenters driven by economic pressures. Imported bar-iron was becoming increasingly expensive while a contemporary song sung in John Wilkinson's works tell its own story of the problems facing the charcoal-based industry:

> That the wood of old England would fail did appear,
> And tough iron was scarce, because charcoal was dear.
> By puddling and stamping he prevented that evil,
> So the Swedes and the Russians may go to the devil.

Since it took 24 hundredweight of charcoal to refine a ton of iron in a forge there was great pressure to find a substitute for this fuel.

Henry Cort

In 1765 twenty-five year old Henry Cort was a navy agent in London. He began experiments in the hope of devising a method of producing better quality wrought iron from British bar-iron. He wanted to produce better quality naval cannons, using British iron rather than the expensive imported iron. In 1775 he erected a forge and a slitting-mill at Fontley, near Fareham in Hampshire. By 1779 Boulton and Watt had erected a steam-engine to pump back the water which turned the wheel which powered the bellows and the forge's hammer. By 1782 Cort had a steam-engine installed to drive the forge-hammer and was in touch with Watt, as we know from letters quoted in Ashton's *Iron and Steel in the Industrial Revolution*:

> On 14 December Watt wrote to his partner, Boulton: 'We had a visit today from a Mr. Cort of Gosport who says he has a forge there and has found out some grand secret in the making of Iron, by which he can make double the quantity at the same expense and in the same time as usual. He says he wants some

kind of Engine but could not tell what, wants some of us to call on him, and says he has had some correspondence with you on the subject. He seems a simple good-natured man not very knowing. He says he does most of the smith work for the King's yard and has a forge and rolling and slitting mill. I think him a brother projector – and have therefore put him off until some of us can view the ground, which he readily agreed to as he has water for most of the year.'

Cort's 'grand secret' consisted of heating the pig-iron in a reverberatory furnace, using coal. The door of the furnace had several openings or slots through which the workmen were able from time to time to stir the molten iron. Then:

After the metal has been for some time in a dissolved state, an ebullition, effervescence or such like intestine motion takes place, during the continuance of which a blueish flame or vapour is emitted; and during the remainder of the process the operation is continued (as occasion may require) of raking, separating, stirring, and spreading the whole about in the furnace till it loses its fusibility, and is flourished or brought into nature. As soon as the iron is sufficiently in nature, it is to be collected together in lumps, called loops, of sizes suited to the intended uses.

Other forge-masters had always taken the metal at this point and stamped it into plates. Cort left the metal in the furnace, brought it up to an even greater heat and then put it under the forge-hammer, which hammered out the slag.

Then came an operation which was certainly original to Cort. Instead of further reheating and hammering the metal Cort passed it, still at welding heat, through the heavy rollers which had been used for many years for rolling and slitting finished iron. This was a much quicker process than the older method of hammering and reheating. It also enabled the production of much larger quantities of iron. A contemporary quoted by Ashton described Cort's method and not surprisingly in agricultural England used an agricultural analogy to help readers understand the new method:

> As the stirring of cream, instead of mixing and uniting the whole together, separates like particles to like, so it is with the Iron; what was at first melted comes out of the furnace in clotted lumps, about as soft as welding heat, with metallic parts and dross mixed together but not incorporated.' These 'great cinders of iron' were put under the forge hammer and then passed through the rollers, 'and by this simple process all the earthy particles are pressed out.'

The Cranages of Coalbrookdale had used a coal-fired reverberatory furnace. John Payne had the idea of using rollers and Onions had developed the process of puddling. But Cort was the first to combine successfully all these improvements. The effect of his work was felt very quickly. Using a forge-hammer it had been possible to produce only 1 ton of bar-iron in about 12 hours. Using rollers 15 tons could be produced in the same time. What was even more important was the high quality of the product. It could be used in place of charcoal-iron for every purpose except the making of steel.

Cort's discovery meant that the forge-masters and founders were now no longer forced to look for supplies of charcoal. Like the blast-furnace owners, they too could site their works on the coalfields. With blast-furnaces and foundries using the same fuel, the two sections of the industry became integrated, ending the high cost of transporting the coal-produced pig-iron to the charcoal-using foundries.

The iron industry was a large consumer of coal so ironmasters extended their investment. They not only integrated blast-furnaces with foundries, rolling-mills and slitting-mills. They also developed their own coal-mines. All this demanded capital. Within a short time the iron industry was dominated by a small number of proprietors, whose works were concentrated in four major areas. New and large towns grew up around the ports and ironworks of Staffordshire, South Yorkshire, the Clyde and South Wales. Here amid the black hills of pit slag and the ever-burning mountains of slag from the ironworks grew up a new breed of workpeople.

The patent

Cort had arranged that any ironmaster using his patented method of puddling and rolling was to pay him a royalty of 10s (50p) for each ton produced. Within a few years Crawshay's works at Merthyr, among the first to introduce the new methods, was producing 200 tons a week in place of the 10 tons it had previously been turning out. If Crawshay and the other imitative iron-masters had paid the royalty Cort would have been a rich man, receiving, it is estimated, a quarter of a million pounds between 1786 and 1789 alone. Cort had borrowed the capital he required to set up Fontley from Adam Jellicoe, who became his partner in the works. Jellicoe was deputy paymaster of seamen's wages. In 1789 it was proved that Jellicoe had stolen the money loaned to Cort from the government funds with which he had been entrusted. Jellicoe committed suicide. The government, seeking to get back the money that the unfortunate man had stolen, took possession of all Jellicoe's property and called on Cort to repay the money he had borrowed. Cort was driven into bankruptcy. The ironmasters paid nothing, while the patent was thrown open to public use.

The Ironmasters

We have seen that the development of the textile industry depended on the application of new methods by thrifty, prudent and hardworking entrepreneurs drawn from all sections of society but coming mainly from relatively humble beginnings. This was not the case in the iron industry. Most of the ironmasters belonged to families that already had some connection with the industry; some of them were merchants who sold metal products and wanted to get control over the industry which produced their goods. Others were producers of metal goods seeking to gain control of the raw material for their works. There were indeed goldsmiths, farmers, medical doctors and clergymen among the ranks of the ironmasters. But the majority came from within the industry; the father of the first Abraham Darby was a locksmith and other early masters had produced spades and shovels, nails, files and hay-rakes. Blacksmiths, clock- and watch-makers had as their examplar Matthew Boulton who had once produced mechanical toys before becoming engineer and ironmaster.

Many of them were Nonconformists with resoundingly biblical names – Abraham Darby, Isaac Hawkins, Shadrach Fox, Jeremiah Homfray and Zephaniah Parker being only a few of the long list quoted in Ashton. The most successful and progressive of the early ironmasters seem to have been Quakers as were the Darby family, Huntsman and so many others. The domination of the industry by a relatively small number of Nonconformists helps to explain the emergence of dynasties – such as the Darbys, Crawshays and others. The men tended to marry daughters of other ironmasters, providing opportunity for the further integration of works and firms. Sons were provided with the know-how and the capital to set themselves up in business – either on their own account or as junior members of a large integrated concern where they would manage one or more of the firm's works.

Some of the successful ironmasters followed the path of social mobility trodden by the rising middle classes from Defoe's time onwards. The Guests of Dowlais had their industrial origin in Josiah Guest who was merely manager of a small charcoal blast-furnace owned by Lewis Van. Within three generations the Guests had become landowners and a Guest had taken the title of Viscount Wimborne in Dorset.

The ironmasters were controllers of vast enterprises. On one site they had their blast-furnaces, forges, rolling- and slitting-mills. Either on the site or near by they had their own coal-mines, opened to produce coal for the works, then expanded to produce coal for sale at home and overseas. Each ironmaster controlled a number of sites, usually in fairly close proximity, sometimes – as with Wilkinsons – scattered over England and Wales. Some of these undertakings were owned by small partnerships, rarely more than three or four sharing the risks, finding the capital and bene-fiting from the profits. Sometimes, as with the Crawshays, the undertaking was owned by one family and the head of the family was in a real sense a local 'king'.

The new iron and its uses

With the chance to use British pig-iron for both cheap and high-quality wrought-iron and cast-iron there was an expansion of all sectors of the industry. The output of pig-iron doubled between 1760 and 1780 and quadrupled again between 1788 and 1806, largely because of the vast increase in demand from the government once it engaged in the long wars against revolu-tionary France. So great was this expansion that by 1812 Britain which had once been a large importer of Swedish and Russian pig-iron and bar-iron was itself a major exporter of both products.

New machines were introduced to help further the expansion which was under way; Wilkinson invented a steam forge-hammer which could strike 150 blows a minute, far in excess of anything which had been achieved by the old water-driven hammers. In the 1780s and 1790s there were new machines for drawing out, cutting and further working the metal. Wilkinson invented a drill for boring cannon, Maudslay produced a lathe for turning metal and other machines were invented for forging nails and turning screws.

The ironmasters had a most valuable product and seemed to be able to produce as much as would ever be wanted. Between 1788 and 1796 the average output from a blast-furnace increased from 800 tons to 1,139 tons. To people who remembered the charcoal-fired blast-furnaces and their output of perhaps 10 tons these new furnaces were indeed the home of Cyclops. But by 1830 the output of the furnaces had further increased to an average of over 3,000 tons. Meanwhile the price of iron tended to fall and by 1800 British bar-iron was selling for about £20 a ton, while Swedish bar-iron sold at around £35 a ton.

It is not surprising that the ironmasters thought of new uses for this product. In 1767 Richard Reynolds, manager of Coalbrookdale, replaced the wooden railway lines with iron ones; the era of the iron railway had dawned. John Wilkinson earned the nickname 'Iron-mad Jack' because of his seeming determination to use iron for everything; he made iron chairs, iron vats for brewers, iron pipes of all sorts and sizes – he even designed an iron coffin in which he was buried.

In 1779 the first cast-iron bridge was built. This required the passing of a private act of Parliament which was sponsored by a number of iron manufacturers, including Abraham Darby of Coalbrookdale, Wilkinson, who had an ironworks at Broseley, and Francis Homfray, brother of the Homfray who owned the ironworks at Penydarren in Dowlais and in whose works Trevithick built his railway engine. The building of a bridge across the Severn had been under discussion since 1776 and it was Wilkinson who persuaded the other promoters of the scheme that it should be built at least in part of iron – the product of the local industry whose expansion had made the building of the bridge a necessity. The framework was cast at Darby's nearby works at Coalbrookdale, and the bridge opened to the public in 1779. It was made entirely of cast iron and attracted widespread interest. A French visitor used the bridge in 1788 and wrote:

We crossed the river by an iron bridge, with a single arch of a hundred-foot span and of a height of forty-five feet above the level of the water. It is eight yards wide and a hundred yards long, and consists of iron parts, each of which has been cast separately, their total weight amounting to fifty tons.

Other countries were not similarly blessed; some had equally good deposits of iron and coal but for example in Germany it was at a great distance from the sea. Others had deposits of coal but not of iron. Only in Britain it seemed had Providence been triply bountiful. But even Providence has to be helped on its way by human agency. Britain was fortunate in having the capitalists who were prepared to invest in the industry, the innovators to provide the means by which the industry could develop and a sufficiency of skilled workmen to operate the new furnaces and foundries. In 1797 Britain became for the first time an exporter of iron. By 1812 exports exceeded imports. By 1830 about one-fifth of British iron was being exported. The number of blast-furnaces continued to increase from under 20 in 1760 to over 80 by 1790. In 1803 there were 177, in 1830, 372 and after 1800 the majority were coke-fired. The production of pig-iron from blast-furnaces rose from about 30,000 tons in 1770 to 250,000 tons in 1805 and to 650,000 tons in 1830. This industry like the textile industry had taken off, as shown in Ashton's table, page 220.

Iron and the Industrial Revolution elsewhere

Britain's share of the world output of pig-iron grew from about 19 per cent in 1800 to 40 per cent in 1820 and about 50 per cent in 1840. The rapid growth of this sector of heavy industry had major effects on other section of British industry. There were in Rostow's terms linkages between development in this industry and subsequent developments in others. There were backward linkages resulting from the demands which the expanding iron industry made on the rest of industry. There was a growth in the demand for iron ore, limestone and coal. Because of the increased demand for coal there was the need to find an improved method

Table 10 *Production of Pig-iron 1788–1806*

District	1788			1796			1806		
	Furnaces	Output tons	%	Furnaces	Output tons	%	Furnaces	Output tons	%
South East	2	300	0.4	1	200	0.2	—	—	—
South West	7	4,700	7.0	8	3,100	2.5	6	4,100	1.6
Midlands	33	31,800	46.8	37	46,200	36.9	84	104,400	41.8
Chester and N. Wales	2	1,000	1.5	4	3,300	2.6	4	2,100	0.8
S. Wales	13	10,800	15.7	25	34,400	27.4	47	75,600	30.2
York and Derby	15	9,600	14.2	25	20,100	16.0	45	37,000	14.8
North West	5	2,800	4.2	4	2,000	1.6	8	4,000	1.6
Scotland	8	7,000	10.2	17	16,100	12.8	27	23,200	9.2
Total	85	68,000	100.0	121	125,400	100.0	221	250,400	100.0

of transport. We have already seen that every successful canal had 'coal at its heels', and over a quarter of the canals were built to carry coals to the furnaces and forges.

The expansion of the industry created a demand for more efficient steam-powered machinery. Water had to be pumped out of coal- and iron-mines. Engines were wanted to crush the ores which had once been slowly broken up by men using hammers, coke-fired furnaces needed a blast which could only be provided by a steam-engine which was also required to drive the larger and more powerful forge-hammers and rolling-mills. By 1830 the iron industry was using about a quarter of all the steam-engines produced in Britain. This provided the engineering industry with a valuable domestic market and a solid base on which to construct its own future. Expansion and booms may be export-led as they were with cotton; but for most industries it is essential to have a secure, prosperous and large domestic market as a springboard for the launch into the export market. The iron industry provided the engineering industry with that base.

The iron industry also had 'forward linkages' with British industry in that it supplied a cheap, tough product suitable for the production of tools for agriculture and industry, for weapons for army and navy, for machine-making and industrial building. Iron was largely a producers' product in that most of the product of forge or mill was sold to manufacturers of all sorts of goods. When these were offered cheaper iron they were able to lower the price of their own product; they were also encouraged to think of ways in which iron could be substituted for other, more expensive materials. A very important linkage in this respect was in the increasing use of iron instead of wood for the manufacture of machinery in the textile industry. The iron machines turned out on lathes by semi-skilled workmen were cheaper than the wooden machines, each of which had to be handmade by highly paid wheelwrights and carpenters. The iron machines were more precisely made than the handmade wooden ones: machine-made parts were replaceable in case of a breakdown. Finally only the iron machines could have stood up to the continuous pounding of the three-shift day.

In the next chapter we will examine the development of the steam-engine and assess the part played by James Watt in British industrial development. We shall see that Watt's steam-engine played a major role in industrial progress. But Watt would not have been able to build the steam-engine for Wilkinson's iron-works if Wilkinson had not been able first to provide metal cylinders bored to an accuracy which had previously been un-attainable. Wilkinson had taken out a patent in 1774 for a new method of boring cannon. He cast the gun as a solid piece. Then, instead of making the boring rod revolve as had been done previously, Wilkinson made the casting rotate around a fixed bar along which travelled a sliding cutter. The result was a uniform bore. Originally intended as a means of producing better weapons, the invention was turned to more peaceful purposes and the production of cylinders which prevented the leakage of steam which had previously been a major defect in the steam-engine. From 1775 until 1795 most engines erected by Boulton and Watt had a Wilkinson cylinder as Watt explained to a customer who wanted to use a cylinder from some other foundry:

> It was only after many expensive Experiments that Mr. Wilkinson attained the degree of perfection in casting and boring which could satisfy us. We in consequence constantly recommended his castings, and in the course of twenty years we have not erected more than three or four Engines the cylinders of which were not of his manufacture.

Flour-milling and beer-brewing were among the more important of the smaller industries of the country. In 1788 there opened the Albion steam-powered flour-mills, built by Rennie from plans drawn by Watt. John Farey wrote in: *A Treatise on Steam Engines* (1827):

> Messrs. Boulton and Watt executed their first and greatest work of this kind in London in 1785 and 1788 at the Albion

Mills which was a new establishment for grinding corn, entirely by the power of Mr. Watt's new rotative engines. The mills were contained in an elegant and commodious building . . . at the foot of Blackfrairs Bridge; and the two engines were made for them at Soho, by Messrs. Boulton and Watt, each rated at 50 horse-power. . . . Each engine worked 10 pairs of millstones. . . .

These mills deserve particular notice, as being the first of those numerous establishments which have since arisen in all the manufacturing districts of England, Scotland and Wales, entirely out of the advantages of Mr. Watt's engines; the unlimited command of power thus attained, enables a manufactory to be placed at once in the vicinity of the market for the purchase of its materials, and for the sale of its produce, instead of carrying the materials to a water-fall.

This was the first important establishment in which every piece of the plant and equipment, all the axles, wheels, pinions and shafts, were made of metal. In the past most machines in these industries had been made of wood and were irregular in motion and quickly worn out. To take just one example of the improvement made by the use of iron, the huge, regularly shaped and machine-turned cog-wheels had the twin advantages of being both powerful and regular in motion. By 1788 when the Albion mills were opened the change to iron machinery in the textile industry was almost complete. In 1786 a French visitor to a Paisley cotton-mill wrote a letter quoted by Mantoux:

I here admired as in all the large factories I have had the chance of seeing in England, their skill in working iron and the great advantage it gives them as regards the motion, lastingness and accuracy of machinery. All driving wheels, and in fact almost all things, are made of cast iron, of such a fine and hard quality that when rubbed it polishes up just like steel. . . . There is no doubt but that the working of iron is one of the most essential of trades and the one in which we are the most deficient. It is the only way by which we can manufacture on a large scale and qualify ourselves to compete on equal terms with the English. For it is impossible for, say, our spinning mills, to attempt to compete with those machines, and for our wooden machinery to try to rival that made of iron.

The coal industry

There was an increasing demand for more coal for use in blast-furnaces, foundries, forges and rolling-mills as well as for fuel for the growing number of steam-engines in use in the textile and other industries. We have seen that by 1760 the coal industry was a highly capitalistic industry facing problems from gas and water in ever-deeper mines. These problems became more acute as mines were driven even further underground in search for more coal. In 1821 there was an explosion at a pit in Wallsend which was reported in the local newspaper:

October 23, (1821) – a dreadful explosion took place in Wallsend colliery, (Russell's), by which fifty-two men lost their lives. The explosion shook the ground like an earthquake, and made the furniture dance in the surrounding houses. This alarming the neighbourhood, the friends and relatives hurried to the spot, when a heart-rending scene of distress ensued. The greatest exertions were instantly made by Mr. Buddle, the viewer, who, as soon as it was practicable, descended with his assistants, when a most melancholy scene presented itself. At the time of the explosion there were fifty-six men in the pit, of which number four only survived. The bodies of the deceased were most dreadfully scorched, and many of them most strangely distorted. Forty-six of the bodies were buried at Wallsend, fourteen of whom, being relations, were buried in one grave; some of the remainder were buried at the Ballast-hills, and some at Wallsend old church, amidst sorrowing spectators.

In 1829 the same Mr Buddle was called to give evidence to a select committee of the House of Lords on the state of the coal trade:

What is the deepest pit you know? – The deepest pit I am acquainted with as a working pit is 180 fathoms of shaft; but they frequently go deeper.

Can you state generally what is the extent of the expense incurred in sinking a single pit? – I have known several cases upwards of £30,000; that includes the machinery for sinking that pit, the steam engine and all its apparatus; that is merely getting to the coal, and it might be called more properly a winning charge than a working charge. I should think that the aggregate capital employed by coal owners on the river Tyne must amount to about a million and a half, exclusive of craft in the river.

Have you any calculations of the number of men and ships employed on the two rivers (Tyne and Wear)? – I have made a summary; there are, seamen, 15,000, pitmen and above ground people employed at the collieries 21,000, keelmen, coal boatmen, casters and trimmers, 2,000, making the total number employed in what I call the Northern coal trade, 38,000.

Do you think that the particular accidents by explosions, which you have described, have been much lessened by the introduction of Sir Humphrey Davy's safety lamp? – They have, I conceive. If we had not had the Davy lamp, these mines could not now have been in existence at all; for the only substitute we had, and that was not a safe one, was what we called steel mills. They were completely superseded by the Davy lamp of the simplest construction; it costs only about 5 or 6 shillings. A steel mill is very hard work; we were obliged to have two persons to relieve each other; and this lamp was introduced in its room. . . . this introduced quite a new era in coal mining, as many collieries are now in existence, and old collieries have been reopened, producing the best coals, which must have lain dormant but for the introduction of the Davy lamp.

The committee and Mr Buddle were aware of the value of the Davy safety-lamp. Humphrey Davy had been brought up in Cornwall, the centre of the British tin-mining industry. By 1810 he was one of Britain's leading scientists, the first professor of chemistry at the Royal Institute. In 1813 he wrote *Elements of Agricultural Chemistry* which helped make British farmers more aware of the need for a scientific approach to the question of soil-improvement. He also carried out a number of experiments with Volta batteries with the aid of an assistant, Michael Faraday, who was to carry on with the work and earn himself the title of father of the British electricity industry.

In 1812 Davy heard of a serious mine disaster which had been caused by an underground explosion, brought about by the defective methods then used for underground lighting. In 1815 he wrote: 'It will give me great satisfaction if my chemical knowledge be of any use in an enquiry so interesting to humanity. ... If you think my visiting the mines can be of any use, I will cheerfully do so.' In 1816 he produced his safety-lamp which made mining somewhat safer.

The expansion of the industry only increased the amount of capital required. Output increased from about 3 million tons in 1700 to 10 million tons in 1800 – coal being the first industry to measure its output in millions. The capital for some of this development came from local landowners as we saw in Chapter 5. Others who invested in the development of the industry were the ironmasters who wanted to control the supply of the raw material needed in their furnaces and foundries.

The development of the coal industry had its 'linkage' with other sectors. It created the demand for more and better steam-pumps to drain mines and haul the coal to the surface; later refinements on the first pump-engines by Watt would not have been possible without these first tentative steps by Savery and Newcomen (see Chapter 13). We have seen the vital part that coal played in the development of the canal system and the effects which that development had on industrial and social life.

The industry also had forward linkages. It provided the fuel for the expanding iron industry which produced the material on which the Industrial Revolution was built. Coal powered the steam-engines in the textile industries, flour-mills and brickyards which produced the building material for the millions of houses needed to accommodate however inadequately the growing population. R. M. Hartwell believes: 'The decisive technological change which freed so many industries from dependence upon organic raw materials was the discovery of a way of using coal where once wood had been essential.' This gives support to the claim that 'Coal was King', a claim that would be denied by the supporters of 'King Cotton'. But there can be little doubt that coal played a major role in Britain's industrializing progress.

13. James Watt and the Steam-engine

Watt's early career

James Watt was born in 1736 the son of a Greenock shipwright. He worked as an apprentice to an instrument-maker in London before becoming Mathematical Instrument-Maker at Glasgow where he later served as the instrument repairer at Glasgow University. While he was neither a scientist nor a university student he did earn the respect and friendship of Dr Joseph Black the professor of chemistry at Glasgow University. He attended many of Black's lectures while Black and several of his colleagues appreciated Watt's ability as a technician.

In 1762 Watt was asked to repair a Newcomen steam-pump. He found that the cylinder for this machine was imperfectly ground. The result was a loss of heat and efficiency. There was little that Watt could do about this. However he also discovered that the loss of heat in the cooling process was the cause of many of the breakdowns. He then experimented in the university laboratory and workshops to find some way of getting round the heating-cooling-heating process which was carried on in the same cylinder.

By 1764 he had worked out a solution to this problem. He made a separate cylinder which he called a condenser in which steam from the main cylinder was drawn and collected. This avoided the wasteful cooling process and cut down the consumption of coal. He described his success: 'In three hours after the idea of condensing in a separate vessel had occurred to me, I had planned the whole Engine in my mind and in three days I had a model at work nearly as perfect ... as any which have been made since that time.'

Watt the laboratory technician had little difficulty in making a simple model. But to produce the life-size boilers, pumps, beams, levers and gearing was a different matter. It was 1769 before he took out a patent. He then had to produce a working model of his new engine. By 1767 Watt had already spent five years at his work of perfecting the Newcomen engine and had run up debts of about £1,000. Roebuck of the Carron works saw the possibilities in Watt's engine and entered into a partnership. He paid Watt's debts and provided the capital needed to complete the invention. In return he was to receive two-thirds of the profits made from the new engine.

In 1769 Roebuck and Watt produced the first engine, although the standard of workmanship was not very high and the engine only partially successful. It is useful to recall again that at that time there were no machine-tools; the development of the lathe and other such tools had to wait for the flowering of the genius of Henry Maudslay in the 1830s. Samuel Smiles, an admirer of all the thrusting men of science and engineering, wrote:

Some may call it an improvement, but it might almost be called a revolution in mechanical engineering which Mr. Maudslay introduced. Before his time no system had been followed in proportioning the number of threads of screws to their diameter. Every bolt and nut was thus a speciality in itself, and neither possessed nor admitted of any community with its neighbours. To such an extent had this practice been carried that all bolts and their corresponding nuts had to be specially marked as belonging to each other. Any intermixture that occurred between them led to endless trouble and expense, as well as inefficiency and confusion – especially when parts of complex machines had to be taken to pieces for repairs.

None but those who lived in the comparatively early days of machine manufacture can form an adequate idea of the annoyance, delay and cost, of this utter want of system, nor can appreciate the vast services rendered to mechanical engineering by Mr. Maudslay, who was the first to introduce the practical measures necessary for its remedy. In his system of screw-cutting machinery, and in his taps and dies, and screw-tackle generally, he set the example and in fact laid the foundation of all that has since been done in this most essential branch of machine construction.

Mathew Boulton

Mathew Boulton was a partner in a toy-making works in Soho, Birmingham The other partner, Fothergill, was also an ironmaster with works in the Merthyr-Dowlaisd valley in South Wales. Boulton had heard of Watt's work, and even while the latter was in partnership with Roebuck had tried to devise a scheme whereby his Soho works might be associated with the new development. All proposals for such an enlarged partnership had always broken down. But in 1773 Roebuck was driven to bankruptcy. Boulton took over Roebuck's share in the partnership and in May 1774 Watt moved to Soho in Birmingham. Fothergill refused to underwrite the new venture for producing the Watt steam-engine. This forced Boulton to set up a new concern, Boulton and Watt. He provided the capital needed for this enterprise from the sale of his estates at Packington. Once again the countryside had come to the rescue of industrial development.

Even before he came to Birmingham, Watt's major problem was to find an iron foundry which would supply the materials he needed, produced to the fine precision his engine required if it were to be more successful than Newcomen's. He had turned to Darby's Coalbrookdale Company first but in 1770 he wrote:

> the people of Colebrook-dell sent us the castings for the circular machine only a month ago. They were unsound and totally useless and done over with some stuff to conceal their defects. An eminent caster has settled during the summer at Bilston. We were obliged to have recourse to him, but he has not yet sent the things, though he says he will in a few days.

The 'eminent caster' referred to in the last line was John Wilkinson whose invention of a new method of boring cannons (1774) found a peaceful application in the production of the accurate cylinders that Watt needed.

Boulton and Watt

Between 1773 and 1776 Boulton and Watt carried on with their experimental work. In 1776 Watt made two full-size engines, one of which was installed at Wilkinson's works where it was used to provide the blast needed for the new coke-fired blast-furnaces. These machines used between a third and a quarter of the fuel used in Newcomen's engines. By this time there were a large number of Newcomen engines in use; some were used to draw up water for the cisterns and fountains in noblemen's houses; others were used by local water companies to help maintain levels in reservoirs. There were a number at work in the iron industry, driving back into a mill-pool the water which worked the water-wheel which powered the bellows and hammers. Most of the engines were used in tin- and coal-mines where they pumped out water, gently, slowly and expensively.

Between 1776 and 1781 Boulton and Watt converted many Newcomen engines where coal was very expensive. They also designed and erected their own engine, acting as consultants for firms which wished to use their invention. Boulton and Watt did not manufacture the engines themselves. Any industrialist who wished to use a Boulton and Watt engine had to make his own arrangements with founders to provide the materials; the Soho firm supplied the skilled labour needed to erect the engine as well as those parts of the engine which required the precision-production which Boulton's men were accustomed to provide in their original toy trade.

They insisted on the use of cylinders bored at the Wilkinson works. Only in this way could they guarantee that the engine would work as they intended. In February 1776 Samuel Garret at the Carron works offered to provide his own cylinder for the engine which Boulton and Watt were to erect at his works. Ashton quotes the letter which Boulton wrote to Garret:

> Wilkinson hath bored us several Cylinders almost without Error; that of 50 Inches diam^r for Bentley & Co., doth not err the thickness of an old shilling in no part, so that you must improve in boring or we must furnish the Cylinder. I am a great lover of truth both moral and Geometrical – Bore your Cylinders as true as Wilkinson's and then say there is no truth in me if we are not good customers to Carron.

If a customer asked Boulton and Watt to supply all the materials needed for the erection of their engine they generally asked Wilkinson to produce all the cast-iron and brass-work. Even when the customer wanted to do the ordering himself the partners tried to get the order put Wilkinson's way, as can be seen from this letter from Boulton to Wilkinson written in November 1779:

> Mr. Watt informs that many new engines will be wanted for Wh^1 Virgin and other mines and begs I would inform you that upwards of 100 fathom of new pump will be wanted for Wh^1 Virgin, but that you must apply yourself to the mine for their order for that part as he can't do it without giving offence to some of the quackers. We will back your application but its most proper you should first apply.

The rotary engine

Until 1781 all the engines that Boulton and Watt produced were, like the Savery and Newcomen engines, merely reciprocating pumping-engines. Wilkinson and other ironmasters used a water-driven hammer in their forges. In 1777 Wilkinson asked Watt to see if he could supply him with an engine to work a hammer weighing 15 hundredweight. Watt experimented with a small engine then decided that it would be more practical if he devised some method of converting the to-and-fro action of the piston on this improvised engine into a rotary motion. He devised a crank-shaft for his purpose but between 1777 and 1780 was so busy with the erecting of the reciprocating engines that he gave little time to the new idea. When he came back to work on the new engine he found that his idea for a crankshaft had already been patented. Ashton quotes this letter from Watt's son:

'The application of the Crank to the Steam Engine for mechanical purposes, was invented by Mr. Watt in the year 1780, and a model by one of our workmen, who betrayed the secret (as he himself afterwards confessed) to a Mr Pickard of Birmingham, and this Mr. Pickard took out a patent for it in the same year. Mr. Watt, instead of contesting the right of the above patentee, then invented the rotative wheels, which, being found to answer much better than a crank, have been constantly used by us ever since; but Mr. Wilkinson and others of our friends who were acquainted with the above circumstances and thought a Crank preferable, have constantly made use of it without molestation, and we should have done the same without any scruple . . . if we had had any occasion for so doing.'

William Murdoch was a Scotsman who had come to work in the Soho works. Watt admitted the debt he owed his fellow-Scot who was not only a reliable and skilled workman but was also able to suggest many improvements to Watt's engines It was Murdoch who suggested the so-called 'sun-and-planet' action which Watt patented in 1781. This allowed the production of the first rotative engine – a forge-engine for use at John Wilkinson's works at Bradely. Other ironmasters asked for the new engine while the cotton-manufacturers became the largest buyers of the new engine which could turn a shaft and so work the machines in a factory. This brought the cotton industry down from the hills and back on to the plains.

Watt's patent expired in 1800 when the field was thrown open to other potential producers of rotative engines. By this time Boulton and Watt had installed over 500 of their engines, reciprocating and rotative, in mines, ironworks, paper-mills, potteries, cotton-mills and breweries. It seems that there might have been even more development if Watt had not been so cautious. Boulton had had to push him into producing the rotative engine. No one pushed him into other experiments so that Watt ignored the opportunity for developing engines for rail traction or for driving ships, and attacked Trevithick for experimenting with a railway engine. By 1790 a number of engineers in almost every industrial region were experimenting with high-pressure engines. Richard Trevithick is perhaps the best remembered of this host of experimental engineers, none of whom had the training or the ability of Watt.

Invention and innovation

During the last twenty years of the eighteenth century there was not only a great acceleration in the rate of economic growth of exports and an increase in the number of important inventions. These changes were both the results and causes of a generally accepted attitude towards change which in turn drove hundreds of engineers to seek ways of making improvements to existing machines and methods of production. The names of the most famous have reached the text-books. But there were hundreds of others who made their own contribution, whose work was invaluable to the success of the work of the well-known but whose names will remain unknown.

Success in this field depended on a number of factors coming together at the same time and in some senses in the same man. To have had the right idea before an advance in some other field made the implementation of that idea possible was to court failure. To have had that idea after techniques in other fields had also advanced was to be hailed as a success. This was true of Watt's dependence on Wilkinson's boring of cylinders. But Watt also needed determination, clever hands, luck, capital and a backer to carry him through the expensive period of testing. While there was some need for formal education there is no evidence that success or failure depended on a formal scientific education. Watt's connection with Glasgow University was fortuitous and what science he learned there was of little use to him in his later work. His ability to make a model of an improved engine was matched later on by the illiterate Stephenson who was an engine-repairer at a colliery in the north-east. He had no formal education of any sort but proved to be as significant an inventor as was Watt.

The list of those who contributed to the innovative progress shows that clock-makers, blacksmiths, wheelwrights or toy-makers played a part equalled only by amateurs such as Arkwright, and both artisans and amateurs played a larger part than men with higher education. When these men were faced with a problem in their own locality or industry they applied themselves to finding a solution to that problem and this solution, if adopted, became a step forward. We have seen that by the end of the nineteenth century industrial development required more than this rule-of-thumb approach but that England's success with its gifted amateurs persuaded many that formal education was not necessary.

The new steam-based technology

Samuel Smiles, the nineteenth-century biographer of success, wrote:

Early inventors yoked wind and water to sails and wheels, and made them work machinery of various kinds, but modern inventors have availed themselves of the far more swift and powerful, yet docile force of steam, which has now laid upon it the heaviest share of the burden of toil, and indeed become the universal drudge. Coal, water, and a little oil, are all that the steam-engine, with its bowels of iron and heart of fire, needs to enable it to go on working night and day, without rest or sleep. Yoked to machinery of almost infinite variety, the results of vast ingenuity and labour, the Steam-engine pumps water, drives spindles, thrashes corn, prints books, hammers iron, ploughs land, saws timber, drives piles, impels ships, works railways, excavates docks; and, in a word, asserts an almost unbounded supremacy over the materials which enter into the daily use of mankind, for clothing, for labour, for defence, for household purposes, for locomotion, for food, or for instruction.

The widespread use of the steam-engine after 1782 changed the face of British industry. Industrialists could now increase the size of factories, ironworks, coal-mines, shipyards or whatever, because of the power they took from the steam-engine. In economists' terms, the fixed costs of industry went up as buildings, machinery and other installations became larger and more expensive. We saw that in the pre-industrial era the amount of fixed capital was small. It had been very important for an industrialist to get hold of some means of financing his short-term need for floating capital. He had usually little need to find large amounts of long-term, fixed, capital. This changed with the setting up of steam-powered industries.

Gradually industry became dominated by individuals and companies which could get control of long-term capital. As the size of the technology increased so the need for even larger amounts of capital made it the more difficult for individuals or even families to fund a development as had once been the case. Industrial development might have slowed down if the law on limited liability had not been changed. The coming of general limited liability was a feature of economic history between 1830 and 1850, and so is outside the scope of this book. However this demand for a change in the law might not have arisen if the steam-engine had not been widely used to increase the size of industrial concerns.

When a firm has a large share of its capital tied up in fixed stocks of buildings, machines or whatever, it becomes essential for this stock to be used as continuously as possible. If a machine costs £1,000 and it is used only eight hours a day, the real cost of the machine is much greater than if it can be used for twenty-four hours a day. This had long been recognized in tin- and coal-mining where fixed capital had always been a significant feature of industry. In these industries the three-shift system was long-established practice. With the introduction of the steam-engine into the textile industry, a similar system was introduced and the leisurely pace at which people had worked in the cottage was replaced by the endless hum of an engine, manned by people who had to learn a new way of life. The larger, more productive furnaces and forges of the steam-powered, coal-using iron industry were more economically used when ironmasters had taught their men to accept the three-shift system which ensured that the expensive fixed capital would be continuously used.

But such continuous work in mill, furnace and forge meant that there was a flood of goods coming from these places. It then became necessary to find markets for these goods. A reduction in price would enable a wider range of buyers to come into the market for these goods; so one result of the continuous work-system was a rise in real living standards for people who could afford to buy the cheaper goods. There was constant pressure on industrialists to seek wider markets and as part of that process to cut their costs as much as they could. Some cut their profit margins, relying on a smaller unit profit from a larger sale rather than a larger unit profit from a smaller volume of sales. Others tried to make themselves more competitive by introducing more

cost-cutting innovations. As a master spinner told a parliamentary
committe in 1833: 'Our profits are extremely low and I do not
see any prospect that we have of improving it except by reducing
the price still further and extending production.'

The increase in output in any one sector of an industry put
pressure on workers and manufacturers in other sectors to find
new ways of coping with the increased supply coming to them.
Thus the development of a chemical industry was hastened
because the traditional processes of bleaching and dyeing could
not cope with the flood of goods coming from the steam-
powered mills. The demands for engines and machines was so
great that manufacturers of screws, nuts and bolts and other
machine parts were put under great pressure to find new ways of
producing their goods. Hence the development of the machine-
tool industry.

On 13 May 1830 the MP for Liverpool, Mr Slaney, spoke to the
House of Commons:

In 1801 the manufacturing population was to the agricultural
as six to five; in 1821 as eight to five; but in 1830 they became
as two to one; thus, in England, the difference was at one
period as two to one, and at another as six to five. In Scotland
in 1808 they were as five to six; in 1821 as nine to six; in 1830,
as two to one. During the last twenty years, the population of
the country generally had increased thirty per cent, the manufacturing population forty per cent. In Manchester the population had increased fifty per cent; Liverpool fifty per cent, and
Coventry the same; Leeds fifty four per cent; Birmingham
fifty per cent and Glasgow 100 per cent. . . . As an evidence of
the extent to which trade and manufactures were carried, he
would remind the House that while the average annual
importation of cotton in 1813 amounted to 79,000,000 pounds,
in 1829 it amounted to 220,000,000 pounds. The importation of
wool in 1813 was 7,000,000 pounds and in 1829 it was
27,500,000 pounds. During that time the increase of machinery

had been without example. Great as was his sense of the services
of the noble Duke who had conducted the military operations
of the country, still, if he were asked to name the person to
whom England was most indebted in bearing up against nearly
all Europe, he should say James Watt was that person. The
suggestions of Watt in the use of steam had been productive of
incalculable benefit to the country. . . . in the space of fourteen
years [1814–1828], the steam-vessels had increased thirty-fold
in number, and sixty-fold in tonnage.

Early railways

For many centuries coal had been taken from collieries to nearby
rivers or ports along wooden rails on which the horses were able
to pull the laden waggons more easily and quickly than would
have been possible on the unmade roads. The first iron railway
was laid at Coalbrookdale where Richard Reynolds laid a track
of cast-iron rails which had flanged edges to hold the waggon-
wheels on the line. The engineer John Smeaton introduced the
idea of putting the flanged edge on the wheels instead of on the
rails.

The first public railway was opened in 1801 when the Surrey
Iron Railway was built between Wandsworth and Croydon for
the transporting of goods. By 1821 there were over twenty railway companies whose railroads acted as links between canals or
between rivers and canals, rather than as really alternative
methods of transport. Both at the mines and ironworks as well as
on the public railways the waggons were pulled by horses. In
1784 Murdoch built a model locomotive but Watt's patent, and
his refusal to consider the possibility of the steam-engine being
adapted for use on railways, prevented Murdoch going any
further.

Fortunately Watt's patent expired in 1801 and in 1803 the
Cornish engineer Richard Trevithick built a steam-carriage which

he took on several journeys through the streets of London. The carriage was very heavy and the road surface unable to cope with it. In 1804 Trevithick ran a steam-engine between Merthyr Tydfil and Abercynon, pulling a load of 20 tons at 5 miles per hour. His 'Uncle Dick's Puffer' was only the first of a long line of experimental locomotives. William Hedley's 'Puffing Billy' was in use at Wylam Colliery near Newcastle in 1813; an illiterate colliery engine-repairer, George Stephenson, improved on Hedley's engine by giving it a more efficient fire-box which enabled greater steam-power to be raised.

In 1821 a group of Quaker industrialists invited Stephenson to build a railway line from Stockton to Darlington. Stephenson persuaded the directors to use steam-engines on their new line. On 27 September 1825 the 27-mile railway was opened for the carriage of passengers and goods traffic. Stephenson's engine, *Locomotion*, pulled a 400-foot train of waggons on which 500 people were perched. When the train arrived at Stockton the crowds cheered and bands played while the cannons boomed out their salutes to the dawn of a new age and the start of a second stage in the story of the industrialization of Britain.

In 1824 a group of merchants and industrialists from Liverpool and Manchester formed the Liverpool and Manchester Railway Company. When Parliament passed the act which permitted the building of the railway line linking the two towns the directors invited George Stephenson to supervise the building of the line which had to be taken across miles of dangerous bog, through cuttings blasted out of rock as well as along viaducts carrying it over valleys and rivers. The labour of thousands of navvies and the skills of civil engineering acquired during the years of canal-building (see Chapter 10) were fully utilized, and in September 1830 the line was opened, Stephenson's *Rocket* pulling a train of carriages and waggons.

While the Stockton-Darlington line was the first to carry passengers and goods, the Liverpool-Manchester line was far more important. It carried over a thousand passengers each day as well as all kinds of goods. It brought great benefits to the merchants, industrialists and consumers of the two large towns which it linked together, provided a much speedier and more efficient service than did the canals and earned very high profits for its shareholders. In the 1830s there were many other investors willing to help promote other railway lines and so usher in the railway age. The opening of the Liverpool-Manchester line provides a fitting end to the first stage of the Industrial Revolution.

14. The Standard of Living 1760-1830

Friedrich Engels (1820-95) was the son of a wealthy German cotton-spinner. He wrote pamphlets in support of Robert Owen's embryonic socialist movement and also supported the Chartists. He became a disciple of Karl Marx after having visited him in Paris. Engels spent much of his life in Manchester where he lived with a succession of Irish working-class girls. Writing in 1845 he noted: 'Before the Industrial Revolution the workers enjoyed a comfortable and peaceful existence. . . . Their standard of life was much better than that of the factory worker today.'

Engels provided no hard evidence to support his assertions. G. R. Porter armed himself with a series of statistics before writing his *Progress of the Nation* (1847) in which he declared:

If we look back to the condition of the mass of the people as it existed in this country, even so recently as the beginning of the present century, and then look around us at the indications of greater comfort and respectability that meet us on every side, it is hardly possible to doubt that here, in England at least, the elements of social improvement have been successfully at work, and that they have been and are producing an increased amount of comfort to the great bulk of the people.

In 1833 a commissioner, Cowell, was investigating conditions among the working class in Lancashire as part of the work of the commission which was due to present a report to Parliament in that year. In one part he noted:

Mrs. B., Manchester. This witness was accidentally met with, 13th May 1844. She was waiting for Dr. Hawkins, to consult him about her niece's health. I took her into a room, and examined her about the customs and comforts of operative families. I consider her evidence to be a specimen, somewhat under the average, of the way in which an operative family lives.

Her husband is a fine spinner, at Mr . . . ., where he has been from 1816; has five children. Her eldest daughter, now going 14, has been her father's piecer for three years. At her present age, her labour is worth 4s 6d a week. At present her husband's earnings and her daughter's together amount to about 25s a week – at least she sees no more than 25s a week; and before her daughter could piece for him, and when he had to pay for a piecer in her stead, he only brought home 19s or 20s a week (N.B. Whatever sum her husband may bring her home, his earnings as a fine spinner at Mr. M's are certainly not less than 28s per week).

Breakfast is generally porridge, bread and milk, lined with flour or oatmeal. On Sunday, a cup of tea and bread and butter. Dinner, on weekdays, potatoes and bacon, and bread, which is generally white. On Sunday a little flesh meat; no butter, egg or pudding. Teatime every day, tea and bread and butter; nothing extra on Sunday at tea. Supper, oatmeal porridge and milk; sometimes potato and milk. Sundays, sometimes a little bread and cheese for supper; never have this on weekdays. Now and then buys eggs when they are as low as a halfpenny apiece and fries them to bacon.

They never taste any other vegetable than potatoes; never use any beer or spirits; now and then may take a gill of beer when ill, which costs a penny. Perhaps she and her husband may have two gills a week. Her husband never drinks any beer or spirits that she knows of beyond this.

The house consists of four rooms, two on each floor; the furniture consists of two beds in the same room, one for themselves and the other for the children; have four chairs, one table in the house, boxes to put clothes into, no chest of drawers, two pans and a tea-kettle for boiling, a gridiron and frying-pan, half-a-dozen large and small plates, four pairs of knives and forks, several pewter spoons.

They subscribe a penny a week for each child to a funeral society for the children.

Two of the children go to school at 3d a week each; they are taught reading for this, but not writing. Have a few books, such as Bible, hymn-book, and several small books that the children have got as prizes at the Sunday school.

This seems to support the view taken by Engels. However Cowell was an honest investigator and his report goes on:

Read over this account to S.L., an operative, and a respectable witness on their side. He thinks it somewhat below the average of comforts possessed by the working family. The generality, he thinks, have tea and coffee for breakfast, instead of porridge, and that their dinners are generally fresh meat; and he says, that factory families may be divided into two classes, in respect of living – those in which the parents work in mills as well as the children, and those in which only the children work in mills. The first class live better than the second.

The modern argument

If contemporaries could not agree as to what was happening it is hardly surprising that modern historians differ in their opinions as to the effects of the Industrial Revolution on working-class living standards. The first of the great historians of the Industrial Revolution set the stage for the modern argument. In his classic work (1884) Toynbee wrote: 'We now approach a darker period –

a period as disastrous and as terrible as any through which a nation ever passed; disastrous and terrible because side by side with a great increase of wealth was seen an enormous increase of pauperism.'

This pessimistic view was generally accepted for many years. It was the view taken by later historians of the calibre of Cunningham, the Webbs and the Hammonds, who based their work mainly on the Blue Books of parliamentary commissions. That these official papers presented a black picture is obvious from some of the quotations used in this present work. However these reports present only one side of a picture; they were always intended to present the black side only and to draw attention to social evils. We have our own modern reports and documents – on poverty, homelessness, child-battering and the like. It would be a monstrous misreading of historical evidence if a future author of *Life in Britain in the 1960s and 1970s* were to use *Cathy Come Home* as the main source on which to base his account of housing in the 1960s. That there are blots on our modern society is clear; that they are untypical is also clear to those of us who live now. That they are atypical would be the argument of a pessimistic historian using only official reports or similarly critical material as his main sources.

In 1925 Mrs Dorothy George wrote *London Life in the Eighteenth Century*. Using mortality statistics as the basis for her work she showed that the standard of life for the London labourer had improved considerably during the eighteenth century. In later works other historians showed that there was a decline in the death rate throughout the country as a whole. This they claimed indicated a rise in general living standards during the period of the first Industrial Revolution. In 1926 Clapham produced what became the leading 'optimistic' history. Using wage-statistics and commodity prices as the main source for his work Clapham showed that the purchasing power of the English labourer in town and country had risen substantially during the period of the first Industrial Revolution.

Here we see a clash between two schools of eminent historians. The one, represented by Toynbee and later by the Hammonds, used Blue Books and contemporary pamphlets as evidence. The other, represented by Mrs George and Clapham, used statistics – on death rates, prices and wages – as the bases for their work. In 1930 J. L. Hammond agreed that the evidence of the statistics was too strong to be ignored. He admitted that it was clear that as a result of the Industrial Revolution people had more food to eat and cheaper clothing to wear. However, he argued, the workers paid a spiritual price for these materials gains.

This is the argument used by E. P. Thompson in his *The Making of the English Working Class* (1963). Unable to deny the evidence presented by Clapham and a host of successors, Thompson has to rely on sociological assertions to prove that the Industrial Revolution was a harmful development. He claims, according to R. M. Hartwell, that: 'workers lost a "more humanely comprehensible way of life" and were thrust into "a competitive scrambling selfish system, a system by which the moral and social aspirations of the noblest human beings are stultified".'

The argument, then, is less about the question of whether or not the material quality of life improved or not. The question posed by the 'pessimists' is: 'Is an Industrial Revolution desirable?' It may seem strange that the majority of the pessimists are Marxists or inclined to Marxist views. That the party of materialism should wish to decry the process which brings the greatest material change seems paradoxical. Having taken this standpoint about the English Industrial Revolution, the Marxist historians then have to become schizoid or worse when writing about the Stalinist Industrial Revolution of the 1920s and 1930s which exacted a far higher cost in human terms than ever did the English classical model.

The case for and against

The truth is that there was a rise in living standards between 1760 and 1830, that this rise was not a marked one and that by 1830 there was still a great deal of very real, harsh and degrading poverty. Against the pessimists who blame government inaction for permitting the existence of child labour, insanitary conditions and the like, there is the argument that during the period from 1760 to 1830 the infrastructure was laid on which the next generation (1830–60) would create a new system of local government, a reformed civil service and an energetic and ambitious trade union movement, and generally erect the structure for a fairer society.

Engels and the Hammonds argued that 'custom was the shield of the poor' in pre-industrial England. They claimed that the Tudor and Stuart legislation ensured that the worker received a fair wage from his employer and that the dismantling of that legislation took place during the Industrial Revolution, so that the free-booting employer was able to drive down wages at his will. There is however abundant evidence that attempts to enforce the wage-clauses of the Statute of Artificers were generally unsuccessful. We do know on the other hand that in pre-industrial England workmen were forbidden to form embryonic trade unions and that magistrates punished journeymen who tried to form 'combinations' of workmen as a means of enforcing employers to pay higher wages. To claim that the pre-industrial worker was in an advantageous position *vis-à-vis* his employer compared with his counterpart in industrialized England is also to ignore the very plain evidence that it was the Industrial Revolution which led to the growth of an independent, self-confident and ambitious wage-earning class which created its own unions and had ever-higher social expectations.

That there was a 'good life' in pre-industrial England is obvious. However it was a life which was enjoyed by a very small number of people, the owners of large estates, the politico-lawyers and others who had very high incomes which enabled them to indulge in that conspicuous consumption which has left England dotted with their grand houses, collections of furniture and paintings.

For the mass of the population – urban and rural – life was appalling. Dorothy George concludes that 'Appalling as was the state of things revealed by the nineteenth-century reports (1840–5) on the sanitary state of towns it can hardly be doubted that the state of London was far worse in the eighteenth century.'

Throughout the nineteenth century the living conditions of rural workers continued to be very primitive, described by F. M. L. Thompson as 'a violation of all decency', 'altogether filthy and disgusting', with people living in overcrowded and insanitary conditions. Things had been no better in pre-industrial England when the people also faced the appalling problems of frequent harvest failures, famines and outbreaks of epidemics.

Reasons for the rising living standards

We know that as a result of industrialization there was a great increase in total production. The British national income rose from about £48 million in 1688 to about £700 million in 1855. During this period the population was also growing. Output grew more radically than population. The result was an increase in *per capita* income from about £8 in 1700 to £12 in the 1750s and £22 in 1800. During the worst period of the Napoleonic Wars there was a slight fall in *per capita* income, but after 1815 and the return to peace there was a speedy recovery and by 1831 average real wages were about 75 per cent up on the levels reached in 1800. It has to be admitted that 'average' is an abstract which disguises the very real suffering of many families. But even the leading 'pessimist' – Engels – was forced to admit: 'It is not, of course, suggested that all London workers are poverty-stricken. . . . There can be no doubt that for every worker who is rendered utterly destitute by society there are ten who are better off.'

By 1830 about one-third of all British national income was being produced by manufacturing industry which had grown between 1780 and 1830 at a rate of 3 to 4 per cent a year. This industrial output – of clothes, furniture and other goods as well as of machinery and capital goods – had to be consumed. Part of it was 'consumed' in the form of capital investment. But until the coming of the railways there was little demand for very large lumps of industrial capital, relative to the productive capacity of British industry and agriculture. Most of the increase in output and of productivity was achieved with low-cost capital. Capital did not take an inordinate or unfair share of the increased output in the first Industrial Revolution. This incidentally was not so in the case of later industrial revolutions such as that experienced by Russia in the 1920s and 1930s. By then the size of the technological units had increased and so had their capital cost. Capital consumed up to half of all Russian output and national income during the 1930s and the Russian people suffered a long period of social deprivation as a consequence.

Part of the increased output left the country as exports. But even in 1830 exports took only 15 per cent of the national income while as a compensation retained imports added about 15 per cent to the national income. The bulk of the increased output was consumed in Britain. There was then a mass production, described by Robert Owen in 1816: 'in my establishment at New Lanark . . . mechanical powers and operations superintended by about two thousand young persons and adults . . . now completed as much work as sixty years before would have required the entire working population of Scotland.' What has too often been ignored is that this mass production had a counterpart in mass consumption. Real living standards were rising as there was more food, clothing, coal, furniture and other goods available for the working population to buy.

We have already seen that there was an almost constant fall in prices throughout this period. This fall was steepest in the period from 1820 to 1830. Throughout the whole period and in particular during the 1820s there was a rise in wages paid to industrial workers, so that their real wages (i.e. the amount they could buy) rose fairly markedly. J. P. Kay painted a horrible picture of life in

Manchester's slums. What he did not go on to say was that the description referred in the main to life among the Irish immigrants. Like all immigrants they had to take the worst jobs with the lowest pay and the longest hours. As Engels admitted, they were not typical of Britain's industrial workers. But even for these slum-dwelling Irish the poverty revealed by Kay and Engels was an improvement on the conditions they had endured in their own country. There, an agriculture-based economy was unable to provide bare subsistence for the mass of the population who were forced by hunger and a land-shortage to look for a better life in industrial England.

Within limits the same was true of Britain's agricultural workers. While there was no great rush from the countryside to the towns, there was a steady drift of the surplus population of smaller villages into the nearest towns where wages were better than those paid to agricultural workers. The Reverend David Davies was Rector of Barkham in Berkshire. In 1795 he published *The Case of Labourers in Husbandry* in which he proved that many of his parishioners were living in dire poverty which had led to a great increase in the Poor Rates. He commented: 'It is well known that in the great trading towns such as Manchester, Sheffield, Birmingham, etc. four days work in a week amply supply the dissolute and the drunken.' Writing in 1826 another contemporary contrasted: 'the "improving" ... knowledge, comfort, and conduct of town workers with the depression of "the peasantry".'

Evidence of rising standards

David Ricardo was one of the early economists. His major contribution to economic thought was his enunciation of a wage-fund theory which argued that the increasing population would tend to drive wage-levels down to mere subsistence levels. Wages would rise or fall with changes in the price of corn. Ricardo's theory was adopted by Marx and other socialists. But even as early as 1820, Ricardo wrote: 'Many of the conveniences enjoyed in an English cottage would have been thought luxuries at an earlier period of our history.' There was a flaw between theory and reality. Far from being driven into mere subsistence, the industrial working class was apparently enjoying a higher standard of living. Indeed if there was a section of the population which had to endure a subsistence-level existence it was to be found in the countryside and in particular in Ireland.

Later economists have been able to show that a rise in capital formation and a rise in output is generally followed in democratic societies by a rise in overall real incomes and standards of living. One indicator of this rise is increased life-expectancy. We have seen in Chapter 1 that there were close links between economic conditions and increases in population. Whether that increase was due to earlier marriages, greater fertility, a higher number of children per marriage or a fall in the death rate – or any combination of all these – is irrelevant to the main point of the argument that economic conditions must have been improving throughout this period. Indeed one may feel some sympathy for Malthus and his supporters who had prophesied a fall in the birth rate as soon as the total population began to 'press' against output. That the population continued to rise surprised the Malthusians who had not taken account of the fact that output could continue to increase even more rapidly than did population.

Evidence for the rise in living standards are the findings of economists and historians on the *per capita* consumption of meat, sugar, tea, beer, eggs, soap, leather, linen, cotton and coal. These claims are supported by the evidence presented by students of import statistics for this period. These show that there were 'persistent upward' trends in the volume imported of tea, sugar and tobacco. The pessimists argument for 'a golden age' in a pre-industrial rural society is somewhat dented by the fact that after 1820 there was a steady stream of steamships from agricultural Ireland to industrializing England, carrying Irish livestock, poultry, meat and eggs. One of the savage ironies of the 1840s was that while the Irish peasants starved, their country was exporting grain and other foodstuffs to prosperous England where the mass of industrial workers enjoyed a standard of living that was the envy of European workers and would have been inconceivable even to their grandparents.

It could have been that the massive increase in food imports was necessary to compensate for a fall in food production in Britain. However we know that during the period after 1760 there was a great increase in domestic food production, that an increasing amount of land was enclosed and mainly for the production of wheat for domestic consumption (see Chapter 4). While domestic production of wheat failed to match the increase in population, the price of wheat remained fairly stable, apart from the war years from 1783 to 1815. After 1815 there was a sharp fall in prices; in 1835 the price fell to 39s 4d per quarter, the lowest it had reached for over fifty years.

In pre-industrial England the price of wheat and hence of bread had been a matter of life and death for the mass of the people who lived on a very limited diet. After 1800 bread played a smaller but still significant part in the diet of the masses. There was an increased consumption of the potato and other vegetables as well as a rise in the import of fruits such as cherries and apples.

In the days before the Agricultural Revolution the mass of the people had consumed little meat. This was still true of the agricultural population of Ireland throughout the nineteenth century. In 1836 a report from the Poor Law commissioners in Ireland noted that the English working class had meat almost daily in contrast to the population of Ireland. About the same time Dickens wrote: 'Next to the Habeas Corpus and the Freedom of the Press, there are few things that the English people have a greater respect for and livelier faith in than beef.'

This is hardly surprising when we consider the improvements that had been made in stock-breeding during the second half of the eighteenth century. Sheep were no longer bred for the wool they might produce but for their meat content. The same was true of cattle and pigs. The increased output of meat from British farms was sold to the increasing population of industrial towns. London naturally took a massive share of the national output with the meat markets at Smithfield, Newgate, Leadenhall, Farringdon and Whitechapel all reporting continually increasing numbers of animals being brought for slaughter. But London was not alone in this. In 1836 most of the fat stock of Gloucester was not going to London as it once had, but to Birmingham, Liverpool and other industrial towns. In 1833 a parliamentary report noted that meat 'sells well in large towns, the mechanics having more money to lay out'.

The work of a large number of modern historians shows that the most striking single fact concerning labour in the period 1815–30 is that money wages declined, in net, very slightly, less even than food prices and much less than other retail goods. This evidence had forced J. L. Hammond to concede in 1930: 'Let us take it that so far as statistics can measure material improvement, there was improvement.' This makes it all the harder to understand why more recent pessimists still try to maintain that the evidence is not sound, does not present an overall picture and that in spite of the evidence the working classes suffered a fall in living standards as a result of the Industrial Revolution.

The wars against revolutionary and Napoleonic France imposed a severe strain on the nation's economic resources and led to a dramatic fall in living standards for the majority of the working population. The increased output of iron foundries and coal-mines, textile-mills and engineering shops no longer went on improving the material life of the people but had to be spent on the fighting of the war. The government borrowed heavily to pay for the prosecution of the war and this led to the increase in indirect taxation which fell heavily on the working classes who consumed the great part of the taxable items.

In 1797 the government realized that there would be a shortage of gold as a result of the policy of subsidizing European Allies against France. To help alleviate the economic problems that would result from a fall in the amount of gold held by the Bank of England the government suspended cash payments so that the Bank of England was no longer obliged to change notes into gold. For the first time Bank of England notes became legal tender and the issue of notes of less value than £5 was legalized. Country banks followed the example of the Bank of England so that gold almost disappeared and the banknote became the major form of currency.

Up until 1797 bankers had been obliged to bear in mind that customers might wish to change their notes for gold. This had imposed some limit on the volume of notes they printed and the amount of credit they extended to customers. Freed from these restraints by the 1797 act bankers extended their lines of credit and over-issued notes. The result was not surprisingly an upsurge in prices which may be described as a bank-induced inflation. There were other factors which added to the inflationary pressure. Bad harvests in 1798 and 1799 as well as the difficulty of importing grain from war-torn Europe helped increase the price of wheat and other foodstuffs.

The terms of trade turned against Britain between 1793 and 1815 as the rise in import prices was greater than the rise in the export prices. For a given volume of imports there had to be an increase in the volume of exports needed to pay for them. This then led to less being available for the domestic market which accentuated and accelerated the tendency to inflation.

We have firm evidence for the rise in food prices. Between 1783 and 1793 the average price for a quarter of wheat had been 47s; between 1793 and 1801 the average price was 77s; between 1803 and 1813 the average was 92s; and in 1812, a particularly bad year, the price was 126s per quarter. While money wages also rose, they did so much more slowly. There was therefore a fall in real wages. There was a fall also in the consumption of non-food items and a reduction in the quality of the type and amount of food consumed.

Writing in 1884 Thorold Rogers, one of the 'pessimists' noted:

'Thousands of homes were starved in order to find means for the great war. . . . the resources on which the struggle was based and without which it would have speedily collapsed, were the stint and starvation of labour, the overtaxed and underfed toils of childhood, the underpaid and uncertain employment of men.' During this period poverty became a real problem; food riots were common and the Luddite movement reached a new peak in 1812. No historian denies that during this long period there was a decline in living standards – due not to the process of industrialization but to the peculiar conditions consequent on fighting such a long and costly war. Indeed it has to be said that industrialization alone made it possible for Britain to stand alone during much of the period from 1793 to 1815 against a Europe dominated by Napoleon. Speaking at the Lord Mayor's banquet on 9 November 1805 a few weeks after the decisive victory of Trafalgar Prime Minister Pitt noted: 'England has saved herself by her exertions; and will, I trust, save Europe by her example.'

He no doubt realized, even if he did not say, that England's exertions had depended on the cannon produced in the ironworks at Carron and Merthyr which in turn were the results of the work of many inventors and innovators in iron, coal and engineering. He might also have added that England did not save Europe merely by her example but by the massive subsidies paid to allies, by loans raised on their behalf on the London money market and by the help in kind sent to less-than-constant members of the Coalitions. None of this aid would have been possible if England had not already undergone a process of industrial transformation which made her the richest country in the world, able to be the paymaster of the anti-Napoleonic forces in Europe.

The period of dislocation lasted until about 1820. Then in the 1820s there was a return to the trends that had become evident before 1793. Prices fell, notably the price of wheat; the wage-levels also fell from their wartime levels but as G. R. Porter noted in 1847: 'the diminution in the wage earnings . . . has been but small in any case, and certainly not commensurate with the diminished cost of most of the necessaries of life, comprehending in this list most articles of food, and every article of clothing.'

Town life

The Hammonds and their pessimistic successors have almost given up the field to the statisticians. They no longer argue that there was a fall in living standards; rather they argue, as does Professor Hobsbawm, that there was no *major rise* in living standards. This is a significant change of ground. However following the example of the Hammonds the pessimists continue to argue that there was a decline in the quality of life in general. They instance the conditions of the new industrial towns where there was poor housing, little sanitation and high death rates.

None of the optimists argue that there was a major rise in living standards. No one would deny that there were millions who suffered a very harsh poverty throughout this period of industrialization. The problems created by the rapid emergence of an industrialized society were very great, numerous and of a kind that defied easy solutions. Until Doulton invented an efficient glazed earthenware pipe in the 1840s there was no method of providing reliable drainage. Until an efficient system of local government was created later in the nineteenth century there was no means of ensuring that standards would be improved.

It is easy with hindsight to criticize the politicians and industrialists who did not create efficient systems of local government, invent better methods of drainage and discover cures for dominant diseases. It would be wiser to concentrate on the achievements of the people faced with the problems of a new, industrialized and urbanized society. One might pay credit to the men in the new urban centres who tried to come to grips with some of the environmental problems facing them. Men in Liverpool, Manchester, Glasgow and other growing towns paid for private acts which set up new bodies, Improvement Commissioners, whose functions varied from place to place and from time to time but in general were concerned with the lighting, paving, cleaning and draining of the new towns.

The Hammonds argued that 'the problem of arranging and controlling the expansion of the towns was thus the most urgent of the problems created by the industrial revolution', and go on to condemn the political and social attitudes of the time. It might be that in an age of facing the problems of urban decay we are less willing to be quite so condemnatory of the people who tried to come to grips with the novel problems of urbanization and industrialization.

The urban working class

The major changes and improvements in urban life had to wait for the creation of an efficient form of local government, for the reform and enlargement of the civil service and for the technological development, such as Doulton's, which would make reform possible. For the urban working-class life was in many respects brutish and short. But for many workers urban life was an improvement on what they had known before – in the English village or the Irish countryside. Urban life and industrial work brought workers into close contact with each other and provided them with opportunities for creating their own social disciplines. They formed embryonic trade unions, which after the emancipating legislation of 1824–5 were no longer regarded as criminal combinations. Through their unions they hoped to work co-operatively to win for themselves a share in the increased wealth they were helping to produce.

Many of the early unions were little more than friendly societies. Members paid a weekly subscription in return for which they received monetary help in times of unemployment and sickness while the societies also provided pensions for retired members and for the widows of deceased members. From 1793

the friendly societies were protected by law and in 1829 a register
of friendly societies was set up in London. The funds of societies
would be deposited with the Commissioners of the National
Debt, so ensuring a safe income for the society and a guarantee
of payments to less fortunate members. By 1801 there were over
700 such societies in England and Wales and by 1850 it was
claimed that two-thirds of the working population of Lancashire
were enrolled in some friendly society or other.

This is evidence at one and the same time that the urban
working class had money to spare over and above what was
needed to pay for that rise in consumption which we have already
noted, and that not all members of this class were concerned only
with the short term. There were millions who eked out a dreadful
existence and for many of whom the ale-house and gin-palace
were refuges. For many others, regularly employed at decent
wages, urban life provided opportunities for self-improvement.
They availed themselves of these opportunities. It was after all the
urban working class who founded the first building societies,
offshoots in many cases of friendly societies and certainly having
their origins in the twin virtues of self-help and thrift.

In 1804 a Miss Priscilla Wakefield of Tottenham founded a
savings bank where the small shopkeepers and craftsmen of the
village were encouraged to hand in their few coppers each week –
and so build up a little nest-egg which they might use for a
wedding feast, in their retirement, to set up a child in trade or
some such reason. By 1817 there were so many of these small
savings banks in different parts of the country that the government
passed two acts to regulate their activities. By the first act the
trustees (who organized the savings bank) were forbidden to
make a profit from the working of their bank; this meant that
they could not make loans to people who might have wanted to
borrow, nor could they issue notes. The second act compelled the
trustees to enrol the rules of their banks with the magistrates. The
trustees of the various savings banks had to send their customers'
money to London where a Fund for the Banks for Savings was

set up. This fund paid sufficient interest on the deposits to cover the expenses of running the savings banks and enabled the trustees to pay interest to their customers. The London-based fund was used by the government to pay off some of the National Debt.

In 1807 it was proposed that the government should set up a network of savings banks, using the post-office organization. This was not done until 1861 when Gladstone set up the Post Office Savings Bank. But as early as 1828 there were 408 savings banks with deposits of £14 million, evidence of working-class thrift and prosperity. This 'will to save' through the savings bank, friendly society and building society was evidence that the urban working class had opportunities not available to their forefathers. As Toynbee admitted: 'The artisan's horizons became indistinct; there was no visible limit to subsistence.'

Compared to their forefathers the urban working class enjoyed a high standard of living, lived longer and more comfortably. But this was not the end of it. It was Bernard Shaw who pointed out that revolutions are led by the half-satisfied; only people whose horizons have been enlarged and whose appetites have been whetted by a taste of betterment can have the concept of even further improvement. There was a psychological change among the urban working class, a growing self-confidence which they shared with their middle-class employers. As the historian Froude pointed out later in the nineteenth century:

> Amidst the varied reflections which the nineteenth century is in the habit of making on its condition and its prospects, there is one common opinion in which all parties coincide – that we live in an era of progress . . . in every department of life – in its business and in its pleasures, in its beliefs and in its theories, in its material developments and in its spiritual convictions – we thank God that we are not like our fathers.

In the 1930s the Hammonds lamented the passing of *The Village labourer* and the onset of 'a new civilization' in *The Town Labourer*.

They did so from the comfort of an environment created by the new civilization, with its brick houses, medical services, sanitary arrangements, water supplies, transport systems and methods of food distribution. There is no evidence that they wished to return to the pre-industrial society themselves. Nor is there any evidence that the urban workers rushed to return to rural England even in times of urban distress. They saw a new golden age in the light of the glare from furnaces, and they increasingly worked to see to it that they and their children enjoyed a better life in that new age.

Lenin thought that electrification and socialism were synonymous. It might be thought fitting to end with a short account of one contribution made by William Murdoch to urban improvement. Murdoch, uneducated mechanic, friend of Watt and Trevithick, had invented many parts of the steam-engine. Perhaps his major contribution to British social development lay in his introduction of lighting by gas. Samuel Smiles wrote:

The inflammable qualities of the air obtained by distillation of coal had long been known, but Murdock was the first to apply the knowledge to practical uses. The subject engaged much of his attention in the year 1792, when he resided at Redruth. As his days were fully occupied in attending to his employer's engine business, it was only in the evenings, after the day's work was over, that he could pursue the subject.

In the paper which he communicated to the Royal Society on the subject of lighting by coal-gas in 1808:

'It is now nearly sixteen years since in the course of experiments I was making at Redruth . . . that I was induced by some observations I had previously made upon the burning of coal, to try the combustible property of the gases produced from it, as well as from peat, wood and other inflammable substances; and being struck with the great quantities of gas which they afforded, as well as the brilliancy of the light, and the facility of its production, I instituted several experiments with a view to ascertaining the cost at which it might be obtained, compared with that of equal quantities of light yielded by oils and tallow. . . . The experiments were made upon coal of different qualities, which I procured from different parts of the kingdom for the purpose of ascertaining which would give the most economical results. The gas was also washed with water, and other means were used to purify it. . . .'

Parliament had some difficulty in accepting the more modest statements of Murdock, as to the uses of coal-gas for lighting purposes.

'Do you mean to tell us,' asked one member, 'that it will be possible to have a light without a wick?' 'Yes, I do indeed,' answered Murdock. 'Ah, my friend,' said the legislator, 'you are trying to prove too much.' It was as surprising and inconceivable to the honourable member as George Stephenson's subsequent evidence before a Parliamentary Committee, to the effect that a carriage might be drawn along a railway at the rate of twelve miles an hour without a horse.

No wonder that strange notions were entertained about gas in those early days. It seemed so incredible a contrivance, to make air that could be sent along pipes for miles from the place at which it was made, to the place at which it issued as jets of fire, that it ran entirely counter to all preconceived notions on the subject of illumination. Even Sir Humphry Davy ridiculed the idea of lighting towns with gas, and asked one of the projectors if it were intended to take the dome of St. Paul's for a gasometer. Sir Walter Scott, also, made many clever jokes about the absurdity of lighting London with smoke, although he shortly after adopted the said 'smoke' for lighting up his own house at Abbotsford. It was popularly supposed that the gas was carried along the pipes on fire and that hence the pipes must be intensely hot. Thus, when the House of Commons was first lighted with gas, the architect insisted on the pipes being placed several inches from the wall in fear of fire, and members might be seen applying their gloved hands to them to ascertain their temperature, expressing the greatest surprise on their being found as cool as the adjoining walls.

The advantages of the new light, however, soon became generally recognised; and gas companies were established in most of the large towns. Had Murdock patented the discovery, it must have proved exceedingly remunerative to him; but he derived no advantage from the extended use of the new system of lighting except the honour of having invented it – though more than one attempt was made to deprive him even of this honour. As he himself modestly said, in his paper before the Royal Society, 'I believe I may, without presuming too much, claim both the first idea of applying, and the first actual application of this gas to economical purposes.'

The London Gas Light and Coke Company was a flourishing concern before Victoria came to the throne in 1837 and the last oil-lamps disappeared from London streets by 1850. We need the danger of war or the threat of a power shortage before our streets are badly lit. Even the blacked-out, dimly lit, streets of wartime Britain were better lit than were the streets of London and other urban centres before Murdock's discovery. If electrification and socialism were synonymous, then maybe gas-lighting and a rise in living standards should be seen as equally synonymous.

15. The Future

1830 – the end?

We have seen that to choose 1760 as a starting date for the Industrial Revolution as Toynbee did is now at best merely to pay lip service to a convention which owes nothing to conviction. To choose to end the story at 1830 is an even more arbitrary decision. Toynbee and Mantoux wrote of *The Industrial Revolution of the Eighteenth Century*; Professor Redford carried his account on to 1850, while some think that 1851, the year of the Great Exhibition, might be a suitable end-date. However Professor Ashton has chosen 1830 as his end-year and there are other good reasons for taking this as a particularly good year at which to finish what now can be seen as only Part 1 of a long-running story.

The opening of the Manchester-Liverpool Railway in 1830 was in itself a significant feature of economic progress. The opening of the Birmingham-London Railway later in the 1830s was even more significant and marks the start of another phase of the ongoing Industrial Revolution. The first stage with which we have been concerned in this book, might be said to have been centred on Watt's rotative steam-engine; the second stage, which we can date fairly accurately as having begun in 1830, was railway-based. The building of the railway network had a great impact on the development of the coal, iron and steel and engineering industries, all of which had to expand to provide the materials for that building. The railway companies were themselves large-scale employers of labour. Perhaps more importantly the railway network affected the nature of the markets opened to farmers, fishermen and newspaper-producers as well as manufacturers of less perishable goods. The branded goods, advertised in the national press and available at stores throughout the country, were themselves a by-product of the quick, cheap and efficient railway service.

All of this lay in the future, in the age of Cobden, who opened his first factory in 1832, and of Chamberlain, born in 1836. The building of the Birmingham-London Railway was a fitting epitaph to the end of the age of Cobbett, who died in 1835. But none of that later and greater progress could have taken place without the changes that had occurred before 1830. It was these changes which provided the springboard from which British industry could take off into self-generating growth.

One major effect of the first stage of the Industrial Revolution was the creation of a new, large and increasingly influential middle class. By 1830 its members were economically more important than the aristocracy and landowners. But, as the *Declaration of the Birmingham Political Union* (1830) pointed out,

> The great aristocratical interests of all kinds are well represented (in the House of Commons). The landed interest, the Church, the law, the monied interest – all these have engrossed the House into their hands, the members of that House being all immediately and closely connected with those great interests. *But the interests of industry and Trade have scarcely any representatives at all!* These, the most vital interests of the nation, the source of all its wealth and of all its strength, are comparatively *unrepresented*.

The modern study of revolution has revealed that, to quote Bernard Shaw, 'Revolutions come from the half-satisfied.' There has to be a correlation between the economic, social and political development of the various classes which make up the nation. By 1830 it was clear that the middle class had made great economic strides; it was also clear that, following the English tradition, they had been allowed to buy themselves the trappings of social progress – housing, estates, titles, schools for their sons and so on. But there was no similar political development. Because of such a dysfunction the French middle classes had risen in a revolution in 1830 to drive the aristocratic Charles x from the throne and to install instead their own middle-class Philippe Egalité, significantly as King of the French. There were signs that the English middle classes, if denied political advance on par with their economic and social development, might follow the French example. The Whig historian and MP Macaulay pointed this out in a speech in the Commons on 2 March 1831 in support of the Reform Bill:

> History is full of revolutions, produced by causes similar to those which are now operating in England. A portion of the community which had been of no account expands and becomes strong. It demands a place in the system suited to its present power. If this is granted, all is well. If this is refused, then comes the struggle between the young energy of the one class and the ancient privileges of another. Such is the struggle which the middle classes of England are maintaining against an aristocracy who have powers witheld from cities renowned for the marvels of their wealth and of their industry.

The passage of the Reform Act in 1832 admitted that new middle class to a share in the political system and the revolution was averted. Almost a generation later in 1867 the franchise was extended to a minority of the male working class and the logic of facts compelled the further widening of the franchise in 1884, 1918, 1928 and 1972. This democratizing process would not have been undertaken if the Industrial Revolution had not taken place.

The passage of the first Reform Act in 1832 marked politically the success of the first stage of that revolution which ended, according to Ashton, in 1830.

It is a truism that those who hold political power use it for their own benefit. The landed aristocracy had done so before 1830, passing Game Laws to protect their estates from the depredations of poachers and the Corn Laws (1815) to maintain the income they had enjoyed up until then, now threatened because of the food shortage resulting from the wars against the French Revolution and Napoleon.

The middle classes imitated their social superiors in this as in all else. The repeal of the Corn Laws in 1846 was an almost inevitable consequence of the newly acquired political power of the industrial middle class. It is somewhat ironic that Peel, the heir of famous factory-owners, as leader of the Conservative Party should have brought in this repeal, seemingly at the behest of the middle-class, led by Cobden. Peel admitted that the repeal would 'alienate a great Party', while to have maintained the Corn Laws would 'have been sure to animate and please a Party.' But Peel's love for his party was less than his willingness to follow the logical course outlined by Cobden and his Anti-Corn Law League. He admitted as much when addressing the Commons on 23 June 1846: 'But, Sir, there is a name which ought to be associated with the success of these measures, the name of a man who acting from disinterested motives and by appeals to reason. . . . the name which will be associated with the success of these measures is the name of Richard Cobden.'

There were those in the Conservative Party in 1846 who agreed with Disraeli, and thought of the repeal as the Great Betrayal. Disraeli was aware of the great industrial changes which had taken place since 1760. He had written about them in *Sybil* (1845), in which he described the formation of the 'Two Nations.' But he wanted to believe that the changes were only temporary. It was he claimed the landed aristocracy which ought to continue to dominate affairs. It was agriculture and not industry which ought to be the government's main concern. During a bitter attack on Peel he noted:

> The agricultural interest is that great body of people who are the cultivators of the earth; and if you materially change the balance between the populations that depend upon the two great interests of this country, you shake to its centre that territorial constitution, you destroy the security for local government, you subvert the guarantee for public liberty; you change, in fact, the character of England; you bring about the social revolution which the Right Hon gentleman always reminded us would be the consequence of following the policy of the school of Manchester.

But by 1850 even the backwoodsmen of the rump of the Tory Party that followed Disraeli had to accept his verdict that 'Protection is dead and damned.' Industry had triumphed over agriculture even in the eyes of the landed gentry and the middle class had replaced the aristocracy as the dominant class – economically and politically.

The first Industrial Revolution did not merely affect British society and politics. It also had international effects. British industrialists went out to capture an even larger share of the world's markets than they had enjoyed before 1760. Britain became at one and the same time the world's largest exporter and largest importer; 'a nation of shopkeepers' indeed, which took in food and raw materials and sent out a growing stream of manufactured goods. Domination of the world's economy led to the growth of that vigorous arrogance which was associated with the foreign policy of Lord Palmerston in particular. Not even his mentor Canning would have treated the world as Palmerston did. Writing to the Governor of Hongkong in 1850 he noted:

> The Time is fast coming when we shall be obliged to strike another Blow to China. These half-civilised Governments such as those of China, Portugal, Spanish America, all require a

dressing every eight or ten years to keep them in order. Their minds are too shallow to receive an Impression that will last longer than some such Period, and warning is of little use. They care little for words and they must not only see the Stick, but actually feel it on their Shoulders.

A century later in 1956 the Eden government tried to give Nasser's Egypt the 'big stick' treatment. The humiliation of the débacle of the Suez venture of 1956 was due in large part to the industrial-political military power of the USA and Russia and to the relative decline of Britain. Palmerston could behave as he did – and succeeded – only because British industry had by 1850 made Britain 'the workshop of the world', well able to dominate world affairs.

But that domination was, we now know, short-lived. British industrialists exported their know-how to whichever foreigners were prepared to pay for it. By 1851 industrialists in the USA were using more advanced techniques than were most of their British counterparts. The British had already slipped into their still-continuing belief that there is little need to invest, to change, to modernize. They had after all become the world's leading industrial nation without much investment but with a great deal of brawn; their progress after 1760 owed little to learning but a great deal to that empirical 'rule of thumb' which could be acquired at the workshop bench and not at the laboratory table. The anti-intellectualism which was a feature of Victorian Britain was a major cause of the refusal to develop the newer technologically-based industries of the late nineteenth century. The earlier success contained within itself the germs of the seeds of the later decline from a position of predominance.

By 1830 the progress of urbanization was well under way and the sprawling conurbations of Manchester, Liverpool, Cardiff and Birmingham were presenting Britain's ruling class with a new set of social problems. These problems – of undrained and uncleansed streets, overcrowded and insanitary housing, a high death rate from preventible causes – were also to be found in the hundreds of small urban areas, smaller than the great conurbations, but very large when compared to the towns of early eighteenth-century England. Before 1830 the solutions to these problems were left a matter for private and local initiative. After 1830 the government began to play a part in finding ways of dealing with the environmental problems caused by urbanization.

At first this government interference confined itself to promoting what has been called 'gas-and-water' socialism. It was empirical and pragmatic, concerned with the creation of a healthy environment and with the provision of such amenities as the individual could not be expected to provide for himself It was Sir William Harcourt, Chancellor of the Exchequer in Gladstone's last ministry, who declared, 'We are all socialists now.' And that before even the Independent Labour Party was formed in 1893.

But the logic of facts once again compelled later governments to widen their horizons. They were forced to turn from merely passing environmental reforms to providing personal-service reforms, such as the provision of old-age pensions, national insurance and subsidized housing. The roots of the modern social-security system are to be found in the urban squalor of the early industrial towns. Without that urbanization there would have been no call for socialist solutions to environmental problems, and no base on which the social-security society could grow. And without the Industrial Revolution there would not have been the wealth needed to provide the means to overcome the environmental problems and to finance the social-security system. Industrialization is the key not merely to economic but to social progress.

The word 'socialism' was first used in English by Robert Owen. Born in Newton, Montgomeryshire, Owen became part-owner of cotton-mills in New Lanark. He was one of the many factory-owners who dealt sympathetically with their workpeople. He opened schools for the younger children, provided evening classes for older children and adults, and instituted a system of co-partnership. Owen was a prime mover of the Factory Act of 1819, co-founder of the Grand National Consolidated Trade Union in the 1830s and the inspiration behind the Co-operative movement which started in the 1840s.

Unlike latter-day Marxist historians Owen did not condemn the industrial system *per se*. It was this system which brought him the wealth which enabled him to devote so much time and energy to his various humanitarian and socialist ventures. He had seen how the first Industrial Revolution had helped Britain fight off the Napoleonic threat. In 1819 he wrote: 'The immediate effects of this manufacturing phenomenon were a rapid increase of the wealth, industry, population, and political influence of the British Empire; and by the aid of which it has been enabled to contend for five-and-twenty years against the most formidable military and immoral power that the world perhaps ever contained.'

However Owen was aware that the spread of industrialization carried with it the danger that there might be a simultaneous spread of that spirit of individualism which was indeed a mainspring of the Industrial Revolution. He noted:

The general diffusion of manufactures throughout a country generates a new character in its inhabitants; and as this character is formed upon a principle quite unfavourable to individual or general happiness, it will produce the most lamentable and permanent evils, unless its tendency be counteracted by legislative interference and direction.

The manufacturing system has already so far extended its influence over the British Empire, as to effect an essential change in the general character of the mass of the people. This alteration is still in rapid progress; and ere long, the comparatively happy simplicity of the agricultural peasant will be wholly lost amongst us. It is even now scarcely anywhere to be found without a mixture of those habits which are the offspring of trade, manufactures, and commerce.

These 'habits' of which Owen spoke were various in quality and effect. On the one hand there were habits of which, one has to suppose, Owen himself approved. He worked hard, saved for investment and in general followed the pattern dictated by the Puritan or Protestant ethic. He was enough of a historian to have realized that this ethic had been partly, if not largely responsible for the first Industrial Revolution through which he lived and was enriched. But his reference to the 'happy simplicity of the agricultural peasant' serves to remind us that it was only a small minority of people who were driven by that ethic. For the vast majority there was an acceptance of life, station and status; there was the resigned expectation that over the centuries life would change slowly, if at all, and that a bad harvest or two would wipe out all the gains of decades of slow progress.

The Industrial Revolution had indeed ended the centuries of uncertainty with regard to economic growth and social progress. The industrial system would lead to self-generating growth which in turn would entangle the whole population in its web. Owen believed that this might lead to fundamental changes in people's behaviour and beliefs:

The inhabitants of every country are trained and formed by its great leading existing circumstances, and the character of the lower orders in Britain is now formed chiefly by circumstances arising from trade, manufactures and commerce, and the governing principle of trade, manufactures and commerce is immediate pecuniary gain, to which on the great scale every other is made to give way. All are sedulously trained to buy cheap and to sell dear; and to succeed in this art, the parties must be taught to acquire strong powers of deception; and thus a spirit is generated through every class of traders, destructive of that open, honest sincerity, without which man cannot make others happy, nor enjoy happiness himself. . . . Strictly speaking however, this defect of character ought not to be attributed to the individuals possessing it, but to the overwhelming effect of the system under which they have been trained.

Such a system of training cannot be expected to produce any other than a population weak in bodily and mental faculties, and with habits generally destructive of their own comforts, of the well-being of those around them, and strongly calculated to subdue all the social affections. Man so circumstanced sees all around him hurrying forward, at a mail-coach speed, to acquire individual wealth, fitted only to steel the heart of man against his fellow, or to form the tyrant and the slave. Today he labours for one master, tomorrow for a second, then for a third and a fourth, until all ties between employers and employed are frittered down to the consideration of what immediate gain each can derive from the other.

The employer regards the employed as mere instruments of gain, while these acquire a gross ferocity of character, which, if legislative measures shall not be judiciously devised to prevent its increase, and ameliorate the condition of this class, will sooner or later plunge the country into a formidable and perhaps inextricable state of danger.

The 'state of danger' or revolution to which Owen referred was averted by a judicious introduction of ameliorating legislation during the nineteenth and twentieth centuries. In 1848 Marx wrote the *Communist Manifesto* in which he confidently predicted the ever-worsening condition of the urban working classes in the industrialized countries. This condition would, he prophesied, cause the masses to rise in revolution against their bourgeois masters and so usher in the dawn of the Communist Age. In fact the working class has become increasingly subject to the process of *embourgeoisement*, acquiring those material possessions which were once luxuries but have become necessities. Now that over 50 per cent of homes are owner-occupied and ownership of cars, televisions, washing-machines and the rest are commonplace, there is little if any danger of a Marxist-inspired rising.

But Owen's vision of the future was correct in at least one

respect, which is more than can be said for Marx's prophesyings. Industrialization has indeed created a society in which each man seeks his own best interests even at the expense of others. Owen wrote of the system which would 'steel the heart of man against his fellows'. There can be little doubt that we have reached this position in our own prosperous times. If the doctrine of brotherhood and worker-fellowship ought to be found anywhere, one would expect to find it in the ranks of the trade union movement. But here we find more attention paid to the argument about maintaining differentials than over sharing of wealth. Members of unions such as ASTMS campaign vigorously for their larger pay packet and ignore the inflationary effects which would follow the success of their campaign to create an aristocracy inside the legendary brotherhood of workers. The utterances of the leaders of the powerful unions – for miners, power-workers, doctors, dentists and others – have made it clear that they seek only a sectional interest, as Owen had foreseen.

Perhaps we might be entitled to seek for an Owenite corrective in the Labour Party. This after all was founded in the 1890s to help the masses. But in the affluent 1970s we find that here too there is more attention paid to party interest – the holding on to power – than to social justice. In our own time both the Labour and Conservative Parties campaign on the slogan of lower taxes; neither pays even lip service to the condition of the minorities who make up the less well-off. Whichever of the two main parties stays in power does so only because it has persuaded the mass of the voters that their interests will be best served by voting for 'us'. A recent opinion poll showed that 85 per cent of the British people think that Britain is now too poor to be able to send aid to underdeveloped countries. The majority of people have certainly managed to 'steel the heart' against the plight of their fellow-men living in dire poverty but far away. They have also managed to ignore the plight of the unemployed, lowly paid workers, battered wives and otherwise socially deprived members of their own community.

Owen was the first to draw attention to the devisive effect of the industrial changes that were still relatively in their infancy in 1819. He wrote at a time when the majority of people still lived in villages and small towns, where there was a high degree of social cohesion. Certainly there was a squire in his castle and a poor man at his gate; certainly there were stations to which people were expected to keep. But there was at the same time a contact between squire and poor man – whether at the gate or in church, in the village street or the graveyard. It is only in the larger urban centres that we have the division between east and west ends, which was so great that by the end of the nineteenth century Booth could write of *The Submerged Tenth* and Jack London entitle his report *People of the Abyss*, and the well-intentioned from Oxbridge and the public schools could open missions in the East End of London almost as if they were venturing into Darkest Africa.

There can be little doubt that on any quantitative analysis the Industrial Revolution was the boon which Professor Ashton claimed it was in his famous passage which I have quoted on page 21. Owen was aware of this and he had no Luddite wish to turn back the clock. He did however see some at least of the dangers inherent in the new industrialized system. He noted that 'the political and moral effects to which we allude well deserve to occupy the best faculties of the greatest and the wisest statesmen'. Today over 150 years later things are if anything worse rather than better and this in spite of the attentions of statesmen.

Some have hoped, and naïvely some still do, to find a solution in Marxism. The dictatorship of the proleteriat it was claimed would lead to a peaceful sharing out of the plenty which the industrial system produces. The Russians have had two generations in which to put Marxism into practice – and have to build a wall to keep the contented proletariat from rushing to the depraved West. Even if the 'sharing out' were being done more equitably in Russia than in the West, and there is little evidence that this is the case, the cost to the human spirit is a great one.

One doubts that Owen, the humanitarian, the co-operator and the philosopher, would have chosen the extermination of political and economic opponents as the right way in which to achieve a goal.

In Britain there was the hope that Fabian-type gradualism would lead to fundamental changes in society. The new philosophy would, claimed the Webbs and their supporters, bring about without violence a new society in which according to William Morris 'everyone will have abundant leisure for following intellectual pursuits congenial to his nature'. Morris wrote that in 1884. We have had almost a century of social progress since then. And we are no nearer the Utopia of which Morris dreamed when founding his Socialist League. Indeed we may be said to be even further advanced along the road of selfishness than we were in the 1880s.

For a while in the 1960s some hoped that Britain's young people, educated in a socially secure state would produce a new society. Making love not war, waving flowers and not guns, confident that they would overcome by means of songs and sit-downs, they held it seemed the hope for a better future. But that hope has faded as those same young have proved to be as selfish as their elders, anxious to acquire the hi-fi and cassette, as vociferously aware of their rights and ignorant of their duties as their parents have been. There seems little hope that the next generation will be any wiser than the last.

The most recent Owenite prophet was Dr Ernest Schumacher, the economist-author of *Small and Beautiful* (1973). Schumacher would have us turn from the conscious acquisition of more – which Owen deplored in 1819 – to a conscious reduction in the nature, scale and degree of what we consider necessary and essential. He would have us become increasingly aware of the fact that the globe is a village in which all of us should share the good things. He would have us realize that the world's resources are limited and are running out at a terrifying rate. He tried to teach the industrialized world that it was taking proportionately too large a part of those resources, was using these wastefully and was therefore depriving others in the village of the necessities of life.

Schumacher tried to do for the world what Owen tried to do for the single country in which he saw the Industrial Revolution get under way. Neither Schumacher or Owen was an enemy to industrialization. Both however were opposed to the evil effects which industrialization, unless checked, would bring. Only the future will show whether Schumacher has any more success than Owen, who was ignored by the legislators to whom he appealed in 1819. It is to be hoped that Schumacher's ideas will not be so readily and speedily dismissed.

Bibliography

General

Ashton, T. S., *The Industrial Revolution* (1948)

Beales, H. L., *The Industrial Revolution* (1958)

Clapham, J. H., *An Economic History of Modern Britain, vol 1* (1939)

Deane, Phyllis, *The First Industrial Revolution* (1969)

Deane, Phyllis, and Cole, W. A., *British Economic Growth, 1688–1959* (1962)

Flinn, M. W., *The Origins of the Industrial Revolution* (1966)

Hartwell, R. M., *The Causes of the Industrial Revolution in England* (1967)

——, *The Industrial Revolution and Economic Growth* (1971)

Hobsbawm, E. J., *Industry and Empire* (1968)

Mantoux, Paul, *The Industrial Revolution in the Eighteenth Century* (12th edn. 1961)

Marshall, Dorothy, *English People in the Eighteenth Century* (1956)

Taylor, P. A. M., *The Industrial Revolution in Britain; a triumph or disaster?* (1958)

Toynbee, Arnold, *The Industrial Revolution* (1884)

Documentary selections

Barker, T. (ed.), *The Long March of Everyman* (1975)

Flinn, M. W. (ed.), *Readings in Economic and Social History* (1964)

Harrison, J. C. F. (ed.), *Society and Politics, 1780–1960* (1965)

Holman, D. (ed.), *Earlier Nineteenth Century, 1783–1867* (1965)

Huggett, Frank E. (ed.), *Factory Life and work* (1973)

Millward, J. S., and Arnold-Croft, H. P. (ed.), *The Eighteenth Century, 1714–1783* (1965)

Pike, E. R. (ed.), *Human Documents of the Industrial Revolution* (1966)

Sanbrook, G. A. (ed.), *English Life in the Nineteenth Century* (1965)

Specialist studies

Ashton, T. S., *Iron and Steel in the Industrial Revolution* (1963)

——, 'The Standard of Life of Workers in England, 1790–1830' in the *Journal of Economic History* (1949)

Carus-Wilson, E. M. (ed.), *Essays in Economic History*, vols 1–3 (1954–62)

Chambers, J. D., 'Population changes in Nottingham, 1700–1800', in *Studies in the Industrial Revolution*, ed. L. Pressnell (1956)

Chambers, J. D., and Mingay, G. E., *The Agricultural Revolution, 1750–1880* (1966)

Chapman, S. D., *The Cotton Industry in the Industrial Revolution* (1972)

George, M. D., *London Life in the eighteenth century* (1930)

Gilboy, E., *Wages in Eighteenth Century England* (1934)

Glass, D. V., 'The population controversy in eighteenth century England', in *Population Studies* (1952)

Hadfield, C., *British Canals* (4th edn. 1969)

Hammond, J. L. and B., *The Rise of Modern Industry* (1925)

——, *The Village labourer* (1911)

——, *The Town labourer* (1920)

——, *The Skilled labourer* (1919)

McKeown, T., and Record, R. G., 'Reasons for the decline of mortality in England and Wales during the nineteenth century', in *Population Studies* (1962)

Mingay, G. E., *English Landed Society in the Eighteenth Century* (1963)

Porter, G. R., *The Progress of the Nation* (1947 edn)

Pressnell, L. S., *Country Banking in the Industrial Revolution* (1956)

Schumpeter, E. B., *English Overseas Trade Statistics, 1697–1808*, ed. T. S. Ashton (1960)

Thompson, E. P., *The Making of the English Working Class* (1963)

Thompson, F. L. M., *English Landed Society in the Nineteenth Century* (1963)

Wadsworth, A. P., and Mann, J. de L., *The Cotton Trade and Industrial Lancashire, 1600–1780* (1931)

Woodham-Smith, C. M., *The Great Hunger* (1962)

Index

Contemporary authorities mentioned or quoted in the text

Historians mentioned or quoted in the text